Living More with Less

30th Anniversary Edition

Doris Janzen Longacre

Updated and edited by Valerie Weaver-Zercher

Living More with Less and the *More-with-Less Cookbook* were originally commissioned by Mennonite Central Committee (MCC) in response to inequities in world resource distribution and to bring a Christian perspective to material consumption.

Herald Press

Scottdale, Pennsylvania
Waterloo, Ontario

Library of Congress Cataloging-in-Publication Data

Living more with less / [edited by] Doris Janzen Longacre ; updated and edited by Valerie Weaver-Zercher.—30th anniversary ed.
  p. cm.
ISBN 978-0-8361-9521-7 (pbk. : alk. paper)
1. Home economics. 2. Cost and standard of living. 3. Conduct of life. 4. Self-reliant living. I. Longacre, Doris Janzen. II. Weaver-Zercher, Valerie, 1973-III. Title.

TX147.L58 2010
640—dc22

2010040673

Environmental Savings

Mennonite Publishing Network saved the following resources by printing the pages of this book on chlorine free paper made with 30% post-consumer waste.

Trees	Water	Solid Waste	Greenhouse Gases
About 34 trees	15,610 gallons	948 pounds	3,241 pounds CO2

LIVING MORE WITH LESS, 30TH ANNIVERSARY EDITION
Copyright © 2010 by Herald Press, Scottdale, PA 15683.
  Released simultaneously in Canada by Herald Press,
  Waterloo, Ont. N2L 6H7. All rights reserved
Library of Congress Control Number: 2010040673
International Standard Book Number: 978-0-8361-9521-7
Printed in United States of America
Cover and book design by Merrill Miller

15 14 13 12 11 10   10 9 8 7 6 5 4 3 2 1

To order or request information please call 1-800-245-7894
or visit www.heraldpress.com.

In memory of Doris Janzen Longacre,
who died of cancer in 1979 at the age of thirty-nine
before she could complete the original
Living More with Less manuscript.
This thirtieth anniversary edition of her book is revised
and updated in her honor.

Contents

• •

Foreword

Nancy Sleeth

● ●

It all began with two simple questions.

A decade ago, I was living out the American dream in a beautiful home filled with beautiful things. My husband was a physician at the top of his career, a chief of staff and director of emergency services.

One winter break, I asked Matthew two questions that would change our lives forever. First, "What is the biggest problem facing the world today?" His answer surprised me: "The world is dying. If we don't have clean air, clean water, and healthy soil to sustain life on earth, the other problems won't really matter."

Then I asked him, "If the world is dying, what do you think we should do about it?" Matthew didn't have an immediate response. But he said he'd get back to me.

So we embarked on a faith journey. Together we read many of the world's great sacred texts, finding much wisdom but not the answers we were seeking. Then, on a slow night in the emergency room, Matthew picked up an orange Gideons Bible. He began reading the Gospels and found the truth he had been seeking. My husband became a believer in Christ. One by one, our entire family followed.

Eventually Matthew got back to me about my second question. His answer: he would quit his job as a physician and spend the rest of his life trying to serve God and save the planet, even if he never earned another cent. *Hmmm,* I thought. *A job without a job description. Or salary. Or benefits.* "Honey," I said, "are you sure we need to do *that* much about it?"

So Matthew and I read through the entire Bible, underlining everything that had to do with nature, creation, and how we are instructed to care for the earth. Matthew 7:3-5 seemed to speak directly to our family: "Why do you see the speck in your neighbor's eye, but do not notice the log in your own eye? . . . You hypocrite, first take the log out of your own eye, and then you will see clearly to take the speck out of your neighbor's eye."

We took Jesus' advice and began cleaning up our own act before worrying about cleaning up the rest of the world. Over the next couple of years, we downsized our lifestyle, giving away half of our possessions and moving to a house the size of our former garage. Contrary to my earlier fears, we found that the more we "gave up" in material things, the more we gained in family unity, purpose, and joy. Eventually, through many small changes, we reduced our energy usage by more than two-thirds and our trash production by nine-tenths.

After we had our own house in order, we felt called to share our journey. Matthew wrote a book called *Serve God, Save the Planet: A Christian Call to Action.* Using stories from our family's life and the emergency room, he communicated why we made these changes. Letters poured in from readers who felt called to change but didn't know where to start. So I wrote *Go Green, Save Green,* sharing stories about what worked, what didn't, and what our family learned in the process.

Living More with Less takes simple living one step further: it addresses not only caring for God's creation, but also four related life standards, all interwoven like threads of the same cloth. Originally published in 1980, *Living More with Less* has served for three decades as a clarion call for the kind of living Matthew and I now follow.

Doris Janzen Longacre and the Anabaptist writers who contributed to her book knew then what many people are just now discovering: living with less can bring more joy and contentment than living with a lot. What I love most about this anniversary edition is the opportunity to hear a chorus of diverse but harmonious voices, singing together for the first time in one volume. *Living More with Less*—both the 1980 volume and this one—is a book filled with hope and encouragement rather than a one-size-fits-all plan. Each reader is challenged to decide which changes work best now and then to keep doing a little bit better every year. Once our hearts are changed, action follows.

Regardless of where you and your family members are on the journey, this book provides practical advice on everything from household cleaners to gardening to fast food, as well as stories about people changing the way they celebrate Christmas, making conscious choices about technology, and finding quiet time with God.

Years ago, two questions launched our family on this journey. Today, when making a purchase or decision, we ask ourselves two questions: Does this bring us closer to God? And does this help us love our neighbors? The answers will always lead us down the right path.

Mennonite Central Committee Preface

Arli Klassen

• •

"Love your neighbor as yourself": Christ's command, rooted in the Hebrew Scriptures, is no easy task. Many of us ask ourselves, "Who are my neighbors, and what does loving them look like?" Love for our neighbors, in a globalized world marked by poverty and climate change, might look a lot like living more with less.

Living more with less has been part of my theology since I was given the *More-with-Less Cookbook* at my wedding thirty years ago. Later that same year, my husband and I purchased our own copy of *Living More with Less*. Both books have had a tremendous influence on me, just as they have had on many people in my generation. These days our young adult daughters are challenging me to live in ways that care for the whole of creation. I need new ideas and inspiration to create new lifestyle habits, new ways of loving my neighbors around the world. This anniversary edition of *Living More with Less* will do exactly that.

Mennonite Central Committee (MCC) is part of this project because we have always believed that the changes we seek to support around the world must include ourselves. MCC is a worldwide ministry of Anabaptist churches, sharing God's love and compassion for all in the name of Christ by responding to basic human needs and working for peace and justice. MCC works in relief, development, and peace in sixty countries around the world.

We envision communities worldwide in right relationship with God, with each other, and with creation. MCC is not just a ministry of the church but a grassroots movement, drawing inspiration and encouragement from the thousands who participate in loving their neighbors in some practical way through MCC. The concrete lifestyle ideas in this book resonate with MCC's vision and purpose.

Much has changed in our world during the thirty years since *Living More with Less* was first published, yet much has also stayed the same.

- Today 1.1 billion people, or 15 percent of the world's population, are chronically hungry. Thirty years ago, 19 percent of the total population was undernourished, which was 853 million people.[1] Thus, the relative number of hungry people has gone down in thirty years, even as the total number has gone up.

- Today about 1.1 billion people lack access to safe water supplies, about 15 percent of the world's population. Thirty years ago, the same number, 1.1 billion people, lacked access to clean water, but that was 25 percent of the total population.[2]

- In 2005 about 1.4 billion people (25 percent of the world's population) lived in deep poverty, on less than $1.25 (U.S.) per day. This is compared to 1.9 billion people (50 percent) in 1981.[3]

We have made some progress on hunger, water, and poverty issues, but these remain huge problems of inequity in our world today. This book is a new version, with fresh ideas, and it will encourage each one of us to try some new things. I pray that it will inspire all of us to live in right relationship with God, with our neighbors near and far, and with creation.

Preface

Valerie Weaver-Zercher

● ●

five years ago I could not have worked on this book.

At that time I was slashing a dazed path through the thicket of early parenthood, with three children under the age of five. I could manage little more than washing diapers and cooking meals. Even those tasks made me angry, because doing them required labor and time that I could not invest in the editorial work to which I felt increasingly drawn.

The pattern for more-with-less living that Doris Janzen Longacre outlined in *Living More with Less*, paired with its classification as a home economics volume, looked to me like one more way to make homemakers (still mostly women, still mostly mothers) feel like they weren't doing enough. The time and energy to "green" one's life, as popular parlance had branded it, felt like privileges I didn't have and couldn't summon. So it was that I spent my days caroming between self-righteousness when I met my more-with-less ideals (full laundry line! local foods for dinner!) and self-reproach when I didn't (countless trips in the gas-hogging minivan! frozen pizza!).

Had I worked on an anniversary edition of *Living More with Less* in those years, my editorial vision would have been blurred by envy of the writers in these pages for achieving what I wasn't and resentment of them for not admitting how much work a more-with-less ethic may require. The 1980 *Living More with Less* sat mutely on my bookshelf, and I avoided cracking its aging spine.

13

A few things have changed since then. I'm realizing that *Living More with Less* is about as close to a theology book as it is a home economics manual (see chapter 4), and that it holds joy and challenge for both women and men, no matter their roles. I still worry about the crazy-making potential of trying to implement all the ideas offered in this volume, and I sometimes feel depleted by guilt over all that I'm *not* doing, rather than energized by joy at the little that I *am*. But I'm learning grace toward myself and others, as well as learning to trust that the momentum of my small actions can carry me toward larger ones.

I still wonder: Is the burgeoning interest in living more with less cheapening it into a fad—or enlarging it exactly the way Doris Janzen Longacre would have hoped? Now that "more with less" has become a slogan for everything from Proctor and Gamble coupon books to corporate downsizing, how do we keep it tethered to faith and authentic concern for the poor and for the planet? And speaking of the poor and the planet: are the concerns of both always aligned, and what's the best course of action when they're not? How do we avoid oversimplifying the complicated economic and ecological realities facing all of us? And how can we pursue more-with-less ideals without settling into self-castigation, smugness, or doomsday sermonizing?

Perhaps there are no good answers to such questions. But perhaps thirty years from now we'll have found a few.

A few notes: Doris Janzen Longacre's chapters have been edited for space and clarity. Occasional sidebars offer updated information to accompany the 1980 writings. Entries from the 1980 edition that appear in part 3 are indicated by the date in parentheses at the end of the entry.

We have added two chapters ("Gardens, Farms, and Markets" and "Technology and Media") and expanded several others. We have not, however, attempted to follow up on the lives or locations of the contributors whose submissions to the 1980 edition are included here. It is likely that many have moved during the past thirty years and that several have passed away. We include, for example, an entry from Peter Dyck, a beloved storyteller and hero of peace and relief work who died January 4, 2010. His entry, for those who knew him, offers a poignant opportunity to hear Peter's distinctive voice surrounded by the voices of the living contributors. Additionally, some contributors to the 1980 volume might live differently now than they did in 1980. Were they to submit updated entries, they may write in very different ways. Yet that fact does not render their words irrelevant or obsolete. Rather, we can allow the stories from thirty years ago to remind us of how much has changed—and how little.

Ultimately, distinguishing between new and old material as you read is not vital. Instead, allow the voices from the past and from the present to merge into a great cloud of witnesses. The path to a sustainable, compassionate life is lovely but rugged, and a cloud of witnesses can buoy you up and cheer you on.

Part 1
The Legacy of *Living More with Less*

1

Living More with Less in Retrospect

Rachel Waltner Goossen

● ●

In early 1978, Doris Janzen Longacre, an advocate for the world's hungry, envisioned a new project that she called "More-With-Less II." Writing to her friend William Snyder, the executive secretary of Mennonite Central Committee (MCC), a worldwide ministry of Anabaptist churches, Longacre noted,

> Having gained the attention of many people with a book on food, we have an opportunity to make another statement. What may be said next? What assets do we have for learning to handle food, energy and other resources so that more may share their values? The thesis of the book here proposed is that the poor, or those living on less, or those very people we try to help, are also a resource for helping us.[1]

The "book on food" she was referring to was the *More-with-Less Cookbook*, which since its publication two years earlier had been a best seller for the Mennonite publisher Herald Press. As part of MCC's effort to address world hunger—including an appeal to its Canadian and U.S. constituents to reduce their food consumption by 10 percent—the book offered healthy, economical recipes submitted by international service workers and others. With nearly 200,000 copies in print at that time, the cookbook—prized for its creative approach to food, thrift, hospitality, and concern for others—was generating royalties for MCC and fostering wide interest in Christian stewardship of food resources.[2]

"So many things I would still like to say"

As the author of the *More-with-Less Cookbook*, Doris had drawn
on her home economics training as well as international experiences with her husband, Paul, with whom she had served with MCC
in Vietnam from 1964 to 1967 and Indonesia from 1971 to 1972.
After the cookbook appeared in 1976, the Longacres and their two
young daughters moved to Manhattan, Kansas, so they could pursue graduate work. While there, Doris was diagnosed with cancer,
and the Longacres terminated their studies and moved back to
Akron, Pennsylvania, where they had previously lived.

In the spring of 1978, reflecting on these life-changing events
in a sermon to her congregation, Akron Mennonite Church,
Longacre framed her family's experiences in theological terms:
"Actually, we ended up going to two schools. One of these was
Kansas State University. The other was a school with a much more
difficult curriculum—the school for finding God's presence in the
experience of having cancer."[3] At around the same time, she told a
friend, "It is, of course, difficult to think that I may be nearing the
end of my life. I am hoping and praying that I may be granted a
few more years with family and to do some more writing. I have so
many things I would still like to say to the churches."[4]

As it turned out, she would have just enough time. Before
her death in 1979 at the age of thirty-nine, Longacre had nearly
completed the manuscript of *Living More with Less*. Her husband,
to whom she had dedicated the volume, readied it for publication with the help of Pat Hostetter Martin, Margaret Reimer, and
Gayle Gerber Koontz. Herald Press released it in 1980. Paul, who
served as MCC's hunger concerns secretary, noted in the preface
the symbolism of the need for others to complete Doris's work,
since "no one person is a final expert on the subject. We need
help from each other."[5] In subsequent interviews, he reiterated
this theme: "Doris said—and I'll say the same—we're not experts.
Many people live more responsibly than we do, and are further
along in conservation efforts than we are."[6]

Practical help for changing habits

In her speeches and writings, Longacre resisted the term *lifestyle*, which she viewed as too faddish; she offered guidance for people to change their habits of daily living by paying attention to what she called "life standards" (see chapters 4–9). Her articulation of these ideas received crucial early support from colleagues at MCC, including Edgar Stoesz, associate executive secretary for overseas services, who encouraged her to think about the long-term influence of the project she was embarking on: "A book is flexible. It has staying power. It is a good way for you to influence a large number of people in a wide variety of circumstances."[7] These were prescient words, particularly given the urgency with which Longacre pursued her work.

As she began gathering materials for the book, Longacre noted that her goal was to "give practical, 'how-to' help to North American Christians who genuinely desire to live more interdependently with the poor" and to "put into understandable, tangible forms those frequent references from cross-cultural workers that 'I learned more than I taught, I received more than I gave.'"[8] She developed an eighteen-month plan to work part time on the book, as health permitted, with mornings writing at the MCC office and afternoons and evenings spent with family and friends. She introduced the volume with a biblically based rationale for sustainable living (see chapter 3), and her writing reflects a deeply spiritual orientation to both the prophetic traditions of the Old Testament and the social and economic justice concerns of Jesus and his disciples.

Longacre solicited counsel from MCC associates on several continents as she drafted the book. For example, to Luis Correa, who served a Colombian Mennonite relief agency in Bogotá, she wrote, "I am particularly interested in your criticism on the chapters 'Do Justice' and 'Learn from the World Community.' This is where I discuss our relationship as wealthy North American Christians to less-affluent people in other countries. Do you approve of the theology? The terminology? The tone?"[9]

As she worked on the manuscript, Longacre replicated the process of amassing readers' ideas that had worked so well with the *More-with-Less Cookbook*. As she explained to her MCC colleagues,

> The process of contributing to a book is as important for many as reading it later. We plan to explain the book's message and call for materials through church papers. Returned MCCers, VSers [Voluntary Service workers], missionaries, exchange students and exchange visitors and their hosts are target contributors. However, the process will allow almost anyone who turns a learning ear to the poor and who wants to conserve resources to contribute.[10]

While soliciting responses from readers of Mennonite and Brethren in Christ publications throughout 1978, Longacre received mixed responses, including from some contributors who worried that acquaintances might interpret their published entries as hypocritical, given inconsistencies in their living habits. She assured them that "reporting a decision which involves money, energy use and spiritual values is tough. . . . But I'm hoping for many responses because I know that people daily grapple with these questions and find solutions."[11] Within a year, she had received more than enough material from hundreds of contributors.[12] Later, one reviewer would write that the result was a "sort of gigantic brainstorming session captured on paper with something for everyone."[13]

Off the press, into reviews

What was the book's immediate impact? When it came off the press, many Canadians and U.S. citizens had experienced the 1970s as a time of disillusionment characterized by the Vietnam War, the political turbulence of the Watergate scandal, problems with runaway inflation in both Canada and the United States, an energy crisis, and continuing political tensions over civil rights for African Americans and Native peoples. All the while, poverty and world hunger remained pressing problems.

MCC Executive Secretary William Snyder noted in 1979 that, given this context, "efforts [to address food issues through the

Longacres' assignments] have been warmly received by churches within and outside of MCC's constituency."[14] In this milieu, *Living More with Less* called for Christians to free themselves from greed, acquisitiveness, and waste. Longacre caught a wave of receptive readers, many of them subscribers to Mennonite and Brethren in Christ periodicals. Calls to simplify one's life and to scale back were part of the times, and with this volume, Longacre had identified concerns that would resonate with readers.[15]

David Anderson, a religion writer for United Press International, noted in a review of *Living More with Less* that "biblical justice, sometimes explicitly, often implied, winds itself like a thread" throughout the work. As MCC officials noted at the time, Anderson "distinguished Longacre's concern for 'simple living' from the faddishness of those who 'turned inward' during the last decade in an anti-urban nostalgia for the rural past."[16]

Not all readers were as positive. One critic wrote to the *Christian Herald* that she regretted the magazine's promotion of the new volume, since "I do not doubt the sincerity of the simplicity buffs . . . but an obsession with poverty is just as idolatrous as an obsession with wealth."[17] In a more substantive critique, Rudolf Dyck of Winnipeg declared in the *Festival Quarterly*, "[Longacre's] examples of simple living will not be attractive to many. They go back in time, appear old-fashioned. . . . Longacre doesn't hold out much hope for the science oriented person."[18]

On the whole, however, *Living More with Less* found a largely appreciative audience. Marketed to both Christian and secular publications—including the *Saturday Evening Post*—it was reviewed in more than six dozen print sources, ranging from the mainline Protestant standard-bearer *The Christian Century* (whose editors encouraged readers to buy the book) to papers in Canada, Australia, the Netherlands, and Great Britain. "St. Francis of Assisi would love this book. . . . Learn how to thumb your nose at rampant consumerism, and how to 'give up' all kinds of superfluous and painful anxieties," advised one reviewer.[19]

Although reviews appeared in some conservative women's magazines, Longacre had never meant to reach a predominantly female audience. A wide potential readership of men and women alike became acquainted with the book through reviews in daily news sources such as the *Wichita Eagle-Beacon* and through the denominational publications of Catholics, Southern Baptists, Lutherans, Methodists, Presbyterians, and others.[20]

A new generation of readers

Within twelve months of its initial appearance, 90,000 copies were in circulation, and *Living More with Less* was on its third printing. Delores Histand Friesen wrote a study guide to accompany the book, which was used by small groups, retreat leaders, and Sunday school teachers. Three decades later, by 2010, sales had reached 115,000 copies, including a Japanese translation completed in 1987. Over the past decade, readers of the book have posted dozens of online reviews of *Living More with Less* on Amazon.com and other sites. As new readers encounter the book, the impact of *Living More with Less* is ongoing.

In 2000, the magazine *The Mennonite* named Doris Janzen Longacre one of the most influential Mennonites of the twentieth century, recognizing that her books encouraged millions of people to engage the seemingly intractable problems of hunger, economic disparity, and overconsumption of resources. "The books reinforced discipleship for many people," the editors noted, "while introducing countless non-Mennonites to the faith."[21] With nearly 860,000 copies of the perennial favorite *More-with-Less Cookbook* sold by 2010, including British and German editions and a twenty-fifth anniversary edition, the influence of Longacre's books spreads to a new generation of readers seeking resources for sustainable living.

2

You Wrote What You Lived: A Letter to My Mother

Cara Longacre Hurst with Marta van Zanten, Paul Longacre, and Nancy Heisey

● ●

om, I think you would be honored to know that this anniversary edition of *Living More with Less* is being published. More than thirty years after you wrote them, your words are still speaking. As I've reread your writings, I have become more aware of your thoughts, your struggles, your joys, and your growing mindfulness of God's presence that you so deeply desired. Self-aware and reflective, you were foremost a seeker of beauty, attuned to your daily surroundings and most loving and appreciative of your family and community.

As you witnessed hunger in Vietnam and Indonesia, your creativity combined with your deep compassion for those with less. I understand now that it was your growing mindfulness and compassion that grounded this book. You declared on April 26, 1979, "Writing this book is my ministry." You wrote what you lived.

From its start, you desired to "write stories of hope, love, and goodness." I know joy and unexpected freedom were your own experiences of living more with less. You wanted to inspire others to live creatively and to find fresh ways of making healthy choices for themselves and this planet. You definitely intended that living more with less be a joy, not a burden: a guilt-free way of choosing life.

Kevin and I, along with your granddaughters Anika and Claire, continue to find inspiration in various ways of living more with less. And we are still seeking. You wrote on June 6, 1979, "I dream of living somewhere where every day I could see open space—especially wooded hills. And where I could walk in meadows and woods." As I live out your dream in the river hills of Lancaster County, Pennsylvania, I am especially inspired by the beauty and light in the trees and hills that I ponder while painting in our backyard. As a family, we find that growing vegetables and fruit, with the care and daily observation they require, has nurtured our spirits as well as our stomachs. The garden is a source of entertainment and investigation for our girls. They report on the nature of wheel bugs, the daily status of our ripening strawberries, or the whereabouts of our latest groundhog threats.

Marta, Erwin, and granddaughter Ruby enjoy living in a community in which the school, grocery stores, businesses, and restaurants are all within easy walking or biking distance. Marta has found her daily walks to public transportation pleasurable and beneficial. Rather than lapsing into a mindset of rushing to her work, she takes in the beauty of neighbors' flower beds and gardens, all the while valuing the daily exercise.

My father, Paul, and my stepmother, Nancy, in Harrisonburg, Virginia, continue to be grateful for your gift of finding joy and celebration in seeking a simpler way of living. Just as you found inspiration in the more-with-less models of your parents, Helene and John Janzen, so too have Paul and Nancy appreciated the approaches and choices of their Longacre and Heisey parents. The Great Depression thrust upon their parents some of their practices of simplicity, but they did not abandon these values when greater affluence came their way.

In recent years, Paul and Nancy have sought to take seriously the cost of the energy they use to travel. Their voluntary gas tax group meets for potlucks and conversation about the miles they've traveled. They assess themselves a tax per gallon and pool the money to contribute to local and international projects designed to care for creation and strengthen community. As they drive back and forth to Pennsylvania to visit family and to care for a small orchard on Paul's brother's farm, Paul and Nancy have found this voluntary tax to be life-giving.

In observing and experiencing the many changes in our world since *Living More with Less* was published thirty years ago, I like to think of our family as seekers. We've absorbed many of the practices of our parents over the years. And in our own small ways we are discovering new opportunities to do justice, learn from the world community, nurture people, cherish the natural order, and nonconform freely. Most importantly, we can involve your grandchildren in celebrating these old and new discoveries as they grow and face the environmental and social challenges of their generation. Mom, as we listen to your invitation to live more with less echoing to us over the years, we share your longing to be mindful of God's presence, guiding us as we find our way.

3
Introduction

Doris Janzen Longacre

● ●

This is a book for people who know something is wrong with the way Canadians and U.S. citizens live and are ready to talk about change. This is a book about rediscovering what is good and true. This is a book about beauty, healing, and hope, a book about getting more, not less.

Volumes can be written on our unbelievable carelessness with God's gifts. We not only neglect the poor, for whom the gospel is to be good news—we exploit them. We nurture purses, professions, cars, and houses more than people. We relinquish freedom and personal productivity in favor of dull conformity. We spoil nature, the only home we have. We don't look beyond predictable, familiar voices for help. We fail to fortify each other in solid communities.

Truth comes only to those who must have it, who want it badly enough. And the gifts of healing come only to those willing to change. Jesus had his demands even for the blind and leprous: *Go, wash in the pool of Siloam. Show yourself to the priest. Sin no more.* He had larger demands for the rich: *Sell all and come.*

There is beauty, but only in the exercise of discipline and the control of waste. Our lives can be redeemed, but only with lasting commitment to live under God's judgment and grace. More with less, then, is no prepackaged way to "simplify your lifestyle." There is no fast, easy way. We can rehearse background facts, share experience, and distill standards to guide future decisions, as this book attempts to do. We can attend workshops and conferences, draw on still more experience, and collect a helpful library. But when we close the books and come home from the discussion, one voice still speaks in the silence. For Christians it is the call to obedience. Without answering that voice, and answering again and again, there is no new way to live.

Styles and standards

A book about lifestyles sounds more appealing than one about life standards. *Style* bears the stamp of the new, the distinctive, the fun. This book makes only limited use of *lifestyle*. *Life standard* more aptly describes a way of life characterized by timeless values and commitments. I admit that *standard* is rather lackluster. It doesn't have the zip and zing of *lifestyle*, and has little to do with the latest models and fads, with chrome on cars or the color of bed sheets. *Standard* is a word that fits a way of life governed by more than fleeting taste. It is permanent and firm without being as tight as *rules*.

Part 2 of this book discusses five life standards. These emerged from the materials that make up part 3: stories about and materials submitted by many people struggling to live faithfully and simply.[1]

In reality these standards cannot be easily separated. To number and analyze that by which we live does it some violence. Following and obeying Jesus Christ is never a list of responsibilities. It is a perpetual response to the living God. Standards are divided and listed here only for ease in handling concepts. My hope is that after you absorb what's in this book, the separate standards will melt together for you into a solid, integrated way of living.

Living by standards sounds like regulation, reminiscent of a private-school catalog that spells out what you dare and dare not do if you want to remain on campus. But it need not mean holding to rigid rules that squeeze and pinch us.

More with less means that by using less we actually gain more for ourselves. The opening page of the *More-with-Less Cookbook* reads, "Put dismal thoughts aside . . . because this book is not about cutting back. This book is about living joyfully, richly, and

creatively."[2] *Living More with Less* is built on the same philosophy.
So how does talk of the discipline of living by standards really fit?

I can answer only this way. The trouble with simple living is
that, though it can be joyful, rich, and creative, it isn't simple. Less
of what? For more of what? And for whom? Every day the average
tradesperson or homekeeper makes a hundred small decisions that,
if you stop to think about what causes what, become maddeningly
complex. This book is unapologetically about such small decisions.
For example:

*Oh, not enough flour! I've got to take the car and run to the store.
No, I'll walk . . . I need the exercise . . . it's only a mile. But I need
the flour now. The bread must start rising or it won't be done in time.
I could buy the bread, but I do want to welcome this family to our
neighborhood with a nice meal . . . they seem lonely . . . the rest of
my meal is rather plain. I'll just grab my purse and go before Ann gets
home from kindergarten . . . oh, there's hardly time!*

*Look, why am I always in a hurry? I've got to slow down, take
more time to think, see the clouds, listen to Ann . . . and walking saves
gasoline, energy. Everybody jumping into a car for simple errands
is one reason we get that statistic . . . what is it . . . 6 percent of the
world's population uses 40 percent of the resources. That way of living
makes other people poor.*

*But the flour. I need it. Now, if the bike were here . . . but Bill
took it to work. What I really ought to have is another bicycle just for
my quick trips. But bikes cost plenty. The flour! If my neighbor were
home I could borrow it . . . but she never has whole wheat anyway.
We want to eat more whole grains. . . . I've got to take the car. No way
out.*

*Wait. Back up. I don't have to make bread today. That can wait
until I shop for the week . . . there's enough flour here for that good
muffin recipe. And, lucky me, I don't have to start that until five
o'clock. Ann and I can take a walk. . . .*

One tiny decision. Nothing that will change the world. But it's
the kind of decision that forms the building blocks of our lives. It's
the sort of decision on which we often falter if we slide unthink-
ingly into the groove of our society. More-with-less standards don't
come naturally right now in the United States and Canada.

Do justice. Cherish the natural order. Nurture people. These and other standards must become second nature for Christians, part of the heredity of our new birth. Many decisions still will be hard. But strong standards rooted in commitment to Christ offer hope for better choices.

The testimonies

Part 3 is a glimpse into the experience of people trying to live by standards of simplicity. The entries in this section invite you to an old-fashioned testimony meeting. Christian response in personal life to world poverty and hunger is the subject, with the voices in print instead of sound. The voices you will hear come largely from the Anabaptist-Mennonite tradition. This focus on Anabaptists, one way of limiting the size of the "meeting," is not meant to imply that we have the answer to more-with-less living.

Testifying isn't easy. I sat in many testimony meetings as a child and still occasionally hear our pastor call for words from the congregation. If I think I should speak, my palms still perspire and my knees tremble. Will people think my ideas foolish? Will they trust my experience? Is my life ever consistent enough that I dare open my mouth publicly? What I have to say is nothing new anyway!

These are the same feelings expressed by those who wrote (and sometimes refused to write) for this book. Entries began in humble tones, often with some version of "undoubtedly you already have these ideas. They may not be usable anyway, but I'll share them just in case." Postscripts frequently read, "I know we haven't arrived" or "I know my living isn't really consistent." People everywhere confided that they *did* have ideas but were afraid others might think them either proud or ridiculous. Some entries came only with firm promises from me that the book would clearly make this statement: no contributor believes his or her idea is right for every reader.

For help, let's look at what a testimony meeting tries to do. Such a meeting does not report how God always acts or how people always respond. It never assumes common experience— otherwise there would be no point at all in holding it. A testimony meeting expects that God gives unique skills and experiences to people and communities, and that sharing stories will strengthen everyone who hears. A testimony meeting believes in "many gifts, one Spirit." Accept in that framework what individuals offer through this book.

I believe the standards discussed here are all rooted in Scripture. That's why the list doesn't begin with "study the Bible." On the other hand, this book is not a thorough biblical study. Here the Bible is used as it traditionally has been used at testimony meetings—with familiarity and love, but with no attempt to look at all passages relevant to a subject. My writing and the entries from others lift up certain texts to show how they motivate action, connect with a story, or illuminate experience.

Part 2
The Life Standards

4
The Five Life Standards: Theology and Household Code

Malinda Elizabeth Berry

• •

t happened again. For the second time, I was minding my own business when five phrases appearing in print caught my attention: *Do justice. Learn from the world community. Nurture people. Cherish the natural order. Nonconform freely.*

It first happened in 2002, when I noticed these phrases on a poster in a Syracuse Cultural Workers' "Tools for Change" catalog. Now, as I perused books on a giveaway table at the seminary where I teach, I saw them again, in a book about simple family celebrations. I snapped it up.

Readers familiar with the 1980 version of *Living More with Less* will recognize these phrases as the five life standards Doris Janzen Longacre developed. These five life standards chart a path of Christian discipleship that seriously *and* joyfully combines faith and action. (Longacre's original essays on each of the five life standards, as well as response essays by contemporary Anabaptists, appear as chapters 5–9.) Doris knew that being a Christian bathed in the waters of Anabaptism means living with what she called "holy frustration." In the *More-with-Less Cookbook*, which was published four years before *Living More with Less*, Longacre described this emotion by summing up the main question many of her contemporaries were asking in the face of the food and fuel crises of the 1970s: "'We want to use less,' they say. 'How do we begin? How do we maintain motivation in our affluent society?'"[1] Holy frustration stands at the center of what we can think of as a more-with-less theology created by the five life standards.

A theology?

What may strike some readers as a leap from the five standards to a theology is really a small step. Theology is the formal name we give to our talk about God. A more-with-less theology, then, is the way we verbalize the connections we make between God's unified presence in the universe and our response to God as we live within the world. More-with-less theology gives special attention to the ways that economic patterns and systems help or hurt this response to God and all that is around us.

Our English term *economic* comes from the Greek roots *oikos* ("house") and *nomos* ("custom" or "law"). Together they form the word *oikonomia*, which refers to the customs and management of households—what we might think of as "homemaking."[2] In other words, doing justice, learning from the world community, nurturing people, cherishing the natural order, and nonconforming freely are part of our "household code" as Christians. In this age of globalization, when our world is both a vibrant village marketplace and a groaning ecosystem, such a household code is more necessary than ever.

This five-part household code invites us to think about *home* in two ways: earth as our planetary home, and the spiritual and physical homes we build as human beings. By understanding home as something that is ecological, spiritual, and physical, more-with-less theology draws on the biblical tradition that speaks of the ways that human beings dwell with and in God.[3] From theory to belief to form, God gives us homes, and how we make them matters.

When I was in high school, a bumper sticker that my mother stuck on one of the thresholds of our house daily reminded me that "world peace begins at home." This was her way of reminding us that the Prince of Peace was ultimately in charge of household management at 19736 Riverview Drive. I am grateful for the more-with-less memories I carry with me from that home:

smelling granola roasting in the oven, kneading food coloring into warm batches of homemade play dough, setting personalized cloth napkins at everyone's place around the dinner table, and understanding that jars of homemade tomato sauce are not simply symbols of thrift.

The One who dines at our tables

Cooking and seasoning homegrown tomatoes, turning them to sauce, filling quart and pint jars with the red liquid, processing them, and listening to them pop as they cool on the countertop— these acts connect us to the productive cycles of life and offer satisfaction in the communal work that feeds our households. These jars of sauce are not simple because they are quick and easy; they are simple because they are authentic. What you see is what you put into it: love and hope for a world where everyone's needs are sustainably and joyfully met.

As you read Doris Janzen Longacre's words and the words of those who join her in this tradition of Anabaptism, I invite you to think of her as a theologian as well as a home economist. Why? Because Longacre, trained in the art and science of household management, practiced her profession in a way that recalls the biblical imagery of the One who lives with us in our homes, dines at our tables, and, in turn, brings us to a table set simply with bread and a cup.

ECONOMICS FROM "OIKOS" & "NOMOS" = "HOMEMAKING"

5

Do Justice

Doris Janzen Longacre

● ●

bertha Beachy, a longtime missionary in East Africa, made this observation: "North Americans find it very hard to believe that their wealthy ways of living affect poor people on other continents. But in Africa, people are fully convinced that North Americans and their actions strongly influence their lives."

We're skilled at screening out and arguing away this connection. We don't believe it, but the poor do. Marie Moyer, a missionary in India, told this story:

> Years ago I was studying the Hindi language with my teacher, Panditji. I especially remember one lesson. It was Christmastime and as I awaited the arrival of Panditji, I quickly opened stacks of delightful cards, discarding the envelopes in the wastebasket. When Panditji entered the room, he sat down soberly and studied the situation. Then he solemnly scolded me in perfect English with these words, "The reverberation of this wasteful act will be felt around the world."

> Stunned, I asked, "What do you mean, Panditji?" "Those envelopes," he said, pointing to the wastebasket. "You could write on the inside of them."

> Chagrined, I apologized and began taking them out of the basket. He carefully helped me, almost caressing each one. For every Hindi lesson he taught thereafter, I took notes on the back

of an envelope. Our class also began sharing envelopes with his growing family, for he could not afford tablets for his children. Today I still carefully save paper in my home and office.

No connection

A typical U.S. or Canadian reaction to that story, however, is probably not to start saving paper. It's likely to be one of these two statements: "Okay, how? How does throwing out blank-on-one-side paper affect people on the other side of the globe? I don't see the connection." Or it may be, "What you say just makes me feel guilty. It's not good to raise all this guilt. We don't know what to do with it."

Let's look at the first reaction. I could now present pages of facts, statistics, and graphs to make a case for the link. This material would show, first, that Canada and the United States actually import a great many of the resources that underpin our way of life. And we import many of those resources at low prices from economically impoverished countries while sending back ever higher-priced manufactured goods. Rich countries like Canada and the United States control the terms of those exchanges.

• •

Complicated enough?

Global trade in the twenty-first century is nothing if not complex, say two professors of economics at Mennonite universities. The rising number of exports of once-lucrative commodities (such as tea and sugar) by low-income countries has continued to drive down prices, says Jim Leaman, associate professor of business and economics at Eastern Mennonite University in Harrisonburg, Virginia. "Thirty years ago, when *Living More with Less* was first published, it might have cost Tanzania thirty tons of sugar to buy one tractor," he says. "Today it might cost 250 tons of sugar to buy that same tractor." Agricultural subsidies in the United States and other wealthy countries also now disadvantage local producers in the Global South, who can't compete against the engineered low prices of the food streaming into their market.

What about the countless cheap manufactured products that Canada and the United States now import from countries in the Global South? Simply boycotting companies like Nike—often offered as a solution—isn't necessarily the answer, according to Leaman. Such a boycott "may actually hurt the Bangladeshi who would rather work for that low wage than nothing at all, and who might be supporting an entire family with it." Advocacy for better working conditions for laborers is a better avenue, says Bluffton (Ohio) University assistant professor of economics Jonathan Andreas. "Political pressure by consumers on multinationals like Nike and Wal-mart can be effective at helping them be better world citizens and can help improve the labor standards of their suppliers." Unfortunately, even that gets complicated, Andreas admits: "How can we influence BP to be a good corporate citizen in Uzbekistan when we can't even get them to behave in our own backyard?"

• • • • • • • • • • • • • •

Current figures

World military spending is now over $4 billion a day. In 2008, the United States ranked first in arms transfer agreements with developing nations, making $30 billion worth of such agreements, which represents 70 percent of the total trade.[1]

And just in case it's *still* not complex enough: what is economically beneficial to poor countries might be spiritually harmful to consumers themselves—not to mention ecologically harmful for all countries involved. "When we purchase products from low-income countries, we're benefiting their economies in a macro sense," says Leaman. "But when we consume at high levels, we're using up resources—often nonrenewable ones—and that is detrimental to the environment."

Second, we must talk about money, minerals, fuel, and human work hours wasted on the arms race, of which the United States is world leader and from which Canada also profits. World military spending is now over one billion dollars a day, up more than 60 percent since 1960, even after allowing for inflation. Exports of weapons to low-income countries have quadrupled since 1960.

Third, we must discuss how giant corporations, neither based in nor controlled by any one country, seize a kind of global power by using the land and labor of the poor to sell products to the rich. The human family is only beginning to understand this new power and to wonder how to deal with it.

To really understand all this is to be awed and even terrified by the complexity of the connections. But we can never conclude that they don't exist. Part of the terror of the situation is that the connections are so tightly strung.

Not guilty

Refusing to accept a connection is one way to back off. Believing it but refusing to accept guilt is another.

"Let's just be careful we don't raise too much guilt," says a world-hunger conference planner. "But you made us feel so guilty

• •

Connections between living patterns and poverty

The witness of Christians around the world about how our living patterns affect world hunger confirms these connections between Canadian and U.S. living patterns and poverty. Doris Janzen Longacre included several examples in the 1980 version; here are some updated ones.

Jon Nofziger of Abbotsford, British Columbia, writes that Canadian mining companies—some of which even appear in "socially responsible" or "ethical" mutual funds—"contribute to the displacement of people, environmental degradation, human rights violations, contamination of water supplies, violence, and armed conflict." He writes that the Christian Council of Tanzania invited Mennonite Central Committee staff and regional partners to visit villages in 2010 to see the detrimental effects of large-scale mining

companies. "Although the conflict is multi-layered," he writes, "a complicating factor at one Canadian-owned mine is the displacement of local villagers and their artisanal mining operations, resulting in a loss of employment and income base."

Samia Khoury, a member of the MCC Palestine advisory committee, writes, "The age of luxury and comfort has created a set pattern of life in countries such as the United States and Canada, where it has become very difficult to dismantle economic and social structures. To retain their popularity, politicians have been consolidating these structures. As a result, the world is faced with a situation where superpowers continue to impose their hegemony over other people and to create havoc in those countries instead of addressing issues of poverty."

about this coffee break," says the food committee chairperson, passing out glazed doughnuts in the middle of the meeting. "I guess we just go out of here feeling guilty," remarks the recreational vehicle manufacturer to his colleague on his way out of the conference.

One thing is sure. How-to books on pop psychology do not generally look fondly upon feeling guilty or raising those feelings in anyone else. But what if you *are* guilty?

Is there no damage to the psyche of one who clearly recognizes wrong in specific actions but refuses to accept responsibility? Can we squash down the guilt and blame it on another? Statements like "This meeting [or this book or that person or the poor of the world] makes me feel guilty" need careful scrutiny. Where does the guilt come from? From those who are poor? That's blaming the victim. From those who shared the information? Or from living the way we do?

Certainly there are those who carry guilt out of its useful function and into paralyzing complexes. But to live as most of us do in the United States and Canada, then to study world poverty and our role in it, and to come away without seeing a need for forgiveness and change—that is unthinkable.

To live as most of us do . . .

If everyone on the planet lived like Canadians, we would need 4.3 earths to support us. If everyone lived like U.S. residents, we would need 5.3.[2]

Do justice must become a standard for living by which Christians make choices. Our guilt must resolve itself into a lasting attentiveness. This means being mindful, conscious, and aware, so that never again can we make a decision about buying and using without thinking of the poor. They lurk in the new-car lot and behind the rack of fall outfits. They sit beside you in the restaurant and wait for you in the voting booth.

This way of responding has a simplicity about it that contrasts with the arguments usually called upon when someone asks, "Does it do any good if I conserve?" Intricate reasoning on the causes and solutions of world hunger has its place. But there are times when the only answer is, "Because they have little, I try to take less."

Remember the story of the Indian teacher who couldn't watch his American student waste paper without honestly exposing his feelings. The point is not only that a wasted envelope reverberates around the world—or how in reality that can happen. The point is that the student heard wasted envelopes reverberate in the soul of her teacher who lacked paper. And she could never be the same.

To make *do justice* a standard is to live by both reason and compassion. The classic, universal truths of the Old and New Testaments make excuses impossible: "He has told you, O mortal, what is good; and what does the Lord require of you but to do justice, and to love kindness, and to walk humbly with your God?" (Mic 6:8). "How does God's love abide in anyone who has the world's goods and sees a brother or sister in need and yet refuses help?" (1 John 3:17).

HOW THE STORIES WE HEAR ABOUT POVERTY CAN CHANGE OUR DECISIONS GOING FORWARD

Simple living isn't enough

I don't apologize for the seeming unimportance of the individual entries that make up this book. All of us should walk more, save hot water, use less aluminum foil. These are small ideas, small acts. But they offer a realistic place to start. Doing justice, however, demands much more. The message here is mainly one of first steps. This collection is about putting our own houses in order. Yet in that process we invariably move on to economic and political issues.

Actually, the two realms—conserving resources at home and taking on economic and political issues—are as inseparable as the yolk and white of a scrambled egg. It never works to say, "I'll stop using paper towels and driving a big car, but I won't take this world hunger thing past my own doorpost." Once an egg yolk breaks into the white, there's no way to remove every tiny gold fleck. Similarly, once you walk into a supermarket or pull up to a gas pump, you *are* part of the economic and political sphere.

Certainly your influence is small. But whether you conserve or waste, it is real. *Many* people using or not using affects things in a *big* way. Gathering up the fragments of our waste—recycling, conserving, sharing—is a logical and authentic beginning. Such actions are the firstfruits of the harvest of justice. They are the promise of more to come.

The fact is that living by the standard *do justice* will draw us more deeply into economics and politics. And for the sake of the poor and hungry, that's good. Solutions for their needs will come primarily through economic and political change.

● ●

Large-scale actions needed

What actions on the international economic and political scene are most needed to alleviate poverty and hunger? Doris Janzen Longacre drew on the ideas of Wayne Nafziger, an economist, and Delton Franz, an MCC staff person in Washington, D.C., to answer this question.[3] The following ideas come from Karen Klassen Harder, an economist at Bluffton (Ohio) University who has worked in five different countries and who studies resource flows between rich and poor nations.

- *Embrace the complexity.* We live in a world where many expect, if not demand, "simple" solutions to every problem. Unfortunately, the vexing problems facing humanity are complex and do not solve themselves. We must acknowledge that the twenty-first-century world is complex and respond accordingly, with patience and with focused attention. For example, in earlier times we could use the terms "first world" and "third world" to fairly accurately describe relative resource attributions. We understood that distributing financial, human, and other tangible resources from one part of the world to the other was a significant part of the development challenge. In contrast, the resource inequalities and deficits we see in the world today are not so clearly differentiated between the "haves" and the "have nots." Poverty today has many different manifestations and trajectories. Informed discussion and reasoned policy advocacy is more challenging than ever.

- *Keep the problems and desired outcomes in view.* The eight United Nations Millennium Development goals created in 2000 and endorsed by 189 nations state clearly what needs to be done. These goals describe the need to end poverty and hunger, support universal education, create gender equality, improve child and maternal health, fight HIV/AIDS, and work for environmental sustainability by the year 2015. One goal states that we will "develop a global partnership for development" between developed and developing countries. This will have implications for how we approach such things as trade policy, governance structures, aid flows, debt relief, technology transfer, and climate management. The problems and outcomes have garnered broad agreement among policy experts

in the field of poverty alleviation, although at the political level much debate remains. Our personal challenge and opportunity is to help keep the problems and desired outcomes in full public view.

- *Connect with organized responders to poverty.* This community of responders is made up of supranational agencies (such as the United Nations and World Trade Organization), national governments, and faith-based and community-based relief, development, and advocacy organizations. Each organization has a particular set of assumptions, capacities, methodologies, and interests. Our challenge is to identify the efforts that most closely resonate with our understanding of the world, while at the same time accepting the complexity associated with material poverty and hunger reduction. We should then listen to what those organizations tell us about what they are doing, how they approach their work, and the experiences they have in accomplishing their goals. Three organizations associated with Mennonites—MCC, Mennonite Economic Development Associates, and Ten Thousand Villages—facilitate resource availability for people in developing countries. Those organizations can connect us directly to those with limited access to resources and help us to respond to those needs.

Guilt: Bringing Us to Our Knees

Hugo Saucedo

I grew up in Brownsville, Texas, during the 1970s and 1980s. This was a significant time to live on the U.S.-Mexico border. Civil war was raging in Nicaragua and El Salvador, and people were seeking sanctuary anywhere they could. Sometime in the early 1980s, soon after Doris Janzen Longacre wrote *Living More with Less*, my community was faced with the daunting task of clothing, housing, and feeding thousands of people. This was the beginning of what later became known as the Sanctuary Movement. We were aided in this struggle by a group of dedicated young people we knew as "Mennonite volunteers."

These volunteers were the first white people I remember seeing. I was eight years old when they came. I wondered where they came from and why they were here. It didn't take me long to find out, because a couple of these young "golden-haired women," as we called them, came to live with me and my family. They told me that they were here to help care for the *refugiados* (refugees). They spoke Spanish and seemed very comfortable around me and my family.

But what really left a lasting impression was their talk about God calling them to do justice and show compassion to those in need. At the time I did not understand why people would come to my community to help people they didn't know and with whom they didn't seem to have anything in common. The volunteers told me stories about how our government was partially responsible for the instability in Central America and how it was their duty to come and prove to these refugees that not every American was like their government. As an eight-year-old, I did not grasp concepts of loving your neighbor or carrying each other's burdens. But as an adult, I have found that these memories have guided my life in profound ways.

As citizens of the United States and Canada, we often see conflict and disaster around the world via our televisions. We pause, say how terrible the situation is, and move on with our lives. We don't stop to think how our way of life contributes to disasters and conflicts around the world. We don't ask ourselves about the human cost of the products we consume. We don't connect the dots when a war rages in the Middle East over the oil on which we depend. We don't ask ourselves about, *Who in Vietnam made my running shoes, and are the workers able to survive on the wages they earn? How much of the one hundred dollars I paid for these shoes really goes to the person putting my shoes together?* When we do ask ourselves these questions, we often feel guilty. As Longacre reminds us, guilt can be a productive emotion; too many times, however, it paralyzes us.

To allow guilt to paralyze us is to ignore God's call for us to love one another and carry each other's burdens. I learned many things as a child growing up in south Texas. I learned that our seemingly indirect actions can actually cause very direct consequences in the lives of many in parts of the world that seem distant. Probably the most important lesson I learned, however, was that to ignore Christ's call to serve others is to be disobedient to God's plan in our lives. As followers of Christ, we are called to a high standard; thus we are held accountable for our actions.

No, guilt is not a good reason to act or react. Yet if redirected, guilt can bring us to our knees. And on our knees is a good place to start praying: for grace, for forgiveness, and for a new understanding of what God means by loving our neighbors as ourselves.

Making Do:
A Perspective from an Urban Dweller

Leonard Dow

I do not recall exactly when I first heard the now-familiar re-
frains of "living simply so that others may simply live" and "living more with less." It was sometime after I was first exposed to
the Mennonite world upon entering ninth grade at Christopher
Dock Mennonite High School in Lansdale, Pennsylvania, in
1978. I graduated from Eastern Mennonite University and later
became part of a Mennonite church in Philadelphia, where I
currently work as pastor. It is in these Anabaptist-Mennonite
communities that I have seen the genuine attempt by many
wonderful people, both in the past and the present, to live simply so that others may simply live. I have much to learn from
them. I truly appreciate Doris Janzen Longacre's willingness to
challenge the status-quo worldview of consumption and to ask
people of faith to "count the costs" of what it means to be rich
Christians in an age of hunger, as Ron Sider calls us.

Yet I would be remiss if I didn't also share my concern as
an African-American urbanite who was raised in a home that
social scientists would describe as "working poor." I have observed that the idea of living more with less has led some into
what I call the "professionalization of poverty." This term is
also used to describe the growth of the field of social work, but
I use it in a different sense. The professionalization of poverty,
as I use it, describes a dynamic whereby those who can choose
to become poor or adopt simple lifestyle measures are praised
for individual acts of self-denial such as going green, buying
organic, biking to work, or purchasing hybrid cars and energy-
efficient appliances. All of these efforts are to be commended
and are needed, but far too often these become the standard by
which attempts to "live simply" are measured and affirmed.

But what do we have to learn from those individuals and
communities whose financial circumstances demand that they

do more with less? For instance, my story as a child was more about *making do with* less than about *choosing* less. For much of my childhood, I was raised in a three-bedroom home. I shared (sometimes reluctantly) this modest living space with my grandmother, who owned the home, and my parents and four siblings. We shared with our neighbors out of necessity. We shared child-care responsibilities, weekend meals, and rides to church and to the hospital. Taking public transit or walking to work, school, or social events was the norm in my neighborhood. Using recycled or discarded materials to play childhood games (such as stick ball, Double Dutch, and kick the can) or to beautify our community (using car tires as flower planters) was routine.

My point is this: living simply, or making do, was and is still part of the daily lives of the underemployed, unemployed, and working poor in our communities. It is also part of the culture of many Mennonite urban congregations whose members live simply by making do with what they have. The working poor do not get to choose this lifestyle. Rather, life circumstances simply demand that we make do.

The difference between *choosing* to live simply and *having* to live simply is important to consider. Yet stories of making do are rarely told or written by us or for us. The professionalization of poverty can easily lead to celebrations of the individual "radical rock stars" who can choose to be poor. Focusing on these stories means we may miss out on those who come from communities of people that have been making do all our lives.

May we continue to value opportunities to listen to and affirm the voices of those who make do as we all faithfully seek to do justice, to love kindness, and to walk humbly with our God.

WE WILL LEARN MORE ABOUT LIVING SIMPLY BY TALKING WITH PEOPLE WHO HAVE HAD TO "MAKE DO" THAN FROM THOSE WHO CHOOSE POVERTY.

6

Learn from the World Community

Doris Janzen Longacre

• •

If you as a Canadian or U.S. citizen travel to an economically poor country such as Haiti or Bangladesh, your first reaction is likely to be shock. You have heard of poverty and seen it in pictures. But to find yourself face to face with hungry people jars your soul with feelings for which you are unprepared.

After a time, shock often gives way to ideas for development projects. These usually promote better education, nutrition, agriculture, sanitation, family planning, small business investments, and, increasingly, a concern that people receive just access to resources. These are the problems we believe need attention, though of course we are always in danger of misreading needs and running ahead of those actually involved.

These reactions are certainly warranted. God help us when poverty no longer shakes us into action. But how rarely we realize that persons from other countries often go through a similar thought process when living with us.

What if we asked them for help with our problems? What if the flow of development assistance became two-way? "We think we know it all, the poor peasants know nothing, and we are going to go and tell them what to do," says Romeo Maione, of the Canadian International Development Agency. "Many of the world's poor survived for thousands of years with none of our technology. That feat takes wisdom worth learning about."[1]

For we have problems too, of course. What if we became as concerned with our overdevelopment or *mal*development as we are with the *under*development of poor nations? Would they have anything to say? Could they help? Consider this list of development projects for Canada and the United States, suggested by Mennonite Central Committee visitors who have lived and worked in Canada or the United States for a year and by other international guests.

● ●

Who do these ideas come from?

The current entries were solicited from participants in the International Visitor Exchange Program (IVEP) during their 2009–2010 terms; the entries marked with "(1980)" came

from MCC Exchange Visitors in the late 1970s, participants in the precursor to IVEP. Seven projects were included in the 1980 book. Based on several submissions by current IVEPers, an eighth project has been added.

Project 1

Build an energy-efficient public transportation network among small towns and cities.

In France we drive smaller cars for sure, and we never have to drive for such long trips as Canadians and U.S. citizens do. Also, our roads are so narrow that a too-big car would just be unable to drive in half the country. Carpooling is more popular in Europe than in Canada and the United States We use public transportation much more; such transportation is not very efficient in the United States and Canada, and I miss that.—*Julie Kauffmann, France*

In my country, fewer people have cars than they do in Canada. I think people [in Canada] should jointly own cars and walk or bike when the weather is nice.—*Manivone Senyavong, Laos*

I think most of the people in the United States and Canada prefer to have a car or truck. In my idea of living simply, I would have a small car for my family. For a short distance like two or three miles, I would choose to walk or ride a bike to school or work.—*Roseta Nou, Cambodia*

Both Canada and the United States are automobile countries. It's quite inconvenient for people who do not have their own.—*Mari Nagao, Japan* (1980)

The large and comfortable cars impress me. People waste lots of energy by using them. They don't like to go ten steps— they always need their cars. They have large cars, although only one person uses them. Some older couples have two big cars. —*Barbara Walz, West Germany* (1980)

Project 2

Learn to cook simple, nutritious meals. This would include conserving meat and fats and accepting more fruits and vegetables, fewer sweets, and less waste.

I feel very sad when I see the kids in school just throwing away their food if they don't like it or if they feel full. And their teachers say, "It's okay if they don't like it!" I think that schools have to make rules about throwing away food so that students will think about their brothers and sisters around the world. Maybe cafeterias could provide a box to keep their food and then the children could take it home.—*Sidha Apsari, Indonesia*

I think Americans always cook big portions and use a lot of meat, butter, and frozen food. In my country, Indonesia, we always buy and use fresh ingredients and cook a little portion for us to eat that day. If we cook too much, we will share it with our neighbor instead of freezing it.—*Debora Supeni, Indonesia*

Americans eat lots of cookies. There is always a can with sweet things nearby—you only have to reach out and put it in your mouth. From the Austrians, Americans could learn to use more "full food" [opposite of "empty calories"] such as whole wheat, raw fruits, and vegetables.—*Sylvia Furgler, Austria* (1980)

On the tables in Canada and the United States you see more than four kinds of food.—*Elias Acosta, Dominican Republic* (1980)

Project 3

Use fewer kitchen appliances. This includes energy-saving skills in cooking such as cutting food in small pieces and cooking only a brief time, stacking kettles on a single heat source, and cooking only once a day.

I think Americans have been spoiled by many kinds of tools to help: choppers, dishwashers, even knives with electricity to cut meat or bread. In my country, Indonesia, we never have those kind of tools; we use our hands to wash, cut, or chop, which I think uses less energy.—*Debora Supeni, Indonesia*

We think Americans could live without appliances like dishwashers, electric knives, and can openers. In Paraguay we don't use as much fuel partly because we don't have so much equipment. When I was in Indiana during an unusually cold winter, we were told to cut back on fuel. One family couldn't find anywhere to cut! But some of our neighbors were able to cut back 20 percent. Why don't they do it all the time?—*Anni Weichselberger, Paraguay (1980)*

Project 4

Live without disposables, setting up community systems for repair and recycling, reducing waste.

America is a wasteful society. In every store you see disposable things. People want everything to go fast, so after using things once, they throw them away.—*Jusef Sumadi, Indonesia (1980)*

People in Canada and the United States don't care to repair things once they are out of order. There are few repair shops. I cannot imagine how TVs and refrigerators that are repairable are put into junk.—*Guillermo Abanco, Philippines (1980)*

Project 5

Plant home and community gardens.

American communities are beautiful. But instead of growing vegetables or fruits, the people prefer grass and spend money taking care of it.—*Guillermo Abanco, Philippines* (1980)

In Germany, urban apartment dwellers like us can rent garden plots situated on the outskirts of cities. For thirty years we enjoyed our plot. We often spent afternoons and evenings there. During summer, the children and I began our hike to the garden immediately after sunrise. We took our food along and sat under a small canopy if it rained. In some areas, gardeners are permitted to sell produce from these plots in the stores. —*Mary Woelke, Germany* (1980)

Project 6

Value family ties and friendship above making money.

Canadian people always seem busy with their jobs, family, property, hobbies, and technology. It is unusual if the neighbor comes over just to visit. In Indonesia we really know who is in our neighborhood. If we are building a new house, we just need two to three weeks, because a lot of volunteers from the neighborhood come and help to build the house.—*Iwan Supriyono, Indonesia*

Citizens of the United States and Canada have to work more in order to buy things. For that reason they spend less time with their families, thinking that to be comfortable is more important for the family than to give them love and time together.—*Inez Morales de Rake, Bolivia* (1980)

Project 7

Build simpler, less expensive facilities for churches.

People in Canada and the United States have more facilities for everything than one can imagine. How can they spend so much knowing there are people even in their own country who need these things?—*Luis Correa, Colombia* (1980)

When we first walked into a North American church, my friend from Indonesia said, "The cost of this carpet alone would build a beautiful church in Indonesia."—*Sammy Sacapano, Philippines* (1980)

Project 8

Pay attention to how one's desires and relationships are affected by advertising and personal media devices.

Americans base too much on advertising from TVs, magazines, and newspapers. I had a chance to visit a wealthy family; they have a big, two-story house. The house has many rooms, but only four people live in it. Each bedroom has a TV and a small refrigerator in it, and the living room has a huge TV. I asked the owner of the house, "Why do you have so many TVs in your house?" "Because we are too lazy to walk down to the living room," he answered. In my family, we have only one TV, and the whole family can watch together.—*Bounpheng Thammavong, Laos*

The emails and text messages here make the human relationships weaker. I know some people who can make a whole conversation just with text messages instead of calling or visiting each other. Dialogue is a very important thing that some people miss here. Some people, even little kids, are used to Googling anything to get any answer instead of thinking first.—*Dina Tharwat, Egypt*

Today Christian churches are solidly rooted in most economically poor countries. Our responsibility to share and tell doesn't necessarily diminish, but something new is added—the responsibility to accept and listen. If we will, we can call it a privilege, an opportunity to grow. Now we have a mirror to hold to ourselves. We have loving brothers and sisters around the world ready to wipe the fog from that mirror and tell us how they see our lives in light of God's kingdom.

To listen is more than good worldwide church politics. It's more than interesting cross-cultural exchange. The best reason for listening to and learning from the poor is that this is one way God is revealed to us. As the conference of Latin American Catholic bishops affirmed in 1979, "The testimony of a poor church can evangelize the rich."

The apostle James's well-known treatise on the relationship of rich and poor can be summarized with these central words: "Listen, my beloved brothers and sisters. Has not God chosen the poor in the world to be rich in faith and to be heirs of the kingdom that he has promised to those who love him?" (James 2:5).

Look carefully at that paragraph in James. There's no way *poor* can be spiritualized. The apostle Paul also repeatedly emphasizes the strength of weakness: "But God chose what is foolish in the world to shame the wise; God chose what is weak in the world to shame the strong" (1 Cor 1:27). In Jesus' parable of the rich man and Lazarus, even the rich man finally decided Lazarus would be the best possible missionary to his affluent brothers, although by the time he figured that out it was too late. Like us, the rich man had no ears for Lazarus while he lived; it took the next world to clarify his thinking. If we cannot learn from the poor, why should we claim to follow one born in a barn and executed with thieves?

• •

The Earth as Seen from Kaguya

Mitsuko and Yorifumi Yaguchi

The bright green globe
Came afloat beyond
The dry surface of the moon.
Looking at it,
One cannot help thinking the people there
Are living quietly, caring for each other.

No one can imagine that
They are competing against each other to

Make deadly weapons, that
They are destroying their environment, and that
If they go on like this,
The earth will be an ark without the living.[2]
—*Yorifumi Yaguchi*

When the Japanese translation of *Living More with Less* was published in 1986, Japan was in the height of a "bubble" economy. As the translator, I (Mitsuko) wrote in the postscript,

We have been enjoying a wealthy and convenient life, which we had never experienced before. Japan is now advanced technologically and economically, but we still want to advance more. We think that natural resources are limitless and that the people in the world are equally enjoying the material wealth. We have forgotten that our convenient lives have come from exploiting nature. I am afraid we will soon suffer from extreme urbanization, depopulation of rural areas, flooding of cars, too much use of agricultural chemicals, enfeeblement of soil, pollution, domestic violence, suicide, wage differences, crimes, etc.

The contemporary situation is far worse. There is more environmental pollution, more dangerous bombs have been invented and used, and more wars have occurred. The gap between the rich and the poor is widening. These things symbolize the avarice and spiritual chaos of human beings. The more we have, the more we want to have, and the less spiritual we become. Yorifumi's poem hints at endless human greed and the danger it produces.

We are seeing the effects of global warming on our climate in Hokkaido. We can feel it physically. It is said that the sky above Sapporo is polluted by the exhaust fumes from the extreme consumption of kerosene for the heating of each household. Indeed, we should not be extravagant. We should learn not to waste but to live in harmony with our environment and global sisters and brothers, many of whom suffer from material shortage. Shouldn't we seek first Jesus' kingdom and righteousness?

Recently we have seen some hopeful signs. Our government started a policy of reducing the use of fossil fuel and utilizing natural energy such as solar and wind. Auto companies are now making hybrid and solar cars. And more people are trying to stop wasting.

Akiko Aratani and Raymond Epp run an organic farm called Menno Village near Sapporo with Akiko's parents and other national and international volunteers. They don't use agricultural chemicals but natural fertilizers of their own making, utilizing the traditional farming method of Japan. They believe that their fields have been entrusted to them by God. They welcome anybody who wants to join them and enjoy working together. About seventy-five families pay a membership fee and receive biweekly deliveries of their produce. And the houses they built in this village are almost perfectly insulated. Noboru Aratani, a specialist of insulation, claims, "A time will come when the oil is gone. Real pleasantness lies not in the effort to conquer heat and coldness by human power, but in the effort to decrease the consumption of energy and respond to the characteristics of each local area."

Another example is a project to renovate a house owned by the Hokkaido Mennonite Conference. Built in the early 1950s as a missionary house by one of the first missionaries to Hokkaido, it was in a state of disrepair. Some church members insisted it needed to be torn down. But other members said that it was a gift from God and they should take good care of it. After a long discussion, they decided to repair it. It required many long hours of work, but the house was reborn! The air inside is not humid but stable and pleasant, and there is far less consumption of energy.

The 1986 Japanese translation of *Living More with Less* included several testimonies that were not included in the English version, written by Japanese Christians who lived the spirit of more with less. When the book was published, it aroused lots of interest not only from Japanese Christians but from people outside the church. As time goes on, however, the impact has lessened.

So it is that we were very pleased to hear of the thirtieth anniversary edition. We want to continue raising our voices for promoting this standard of living. We want to be witnesses to God's guidance.

Celebrating the Fruit of the *Mkhuna*

Doris Dube

Rural Matopo in Zimbabwe is the home of the *mkhuna* tree. Many people value it for its wonderful shade. It produces fruit, but most people don't care much for its taste or smell. During normal years, when there is food in abundance, its fruit ripens and falls to the ground, where animals eat it or it simply rots or dries up. In 2008, however, a year of great difficulty, the *mkhuna* tree made a difference to the lives of many. It was the one source of nourishment that held the thread of life for those who consumed it.

My husband, Jethro, and I now live in Lesotho, but in December 2008, I visited my family in Zimbabwe. Zimbabwe is experiencing one of the saddest periods of its history. The years 2007 and 2008 were particularly difficult. Officially 80 percent of the population was not employed. Even those who were employed received such low wages that most could not keep their families fed or clothed.

My friend and neighbor MaDube was among the survivors. When we arrived at the village that December, she greeted me with her usual smile and bear hug. Yet something was different.

"Wife of my brother, we nearly died this year. Heaven withheld its dew, and there was little or no harvest for most of us. We could have had many deaths, but God provided for us in an amazing way. [She pointed up.] You know, he is an amazing God."

"I know."

"I have never seen such. We survived on *mkhuna*."

"Don't tell me!"

"I'm telling you. Each day we took turns to go out and gather *mkhuna* to feed the family. In most cases we woke up early and set out to gather our day's supply. Sometimes we stayed out there the whole day, just searching for more trees to collect from. We would eat as much as we could manage, drink some water, then carry the rest home for the children and those who could not go out. It became our manna."

"How about babies and the younger children?"

"They too depended on *mkhuna*. For them we boiled the fruit and then let the children drink the 'soup' of it. We did the same for the sick."

"Day after day?"

"Day after day. God gave us our daily food like the children of Israel. Sometimes we got tired of this same food. We then boiled *chou moellier* or spinach from the garden and ate that. This was no better option, because sometimes we did not even have oil for the vegetables. In any case we got tired of these green vegetables. We felt like our intestines had probably turned green. But as I say, God is a wonderful provider. He always gave us enough for the day."

I looked at her as she said this: she had lost so much weight and looked so gaunt. She had aged many years in just one year, but her faith was very much alive.

In our years as MCC co-representatives in Zimbabwe, we never ceased to marvel at the small things of life that brought joy to individuals. The quality of life was not measured by material abundance. It was in affirming each other, looking out for one's neighbor, and celebrating small things. It was in the joy of having electricity in the classroom block so that students and teachers could have light to read after sunset. It was in the faces of students sharing a textbook, marveling at their new uniforms, or wearing shoes for the first time. It was in the hope expressed by a person affected by HIV and in the positive attitude of one facing certain death. It was in giving a ride to a stranger.

In countries like the United Kingdom, Canada, and the United States, which we have been privileged to visit, the picture is different. At peak hours the roads are often crowded with many vehicles, but unlike the sardine-packed loading we know back home, each vehicle usually only contains one or two people. Buying bread or any other commodity means choosing from a whole shelf and variety. What often broke our hearts, however, was seeing books being shredded because no one had any more use for them. Oh, to have those books for African children who share one book between six!

The difference in the distribution of earth's resources is a mystery we will never understand or have the means to change. "Our fingers are not the same size," one African saying goes. We can only rejoice in the support systems of our heritage as a people. We look out for each other.

7
Nurture People

Doris Janzen Longacre

• •

In the hard decisions of living, to choose that which *nurtures people* is another guiding standard. Nurturing is feeding, but it is more than feeding. In the musical words of invitation that open Isaiah 55, the writer begins by offering food and drink: "Ho, everyone who thirsts, come to the waters; and you that have no money, come, buy and eat!"

The call is to come to a bountifully stocked grocery store—but then the twist: *the store has no cash register.* The food is free. Now Isaiah poses his real question: "Why spend money on what is not bread, and your labor on what does not satisfy? . . . Eat what is good, and your *soul* will delight in the richest of fare" (vv. 2-3 NIV, emphasis added). Then follows a glorious vision of what can be—living by covenant and love, with peace, and culminating in redemption of the natural order. Nurturing includes all actions that bring others to this full life and growth in the kingdom of God.

Kentucky farmer and poet Wendell Berry says that to understand our own time and predicament, we can view ourselves as divided between exploitation and nurture. He describes a division not only between but also within persons.

The standard of the exploiter is efficiency; the standard of the nurturer is care. The exploiter's goal is money, profit; the nurturer's goal is health—his land's health, his own, his family's,

61

his community's, his country's. . . . The exploiter wishes to earn as much as possible by as little work as possible; the nurturer expects, certainly, to have a decent living from his work, but his characteristic wish is to work *as well* as possible. The competence of the exploiter is in organization; that of the nurturer is in order. . . . The exploiter typically serves an institution or organization; the nurturer serves land, household, community, place. The exploiter thinks in terms of numbers, quantities, "hard facts"; the nurturer in terms of character, condition, quality, kind. . . . The exploitive always involves the abuse or the perversion of nurture.[1]

To make choices that nurture each other, we must always be asking the question, What do we want for ourselves and the persons we love? That's hard enough to answer. But then comes another question: Is what we say we want borne out by our choices? For example, in the previous chapter Inez Morales de Rake from Bolivia said that Americans think comfort is more important than time for family fellowship. Few people Inez learned to know in her visit would say that. But actions define their values more clearly than words.

Work and getting out of it

One common trap in our society leads people to make choices that at first seem to nurture people but in the end erode human productivity. This is the trap of buying more and more labor-saving devices.

Work-saving inventions can be good for people. My mother shuddered every time she saw an old-fashioned washboard refinished and turned into a wall hanging, because she remembered her bleeding fingers as she struggled at age fourteen to finish the laundry piled up by eight brothers. She thanked God for Maytag.

In an earlier time, to sweat and labor to stay alive was the only option, except for a few of the elite. This is how life still orders itself for most people in poor countries.

What we forget today is that while labor-saving devices are not all bad, neither is labor. The danger now in Canada and the United States is that too many labor-saving devices will atrophy

HAVING ALL OUR NEEDS MET INSTANTLY KEEPS US FROM BEING RESOURCEFUL OR SOLVING PROBLEMS CREATIVELY.

our ability to respond resourcefully to the environment. Without electricity, people no longer know how to warm a room, cook a meal, or keep themselves happy through an evening at home. Without an engine, they have no way to raise food or to travel.

Genuine need to respond to the environment brings out a creative response in people. The Creator fashioned us in his image; therefore, to be fully human, we also must create. Our moral and physical sense should always be at work in a situation to tell us what we need and what to do about it. But when every possible need is satisfied before we even have a chance to perceive and respond to it, creativity and resourcefulness can't flourish. We become victims of the great disease of technological society—meaninglessness. This disease is not caused by bacteria, virus, or vitamin deficiency. It's caused by having nothing important to do.

Sedentary and sick

Authors of a 2001 study claim that "the American sedentary lifestyle" is linked to at least seventeen chronic diseases and other health conditions. Frank Booth, one of the authors, points to society's increasing use of labor-saving devices as one of the roots of these health problems.[2]

Besides damaging the human spirit, unquestioning dependence on machines is bad for the human body. One of the big jokes of the century is the way we as U.S. citizens and Canadians have to step out of our comfortable cars and run to stay alive. Henry Fairlie, essayist for the *Washington Post*, analyzed it like this: "The American people may be the first to make a complete dissociation between living and leisure, regarding it as wrong to have to make any physical effort in order to live, but quite right to compensate by straining themselves in exercise."[3]

LIKE PARKING CLOSE TO THE GYM.

Another way in which labor-saving devices defy nurture is that they can be offered as imitation love. A husband gives a food processor for his wife's birthday instead of regularly helping her cook. She gives him a cordless weed trimmer to clean the lawn's edge instead of joining him outdoors with a grass clipper or hoe. Together they offer bedroom television sets to their children instead of hikes or the

Kids asleep yet?

Some studies estimate that half of all children in the United States have televisions in their bedrooms. One study of third-graders put the number at 70 percent.[4]

GIVING TIME-SAVING DEVICES INSTEAD OF GIVING TIME.

opportunity to talk. They can choose to cook, garden, and relax with others and nature, or substitute machines. Which choice nurtures people?

"But we haven't got time" is the certain cry. True, the choice is ambiguous. A dishwasher may mean a family can spend time reading aloud or helping a neighbor garden. And a strong desire to do everything "by hand" may mean that a person has less time to spend with a child or grandparent. Observation tells me, however, that those with many machines are not less harried. A machine itself must be nurtured—selected, worked for, oiled, kept clean, repaired, and stored. Labor-saving devices soon become labor-making devices.

Some families, especially those in which the adults are called by vocation or necessity to work outside the home, are exploring other alternatives. Rather than buying more machines, some hire people who need or want work to help with household tasks. Neighbors and church members trade labor and goods. Others deliberately choose to work part time or to arrange for one adult to work at home to free the household to nurture others. We often forget that laughing, crying people can, by nurture, redeem an otherwise menial job.

Contentment, health, and security

After two years as a volunteer in Nepal, Willard Unruh visited his hometown and wrote these words: "Just about everyone is busy. I began wondering if Western society is overstimulated. We see a good play on Friday night that moves us deeply. Before we have a chance to digest it, there's a sports event on Saturday night, a probing sermon on Sunday morning. We get the same glassy feeling one has from driving too long a stretch at one time."[5]

As medicine for the problem Unruh describes, meditation groups and silent retreats are popping up in every community. This treatment will help, if getting to these events doesn't cause more stress than it cures. But we should also look for prevention.

How do we nurture each other with choices that offer more calm, quiet, and time to reflect on and integrate life? Nurturing people surely involves a commitment to reduce stress.

STAYING HOME AND BEING CONTENT WITH THAT → LEADS TO MORE HAPPINESS?

We have the options of going and doing and being. Our heavy energy investment provides the ever-ready car and airplane. Most people in our generation don't have to milk the cows or keep the hearth fire burning or stay home to cook for Grandpa. We can run. But accepting these options without control is destructive.

It sounds too simple, even for a book on simple living. But when we are more content to stay at home, to think, and to pray, we are better able to nurture each other.

For many people, security is the life insurance policy, the pre-paid college education, the expanding business, the comfortable retirement plan. All these are choices that seem to nurture. Yet too often these choices mean second jobs, late working hours, frequent long-distance travel, and no one at home when children come home from school. When does time spent nurturing children to be strong and responsible become the better part—better even than an ensured higher education? Might time used to build family and community ties offer more security than life insurance? Finally, how can people dependent on money for security be nurtured to depend on God? Do they need God at all?

• •

What If We Snapped Beans Together?

Dorcas Smucker

I wanted fifty quarts of green beans in the pantry before fall, and my garden had produced only ten. So on my way home from town, I stopped at a farm stand and asked for three bags of beans.

"Do you want them snapped and washed?" the owner asked me. "It's twenty-five cents a pound more." I calculated quickly—supper to cook, company coming in two days, everything busy and dusty at harvest time, and applesauce to make before the apples went bad—and sided with efficiency. "Yes, please," I said, "snapped and washed." I'd throw them in jars as soon as I got home and have them out of the pressure canner before bedtime.

When I marched into the kitchen and plopped the long,

stiff bags on the counter, Jenny, my red-headed five-year-old, took one look at them and burst into tears. "But Mom, I *like* to snap green beans! Didn't you buy *any* that I can snap for you?" My efficient reasons wilted before her disappointment, and she would not be comforted.

I like to think I have the right priorities, clearly defined and dutifully lived. People before things; family and community over self; God's kingdom over all. Stewardship and responsibility before personal pleasures; love foremost. But even well-defined priorities don't necessarily make for easy decisions.

Life cannot be divided and organized like jars on the pantry shelf—cherries, beans, applesauce, tomatoes; faith, house, family, neighbors. Jesus did not divide life into jars. His opponents liked to challenge him with stark choices: "A or B," they would say, in effect. "Which is it?" But Jesus always came up with option C, outside the narrow dimensions, the right answer to what should have been the right question. He neither pursued material things for their own sake nor rejected them as unspiritual, but used everyday things—loaves and fish, a boat on the lake, jugs of water—to minister to the people he loved and to gently integrate God's kingdom into everyday life.

I tend to think like a Pharisee. Which will it be: efficiency and a disappointed daughter, or pleasing Jenny and getting further behind in my work? Neither one is a pleasant option. Instead, I want to think like Jesus—creatively, seeing the truth in the dilemma. What if we all sat around the table, snapped the beans together, and left the dusting for another day? Or perhaps the guests could help make applesauce rather than sitting stiffly in a clean house.

It evidently wasn't meant to be easy for us, this following the Master while constantly sorting out how to minister to others without neglecting the daily tasks. God could have spelled out all the details, but he didn't. So we must conclude that the struggle itself has value, the backing up and trying again, the finding our way back after wrong turns.

Meanwhile, the beautiful winds of grace blow through our mistakes. The green-bean episode becomes a bell that rings clar-

THIS STORY IS LIKE ANY TIME EVERETT WANTS TO HELP ME WITH SOMETHING BUT I DO IT WHILE HE'S AT SCHOOL TO SAVE TIME.

ity into future decisions. It becomes a story, told and retold as
a reminder that nurture and work must not always be at odds.
This is how the spiritual and eternal flows into the physical
and temporal, and this is our calling: to breathe this grace on
others, to use the beans of life to feed the hungry with joy and
hope and love.

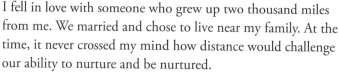

Fragments from the Feast

Carol Penner

I fell in love with someone who grew up two thousand miles
from me. We married and chose to live near my family. At the
time, it never crossed my mind how distance would challenge
our ability to nurture and be nurtured.

Having children, I suddenly became very needy: I needed
a mother-in-law who could share the joy of my children and
babysit, and she needed to do that. For years, we spent almost
all our disposable income on flights to visit my husband's family. Even then I didn't foresee that the needs would become
greater as my in-laws' health deteriorated. One year my husband flew six times to help them in various ways, and still he
felt that he was not able to do enough. These flights put a strain
on our finances, on our time together as a nuclear family, and
on the environment.

We live in a long-distance world. Sometimes people go
home; sometimes they can't. Sometimes the parents move to
them; sometimes they can't. Sometimes new surrogate family
relationships are forged, but sometimes not. We live in a frag-
mented world in which we frequently ask ourselves, *Do I have
enough energy to care for this person? Can I take the time to follow
Christ's command to help out? What if I don't have enough strength
left to care for my own family?*

But nurturing people is not something we do because we
are commanded. It is not a series of good deeds we bestow on
the needy world or something we do for the hope of a heavenly

reward. We nurture because it is our nature; it is who we are as God's children. God nurtures us by creating, redeeming, sustaining. Made in God's image, nurturing is the way we become fully human. It is our identity.

The examples that Doris Janzen Longacre provided in 1980 are not outdated. Choices about whether or not to nurture others still permeate our lives, perhaps with new twists. This way of being is still profoundly contrary to the prevailing Canadian and U.S. worldview, which puts the self on center stage: self-fulfillment, self-promotion, self-actualization, self-indulgence. How revolutionary to put the self aside, to put Christ at the center, and to listen to Jesus' invitation, "Feed my sheep." Even when we think we have no sustenance left to offer anyone else, we may find that our resources are surprisingly, perhaps miraculously, refreshed.

My mother-in-law was a nurturing person. Years ago her husband was in a car accident and sustained head injuries, which left him with significant intellectual and physical disabilities. She took care of him for thirty-three years, until her death. In today's world, I've seen many marriages dissolve because people felt they weren't getting what they needed. They weren't feeling loved or fulfilled. My mother-in-law was a faithful, nurturing person, regardless of whether the person she cared for fulfilled her needs.

This long view—this deep identity of a nurturer, forged in long weeks, months, and years of caring for others—is at odds with our society, which focuses on speed and instant gratification. We even have new tools that seem to speed up and streamline nurturing. Email, Facebook, and Skype can help us nurture each other across distances in the midst of busy lives. But while text messages may keep us "in touch" with our relatives, it's not the same as holding hands around the dinner table. An email can convey words to a friend whose mother-in-law has died, but it lacks the comfort of face time. Technology is not a quick fix for the fragmentation we feel.

More than ever, especially with these new tools all around us, we need to know our deep identity—who we are as nurturers. Early Anabaptists spoke of *Gelassenheit,* which means "yieldedness" to the will of God. It can also be translated as "self-surrender": those who lose their lives will find them. We are in danger of losing our lives to the values all around us, to messages that say, "Put yourself first! You deserve it! Your career, your financial security, your pleasure are your number-one priority!"

But instead of yielding to this barrage of messages, we yield to God's way in us. God will help us face today's choices— choices to nurture our families, but also choices to nurture the stranger on the side of the road, who turns out to be family too.

In fact, that's God's inside joke: when nurturing our own family seems a monumental task, God turns the world upside-down by saying *everyone* is our brother and our sister. "But we don't have the resources" is our response. "I don't have time." That's when God provides the feast from only five loaves. Surprisingly, the more we share, the more there is to share. It may take a long time to pick up all the fragments.

8
Cherish the Natural Order

Doris Janzen Longacre

● ●

When I was a child, farmhouse walls in our Kansas community were decorated mainly with calendar pictures provided by the co-op or grain elevator. Summer-month pages usually treated us to nature scenes of pristine beauty. Purple-blue mountains, always snowcapped, towered behind cool reflecting lakes framed with pine trees.

My father, with prairie grime trickling down his neck from a hot morning at the thresher, would stand in the even hotter kitchen at noon, look at that calendar, and contemplate that somewhere there was land so beautiful that its only purpose was to be viewed. It must have been at such times that he planned our family vacations.

When work slacked off, regular August trips took us to every national park in the West. In our 1950 Pontiac, we took every mountain pass on the maps, peering through the windshield for signs announcing a scenic view ahead. Later I loved looking at the photographs Daddy carefully snapped at those stops. Sometimes he captured mountains, lakes, and pine trees in perfect composition—just like the calendars. A few photographs did show our somewhat rumpled family in the foreground. But my favorites were always pure nature, empty of people.

Today people still hope to preserve those untouched places, those scenic resources that remind us of what nature is like before humans take over. We badly need untracked wilderness as a checkpoint from which civilization is taking us. Mostly we need it to give us the humbling experience of leaving something alone.[1]

But the still bigger task is to put people successfully into our nature pictures. Not just dreamy-eyed lovers strolling a lonely beach. Not three hikers with backpacks on a mountain trail, or children gathering wildflowers. We need nature pictures that can include without being ruined what we honestly need in order to live: farms, factories, roads, homes, places to live and work and relax. Right now we seem to know instinctively that the way we do these things often spoils the scene. *THINK ARCHITECTURE LIKE FALLING WATER*

A peace treaty with nature *OR INCORPORATING NATURE INTO OUR ARCHITECTURE*

Humankind's most violent acts against the environment took place in the past two hundred years. Today we have the means to make our home totally uninhabitable. One standard for living for modern Christians must be to *cherish the natural order.* Even if our environment were not in present danger, simply obeying what the Bible says about our relationship to the earth requires such care.

The following ideas on people and nature are mainly from Willard Swartley's study "Biblical Sources of Stewardship."[2]

First, Scripture clearly states that because God created everything, God is owner of all. "The earth is the Lord's and all that is in it, the world, and those who live in it" (Ps 24:1). In the church, we talk about stewardship of land and possessions. It must be clear that, according to the Bible, this never means judicious use of what is *ours.* Faithful care of what actually belongs to God is the only biblical perspective.

Second, the truth that we are created in God's image has bearing on our relationship to the earth. We are to care for the natural order as God cares for it. In the biblical Hebrew, "to till" means to serve the land. But Genesis 3 and 4 record that humankind's first and lasting sin is refusal to *be* God's image. Instead of representing God's rule, we choose to be like God. We act not as caretakers but as owners. We usurp the right to exploit and waste. With shameless greed for profit, we proceed in pushing the limits, doing what nature never intended.

This Old Testament creation theology must be seen in the context of God's covenant with Israel. That God owns the land was fundamental: "The land shall not be sold in perpetuity, for the land is mine; with me you are but aliens and tenants. Throughout the land that you hold, you shall provide for the redemption of the land" (Lev 25:23–24). In the covenant, this divine claim was the basis for sabbatical and jubilee years to ensure that land would be well cared for and that privilege for its use could never center in the hands of a few wealthy people. In the context of such radical social legislation, we can understand Isaiah's indignation at those who "join house to house, who add field to field" and Amos's golden text of the prophetic ethic, "But let justice roll down like waters, and righteousness like an ever-flowing stream" (Isa 5:8; Amos 5:24).

Swartley shows how the Old Testament vision of justice and righteousness finds fulfillment in Jesus' teachings and actions. The poor inherit God's kingdom, the blind see, the lame walk, prisoners go free. The image lost at the fall is restored through Christ.

Modern and organic

If we accept the demands of living in God's image, we will cherish the natural order. Grabbing and exploiting will give way to sharing. We can learn much about doing this by looking back at the life patterns of the original occupants of Canada and the United States before Europeans arrived on this continent. We can observe indigenous systems around the world in which private ownership bows to the communal good. Grandparents raised here many years ago can also help.

Earlier, human ways conformed to nature because nature was in control; humans lacked the power to act otherwise. Only if they accommodated did they survive. Although this is ultimately true for us also, judgment on failure to accommodate is not quite so immediate.

Today we own the machines for full-scale plunder of our environment. For our future we need a modern "organic technology." We need a blend between the peasant's ecological skill and our contemporary knowledge of what is possible. The answer in housing is likely not a teepee or log house, but a small, sturdily built, comfortable structure heated by the sun. The answer to the litter problem is not an end to ketchup or grape juice sold in glass bottles, but standard sizes that must be returned and will be re-filled by any company. The answer to lung-choking smog in cities is not moving everybody to the countryside, but strong restrictions on private cars and adequate public systems for moving around. We need not give up manufacturing, but we must make ethical choices between factory pollution and human health.

Finding these blends means that we consciously choose to fit the way we live to the environment, not trying to reshape the environment to our whims. Sometimes this will cost more initially than the old system of using up, throwing away, and destroying. Certainly it will take more imagination. Above all, cherishing the natural order requires a willingness to live in God's image and live peacefully with the earth.

Waiting for the big answer

Right now, depletion of energy sources is one of our biggest environmental headaches.

Once on a plane trip, I sat next to an amiable young man from Canton, Ohio. Somehow he seemed different from the usual three-piece-suit crowd who sips cocktails and studies profit-and-loss sheets. This man pulled out pictures of his family, with whom he was eager to be reunited. He explained his business and asked me about my work. But when I told him I was returning from a church conference at which I had spoken about conserving food and energy, his smile became indulgent.

"That's really nice of you," he said. "I know we could all do better. But you know, science is going to get us out of this energy problem somehow. When you think about the things we didn't know thirty years ago! I believe that by the year 2000 some new innovation we've never even dreamed of will be our main source of energy." In the half-hour before we landed, my scariest questions on where we will be if that doesn't happen never dented his optimism.

My airplane seatmate has company everywhere, for doomsday books make tiresome reading. It's hard to put them down with a smile. And for those who don't worry about violent consequences, there actually may be temporary solutions in sight. If the Middle East won't sell us the oil we want at a price we can pay, we can try taking it by military force. We also can build nuclear power systems to help meet our wasteful habits, although we still don't know how to dispose of unimaginably dangerous radioactive by-products.

Although we can scrape together the energy to continue, our waste steals from other countries that cannot pay high prices for fuel to meet even the barest human needs. Luann Habegger Martin wrote from Accra, Ghana,

> The real energy crisis for the poor in developing countries is the growing scarcity of firewood. Most people in these countries depend primarily on firewood to cook their food and in colder climates to provide some warmth. Due to deforestation, women are walking farther and farther to get enough firewood to cook their family's meals. If we as Canadians and U.S. citizens had to go to such efforts to get our fuel and water, I'm sure we would use these resources more judiciously.

Of any course of action, Christians must never ask first, "Is it scientifically possible?" and "Can we pay for it?" When asked first, those are conformed-to-the-world questions. Inquiry tends to stop right there.

"Does it nurture people?" and "Does it protect our environment?" are the conformed-to-God's-image questions. If the answers are yes, the other questions about science and cost also need to be researched. But the order in which we ask them shows who and what we serve.

Finding the Point in a Cornfield

David Kline

Yesterday I was cultivating corn with what Nate Shaw in *All God's Dangers* would call a *good* team—Hank, Kenny, and Dick. After a week of rest, the team was full of vigor, and they knew where to walk between the rows of six-inch-high corn. We were favored with a few days of sunshine along with cooler temperatures following a week of endless rain and humidity. The soil had just dried enough to be worked.

The first cultivation of corn is crucial for an organic farmer if he or she desires weed-free corn, so the team and I set our energies toward getting the job done by sunset. The work at hand wasn't so urgent, however, that I didn't have time to savor the pure pleasure of being in a field of good land. We stopped often to give the horses rest, to unclog the rolling shields protecting the tender plants from the roiling soil, and to pull curly dock plants that had survived the harrowing prior to planting. It was on one of these frequent stops that I found the point.

I had just stepped off the cultivator when I saw the small arrowhead. The point was less than an inch long and perfectly crafted from black Coshocton County flint. As I held it in my hand and cleaned it with my thumb, I was humbled to think that the last human to hold the fine little point was an American Indian. Was he from the Iroquois nation, Shawnee, Delaware, or perhaps an Erie hunter from the vanquished Cat Nation along the south shore of Lake Erie? I have no way of knowing. But I do know his people are gone from this part of the country. I know, too, that I am here for only a season as a steward of the mysteries of God.

The words of farmer and poet Wendell Berry came to my mind:

> Be thankful and repay
> Growth with good work and care.

Work done in gratitude
Kindly, and well, is prayer.[3]

Later in the day I found a hide-scraper: a larger, more coarsely
worked piece of the same dark flint. Now as I write, both pieces
are resting on Doris Janzen Longacre's book *Living More with
Less*. A visitor from Wiesbaden, Germany, gave us a copy soon
after it was published. Our friend knew that we could relate to
Longacre's belief in living simply, in living on the land instead of
merely residing there.

Rereading the 1980 version of *Living More with Less* today
reminds me that Longacre's words are even more applicable
now than they were thirty years ago. She wrote when the
nation was reeling from the 1970s oil crisis. Soon after that,
the North Slope and North Sea oil discoveries began flowing
through the pipelines, and we lapsed back into complacency.
Thoughts of simple living were relegated to the far corners of
most people's minds. Now, however, hardly a day passes that
we aren't reminded that high living can have a tremendous
environmental cost. In 2010 we have watched as the crude oil
spill in the Gulf of Mexico wrecked fisheries and desecrated the
shoreline and bird life. Is this the United States' Chernobyl?

We need to reconsider the wise words of Doris Longacre
and recognize that simplicity is not bondage. It is emancipation. For me, it is the freedom to live at home, where most
of our food travels less than half a mile from its roots to our
dinner plate. It is the freedom to live on 120 acres, where I do
most of my traveling and never fail to be delighted by small
discoveries in the fields, meadows, and woodlands.

I am reluctant to use the term *our* farm. Even though a sheet
of paper tells me that my wife and I are the legal owners of this
place and we pay taxes on it, the small obsidian point by my
left hand tells me I am caretaker only for a season. It reminds
me that I have to act responsibly toward creation. The writer of
Revelation says that God created the earth for his pleasure (see
Rev 4:11). We need to take care of it for his sake.

Just as Revelation speaks of the future, the point in the field calls to mind what is to come. Perhaps someday a person stirring and then dropping seeds into the soil will find a small pocketknife and ponder the same questions I had.

• •

How Many Chickens Can You Cherish?

Bethany Spicher Schonberg

Last spring, the town where I went to college fought a months-long battle over chickens. Not the lethargic, large-breasted variety trucked in daily to the city's poultry plants, but back-yard chickens—the kind that might scratch in the grass and supply a family's eggs. In the end, the anti-chicken crowd won with the contention that, besides being noisy and smelly, hens carry diseases. At a crowded town hall meeting, one mother demanded a ban on backyard layers to protect her child from ever touching a chicken.

This story isn't about the poultry industry, with its manure lagoons and labor violations, or even about our society's collective effort to forget that our food was once alive. Instead, this is about that child, who will never know the sound of a contented hen settling down for the night.

I have a forester friend who insists that conservation does not mean leaving vast tracts of forest untouched. He counsels landowners to cut roads through their woods, to harvest valuable trees when they grow tall, to clear out invasive shrubs, and most of all to walk—often—through the forest. If you don't know your woods, he says, all those trees will just look like cash when hard times or the next generation comes along.

My husband and I are in our second year of growing vegetables in central Pennsylvania. We live in my parents' basement and spend most of our waking hours on two acres of soil that my great-grandfather once farmed with horses. It's becoming clear to us that our pair of draft ponies, our small field, and the countless teeming ecosystems it contains may take more than a lifetime to get to know.

Some days I come in exhausted after flea beetles have chewed the kale or weeds have swallowed up the carrots. "It's like a war out there!" I tell Micah. It's true that industrial agriculture's tank-like tractors and arsenal of pesticides are legacies of the last world war. But we named our farm Plowshare Produce after Micah 4:3—"They shall beat their swords into plowshares, and their spears into pruning hooks"—resolving to tend it, over time, with fewer weapons. So before we spray, we hear the flea beetles saying that our soil nutrients are out of balance. We listen to the weeds asking for cover crops and the eroded hillside crying out for apple trees.

Most mornings, after chores and breakfast, Micah and I read the lectionary and pray before we discuss the day's work. Sunday evenings we walk through the gardens with a notebook and pen, and in the winter we retreat for a weekend to reflect on the season past. Neither of us is naturally disciplined, but we're finding that without these rituals, we become more angry or fretful, we respond less creatively to distraction or disaster, and we forget to listen to the bugs.

It's easier not to know. Where my food comes from and my trash goes. Whether my lights burn on West Virginia coal or my car runs on oil from the Gulf of Mexico. What toxins lurk in the water I drink or in the body of the Indian child who dismantles my discarded computer. Just how irrevocably we humans have altered the climate in the past two generations. All the stories I don't know gather and settle like fog over my days.

How many acres of forest can one person steward? How many chickens can you cherish? How many tremors does your life send down the shimmering strands of earth's web, and how many can you bear to trace? Last spring I gave up plastic for Lent, read a book about garbage, and called around to find the name and location of my landfill. Small things, but I think that getting to know my trash is changing me.

Saving "the environment" may not be a useful aspiration. Instead, the journey toward knowing a particular place, a particular story, and maybe even a particular chicken instills in us nature's sense of scale, habits of renewal, and longing for the day when all God's creatures know their places. Some fog lifts. Like the apostle Paul writes in 1 Corinthians 13:12, we find ourselves more fully known.

9
Nonconform Freely

Doris Janzen Longacre

• •

"If it hasn't already done so, the church . . . must recognize that it lives in a pagan society," New Testament scholar Willard Swartley has written. "It must seek for values and norms not shared by society. In short, it will either recover the Christian doctrine of nonconformity or cease to have any authentic Christian voice."[1]

"Do not be conformed to this world," writes Paul to the Romans, "but be transformed by the renewing of your minds" (Rom 12:2).

But nonconforming is a complicated endeavor. The subject is loaded with touchy, two-sided questions. Words such as *easy* and *hard*, *liberty* and *law*, *freedom* and *slavery*, *independence* and *submission* volley back and forth like ping-pong balls through New Testament discussions. Jesus, who warned that the gate to life is small, the road narrow, and those who find it few, also said, "My yoke is easy, and my burden is light" (Matt 11:30). When early Christian leaders had to respond to problems faced by new congregations, the epistle writers wrestled further with apparently conflicting principles. "So speak and so act as those who are to be judged by the law of liberty," says James (James 2:12). "As servants of God, live as free people, yet do not use your freedom as a pretext for evil," adds Peter (1 Pet 2:16). After a long discussion of all sorts of immorality, including greed, Paul states, "'All things are lawful for me,' but not all things are beneficial" (1 Cor 6:12).

Striking a balance

How can Christians committed to simplicity keep their balance? Mennonites have long seen a link between faithfulness and non-conformity, but everyone knows that sometimes we failed to balance this emphasis with freedom. We quoted, "Be not conformed to the world" to the point that our children wanted nothing more than freedom *from* nonconformity. Those who were denied choices in their youth by poverty or rules seem particularly susceptible later to the pulls of respectability, security, and the good life. Many grew up when "Can we afford what we need?" was the legitimate question, and they aren't able to reverse their thinking to "Do we need what we can afford?"

On the other hand, those who grew up floundering for direction and discipline may be the first to sign up under a new legalism. U.S. and Canadian Christendom offers good examples with its blind personality cults and models of education in which all answers are either right or wrong.

Today we need to be always on the alert not to become carried away with the "bigger and better" slogans of our society. We have the example of Christ and a higher purpose for our earthly life. The young must be taught to appreciate the freedom of not being enslaved to material things.

Slavery in the free world

There is another side of the freedom-slavery paradox. Citizens of Canada and the United States seem to have almost unlimited political, economic, and personal freedom. We live in the "free world." In fact, Canadians and U.S. residents believe we lead the way to liberty for everyone else. Yet we submit daily to brainwashing by commercial interests that must be equal to, if not more powerful than, the political posters and slogans of totalitarian governments. One North American who visited China said that at first he wondered how people could tolerate the constant barrage of slogans on walls and radio, telling everybody what to think. Then he realized that his own society reels under nonstop messages just as inane.

We can't get away from advertising. Our children's values are programmed through television commercials just as surely as they would be if they chanted political lines in nursery school. Advertising covers many of the surfaces that we see. It claims most of the space in our newspapers and has taken over our personal mail. It infiltrates educational materials used in public schools.

Ads all around

Children in the United States view approximately 40,000 advertisements each year; in 2004, some $15 billion (U.S.) was spent in marketing to children. Canadians are barraged with $19 billion (Can.) worth of advertising each year.[2]

In a panel discussion at the 1978 Mennonite World Conference, participants asked a pastor from Latin America about how he carried on church activities and evangelism under a repressive political system. "Frankly, I feel the affluence of Christian people in North America is a more serious threat to the church here than political repression is to ours," came his piercing reply. At the same meeting, Bishop Festo Kivengere, who escaped a tyrannical regime in Uganda, said, "Technology and material things can never liberate you. They have a tendency to squeeze you into their own image."

Surprised by freedom

From nonconformity's paradox we can distill at least this much: Simplicity is a narrow road of self-discipline, but the alternative—money and materialism—is only another master. With marvelous elements of surprise and mystery, disciplined simplicity offers freedom.

The Upside-Down Kingdom, a book by sociologist Donald B. Kraybill, is really all about nonconformity. It's a biblical study showing how everything about God's new kingdom is reversed from what society expects. Kraybill writes that Jesus never said material things are evil in themselves, but rather warned that they threaten our freedom. In this context, simplicity is not restriction, sacrifice, or denial. It is emancipation. We are back to more with less.

Mennonite communities in Kansas may remember the witness of Andrew and Viola Shelly, more-with-less prophets long before simple living was a popular subject. This family consistently culled excess baggage. Their daughter Linda recalled the liberation of their lives:

My parents always made it clear that we were living simply by choice rather than necessity. They gave the money we did not spend on ourselves to help others. As children we became involved by contributing our money to family Bible Society projects and CROP drives. We learned to know missionaries in family devotions. My parents stressed the biblical importance of stewardship. It wasn't until I began filling out forms for college that I realized my parents were giving away over 20 percent of an income that was already below the median national level. Knowing that we were keeping expenses low for a cause made it all the more challenging and fun to go to garage sales to buy clothes and games or to learn to sew and make useful items at home. It actually felt liberating—we were free from the spending patterns dictated by the availability of money.

More with less means choosing limitations. Few of us, however, can live alone by new standards. Taking the narrow way is too risky. As the preacher in Ecclesiastes puts it: "Two are better than one, because they have a good reward for their toil. For if they fall, one will lift up the other; but woe to one who is alone and falls and does not have another to help. Again, if two lie together, they keep warm; but how can one keep warm alone? And though one might prevail against another, two will withstand one. A threefold cord is not quickly broken" (Eccles 4:9–12).

"If I were a super-strong, determined, stubborn, disciplined, organized person, I could single-handedly overthrow a lifetime of captivity to the North American consumer culture," wrote Jim Stentzel from the Sojourners community in Washington, D.C. "But I'm one who makes New Year's resolutions that last about a week. I buy into the televised good life even as I profess my belief in higher things. I am a creature of the fall whose appetite has moved far beyond mere apples. I need help when it comes to more responsible use of God-given resources."

Elsie Dyck, who spent three years in voluntary service away from home after living thirty-two years in one city, emphasized how hard it is to keep a resolution to live more simply upon returning home: "Whether we will now be able to keep a simple lifestyle with all the pressure to conform to dishwashers, big cars, cottages, cleaning ladies, fancy homes, and pools remains to be seen. You do get a feeling of not being in the same league with your friends."

When the first signals of a new king and a new kingdom came to Mary, Jesus' mother, she sought out Elizabeth for confirmation and courage. Jesus himself gathered a core of disciples and sent them out two by two to spread the good news. Believers from the young churches of Acts clustered for mutual support throughout the Mediterranean world and beyond. From then until now the practice of *church*, or *congregation*, and of *Christian community* has never ceased. God is building his kingdom with people whose relationships are being redeemed and who are thus stronger together than any of them ever could be separately.

Lonely freedom

In the past, Christians needed each other to lock arms against the crowd. But today when we try to live obediently in the midst of affluence, new forces tug at us: mobility and personal independence. The fact that we feel so free to move from place to place makes it more important than ever that we check our sources of support.

Mobility has implications for Christians who know they must support each other. Many of us move every two or three years. There may be no one with whom we work or worship who knows our grandmother's name, our father's values, or the community expectations that shaped us. Consequently, no one feels well enough informed or responsible to hold us to specific life standards.

Moving to a new town often provides financial advancement; people follow a better-paying job, a bigger house, access to shopping malls and recreational sites. A father-mother-two children family in a new suburban location may have new carpeting, three bathrooms, and the latest gadgets. But one spouse and the children have no contact with the other spouse's workplace. Grandparents, cousins, and high school friends were left behind two moves earlier. In such settings, a parent at home all day with small children may suffer acutely. Responses include child abuse and addiction to TV, antidepressants, alcohol, and shopping. All things considered, a mother who spends the morning at the mall buying something new for herself, the house, or the children is taking the safest temporary "high" available.

● ● ● ● ● ● ● ● ● ● ● ● ● ●

On the move

More than 37 million people, age one and over, changed residences in the United States during 2009.[3]

Both parents working full time is the usual way out. This becomes necessary to provide for the high cost of material comforts and may alleviate loneliness for the adults. But it can be a poor solution for young children if they have no permanent relationships with other caring adults. In a mobile society, children also battle loneliness. If the marriage itself cracks and breaks under the strain, problems multiply.

Where is help?

Finding a nice church with warm handshakes and well-planned programs is not enough. Friendships developed in many churches will provide tennis partners and dinner invitations, but not the level of support needed for living the standards discussed here. Even small groups within churches easily falter. Most of these are fine at carrying in meals after you have surgery but are less ready to caution you about buying too big a car. Money and how we get and spend it remains the single great privacy from which few dare lift the cover. It's the area in which our individualism sprouts most persistently.

Intentional Christian communities give the problem the most attention. Building a common life as a solution to personal greed is an old and well-tested practice. Although such groups formed here and there all through church history—and not only in the Catholic monastery setting—many contemporary Christians look askance at such communities. People watch and cluck their tongues and wait for these experiments to fall apart. Today intentional communities have proved themselves. Just as with traditional congregations,

● ● ● ● ● ● ● ● ● ● ● ●

New monasticism

Intentional Christian communities are thriving in the twenty-first century. New monasticism is a movement of Christians committed to communal living, simplicity, hospitality, and worship in areas of high poverty. Examples of new monastic communities include The Simple Way in Philadelphia and Rutba House in Durham, North Carolina.

some have not lasted. But many others are solid, viable, and well beyond their early growing pains.

Not all Christians who take simpler living seriously will choose an intentional community for support. I know people who, although they would not claim success in living by more-with-less standards, have actually governed their lives this way for decades. They've done it in one-family homes, at ordinary jobs, with personal bank accounts, and while attending middle-class churches. If most of us lived as they do, I wouldn't have bothered compiling this book.

One such friend wrote:

> For many years we tried to make choices with needs, rather than what-everybody-else-has, as our criteria. Now that simple living has become popular, I hear a lot of talk about support groups being necessary to assume a lifestyle of this sort. But it seems to me that there is no scriptural justification for needing to have consensus before acting in ways consistent with kingdom-building principles. None of the prophets waited for others to agree before they set out to proclaim by their actions what God had spoken to them. When Jesus called his disciples he didn't say, "When we get our group together we'll decide what we ought to do."

Her warning, which is valid only in light of the fact that she has long lived obediently, adds balance to our perspective. With mercy, God speaks through close-knit groups and through prophets who stand alone. God is unlikely to be limited to a single model.

Experiments in Nonconformity

Aiden Enns

Thirty years ago, when *Living More with Less* was first published, I was eighteen years old and a zealous Mennonite Christian living in Vancouver, British Columbia. While the Jesus I knew wanted me to love my neighbor, the best thing I could offer was eternal life in Christ. As the saying goes, I was so heaven-focused I was little earthly good.

Early on, my bias toward a social gospel was nurtured, maybe even triggered, in a Bible study group in which we read *The Upside-Down Kingdom* by Donald B. Kraybill, which Doris Janzen Longacre cites. Yet I failed to grasp the full weight of Christian nonconformity; I still thought it was primarily a spiritual orientation. The material aspect of the gospel was secondary at best, a platform for the delivery of words and metaphysical formulas.

For a couple of decades I wandered in theological spirals—liberation theology, feminist readings of Scripture, social construction of reality—and ended up flipping my priorities. I came to see that the material dimension of the gospel (food, clothing, shelter, redistribution of wealth) is primary. It's not that the spiritual is secondary, but that the spiritual resides in everything anyway—that the spiritual is kind of pre-primary.

Now when I revisit *Living More with Less*, I see it as a manual for living radical lives of resistance to overconsumption and greed. My marriage partner, Karen, and I have lived most of our years together in community with others. We have not had a television for over a decade, eat vegetarian, ride bikes, and are experimenting with a humanure composting toilet. It's not only possible but rewarding and freeing to live a nonconforming life as we join a community of folks with similar values and ethics.

For example, back in 1999, when apocalyptic tension was growing at the brink of the new millennium, I saw a photo of a California highway dotted with cars in a gridlock of traffic. Freshly shocked at the toxic nature of our culture, a culture that not only tolerates the car but celebrates it, I said, "We need to do something about car culture. Let's see if we can go for a whole year without our van." Karen was up for the experiment.

We announced our decision to members of our small Mennonite congregation. In the weeks that followed, another couple said they were retiring their old car. With money from a provincial incentive program, they went car-free and bought bus tickets. Another couple sent around an email and said they

intended to keep their car but set up a borrowing policy for
those who need it. This was handy for our out-of-town family
visits. With these actions in our small, faith-based community,
we were embodying a hint of what a more sustainable, interde-
pendent society could look like.

Such countercultural experiments can become contagious. A
few years later, one woman in our church announced that she
wanted to address unjust food production. She was part of a
group that was seeking to assemble one hundred people to eat
food grown within one hundred miles for one hundred days. I
knew it would require sacrifices, like giving up coffee, beer, and
ice cream, but our intentional community joined the effort.
We struggled together, "cheated" together, and found grace
together.

Nonconformity is easier when done in community. A new
"normal" develops: that which was formerly weird is valued and
the previously conventional is questioned. In our community
it's normal not to have a television, to avoid airplane travel, and
for newlyweds to share an apartment with a single person.

For peacemaking- and global-justice-oriented Mennonites,
nonconformity today has a twofold emphasis. First, it attends
to the prevailing cultural and political forces that fortify injustice. For example, Hollywood films, commercial media, and
major political parties condone the current levels of consumption and violence. By living simple, peace-oriented lives, we
embody our critique of culture.

Second, nonconformity involves a break with the lifestyles
typified by many Canadian and U.S. churchgoers. Christians
seem as capable as others of promoting needless consumerism
and varieties of products, whether it's a new style of Bible or a
Christian exercise video or diet book. We embrace the values
of the dominant culture when we hold travel-intense national
conventions and use the language of advertising and the mentality of consumerism to promote our products.

More than ever, this is a time for more experiments in
simple living. As we purchase fewer new things, grow more
of our own food, and share more with our neighbors, we are

released from the bondage of needing more. Such experiments literally become part of our salvation. They can be our response to the urgings of the ever-present Spirit that moves us toward freedom, hope, and peace.

Confident Enough to Be Compassionate

Nekeisha Alexis-Baker

Super-Christian. That was one of the nicknames I received at my New York City high school. I claimed it as a badge of honor. Although I was given the moniker as a friendly joke, it reflected the straightforward way I wore my faith on my sleeve. After being baptized at age fourteen, I became increasingly determined to avoid being the stereotypical teenager. While I was far from perfect, I was a good student who didn't do drugs, dabble in premarital sexual dalliances, or party—and I wasn't shy about criticizing those activities to everyone in earshot.

It took me a while to discover the hidden cost of the way I exercised my principles among my peers. The wakeup call came after I confronted a good friend regarding his own youthful experimentation. As we talked, he expressed that he had been scared to confide in me because he had worried that I would abandon our friendship. It was disconcerting to realize that when he had needed a listener and a safe space to share his struggles, I had only fostered fear and condemnation. I had rejected conformity and made my values evident to others—and to this day I am glad I did. Yet somewhere along the way, I had failed to be a good and compassionate friend.

Although this experience did not completely quiet my clanging cymbal, I have allowed it and other "noisy gong" moments with family and friends to shift how I live in the world without being of it. Reflecting on Doris Janzen Longacre's call to nonconform freely, in light of my growth as an activist and an agitator, has convinced me that this life standard entails more than seeking liberation from consumerism, materialism, and other social bindings. It also means being free from the need to dominate others and demand that they accept my point of view. The more confident I am in my convictions and practices—whether it is being vegan, abstaining from voting, being pacifist, growing food with my husband, learning to reduce and reuse, or working toward racial justice—the more I can interact with dissimilar perspectives without feeling threatened or asserting my will.

Holding together conviction and conversation without sacrificing faithfulness is not an easy task. As Longacre demonstrated, being either too rigid or too lenient can push people to damaging extremes. Being so closed to another perspective that I never risk the possibility of being wrong sends people running in the opposite direction and limits my own growth. On the other hand, uncritically adopting every idea or activity that I come across without having a core identity as a guide can further entrap me in our hyperactive and alienated society. Being tethered too tightly to one position without seeking a fresh outpouring of the Spirit and being tethered too loosely to my peculiar foundation in Christ are two sides of the same kind of bondage. Either way, we flounder. To echo Longacre, "The balancing act is not easy to perform." But perform it we must if we are to be truly free from the ways of this world *and* from the sins of self-righteousness and misplaced pride.

Christians are called to resist consumerism, nationalism, militarism, individualism, racism, and a host of other social sins not to boost ourselves and stroke our egos. We do so first and foremost because God has shown Godself to us in Jesus, and because we have committed ourselves to the way of peace, justice, love, and reconciliation he embodied while on earth. In nonconforming freely, we can draw others toward a way of living that releases them from isolation, busyness, and the insatiable need for more.

Longacre recognized this when she penned her influential work. Now is the time for a new and diverse generation of Mennonites and Christians around the globe to catch this vision once again.

Part 3
Living Testimonies

10
Money and Stewardship

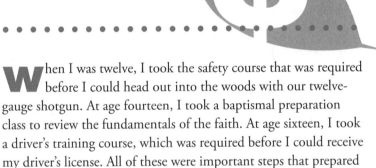

Beryl Jantzi

● ●

When I was twelve, I took the safety course that was required before I could head out into the woods with our twelve-gauge shotgun. At age fourteen, I took a baptismal preparation class to review the fundamentals of the faith. At age sixteen, I took a driver's training course, which was required before I could receive my driver's license. All of these were important steps that prepared me for increased responsibility in life.

The training I received in managing money was, by comparison, very limited. I picked up basic principles along the way from my parents and a class in school, but the question remains: whose job is it to train up a child in the ways of responsible financial management? Who is responsible to teach young people to be good stewards? And, just as importantly, if 40 percent of U.S. households are spending more than they are earning, as the Federal Reserve reported in 2008, how do we expect our children to live any differently?[1]

While we're talking about scary statistics, here are a few more: Adults ages 25 through 34 are experiencing the highest increase in personal bankruptcy claims of any age group in the United States.[2] College seniors have, on average, four credit cards and graduate with between three and four thousand dollars in credit card debt.[3] (This is consumer debt, which does not include debt related to the actual expense of going to college.) These statistics make apparent the fact that money management is not an innate skill, like breathing and sleeping. To be wise stewards, we need training and education.

Thousands of verses

Proverbs 22:6 is one of the most well-known proverbs in the Bible: "Train children in the right way, and when old, they will not stray." But how many of us can quote the verse that follows? "The rich rules over the poor, and the borrower is the slave of the lender" (v. 6). Why have we highlighted verse 6 on training up a child, only to neglect what it is we are called to instruct our children about—namely, the dangers of going into debt and becoming a servant of the lender? In fact, more than one-third of the verses in this chapter on training our children refer to our use and understanding of money.

Since the writer of Proverbs speaks about this throughout his book, and since Jesus, the writers of the epistles, and the prophets addressed the issue of money more than 2,300 times, maybe we should be talking about it as well. "We'll never exhaust Bible study on the subject of money," Doris Janzen Longacre wrote. "There's too much material and too many possibilities for creatively applying it to our own time."

Here are a few places to start:

- *Start talking about the 90 percent.* What little we do hear about money in our congregations tends to center on the importance of giving and the principles surrounding tithing. As important as this subject is, it may not be the best place to begin the discussion. Maybe we need to begin talking about the 90 percent before we talk about giving away 10 percent. One main reason we are unable or unwilling to give generously is because we

> "Today I still grapple with the paradoxes that envelop thrift and simple living. On the one hand, pure frugality is a rare bird, an endangered species in our waste-crazed society. . . . But living more with less is more than thrift. Partly, it's putting what you save to some good use for others. . . . But even with that, we dare not be satisfied. Increasingly it means asking questions such as: Where did this come from? Who benefited and who got hurt in its production? Ought I to be gloating over its cheap price, or not buying it at all?"—Doris Janzen Longacre

have failed to develop a sustainable financial plan for what we decide to keep. As someone once said, we have bought into the foolish obsession of buying stuff we don't need, with money we don't have, to impress people we don't even know.

- *Live below your means.* We have three choices when it comes to personal finances. We can live above our means, within our means, or below our means. The third option is the wisest choice. Living below our income allows us to establish the cushion needed for both responsible savings and intentional and joyful giving. There are four key benefits to living below our means: we can eliminate debt, build savings, experience financial flexibility for the future, and participate in joyful generosity.

- *Commit to passing along to the next generation, in word and deed, the stewardship values you have owned for yourself.* Unfortunately, too many people in our churches have bought into the allure of consumerism, which says more stuff is better than less. We need a new commitment to challenging the voices that draw us away from the biblical call to responsible and wise stewardship. Following Jesus requires no less.

As you read the stories and reflections that follow, I encourage you to ask yourself what steps you are prepared to take to align your financial values with your spiritual ones. In the same way, as we enter new stages of life that require new skills and understandings, let us commit ourselves to seeking out the expertise of others and entering into conversations on this often-neglected subject.

Budgeting. I have the bad habit of impulse buying. Recently I took a hard look at my buying patterns and did the following: (1) I accounted, penny for penny, for an entire month's salary. I was amazed at the amount I frittered away on trivia. (2) My future husband and I tested our compatibility by showing each other our budgets. When I realized I didn't trust him to decide what he needed for himself, I wondered how I could trust myself. (3) I decided that, having lived with an Amish family and in Costa Rica, I could do without a television, blender, electric blanket, expensive stereo system, and curling iron. (4) I read 1 John 3:17 ("How does God's love abide in anyone who has the world's goods and sees a brother or sister in need yet refuses help?"). (5) I invited a friend to be my budget partner. We consult with each other regarding the necessity, practicality, and economics of any purchase not in the regular budget.—*Marti Stockdale, Canton, Ohio* (1980)

Upping the tithe. I've decided to increase my monthly church tithe. Sure, I could use that extra money: it just about equals the university registration fee or the money I promised my daughter toward the price of her wedding dress. It also represents almost half of the car insurance premium heading my way soon. But giving that money away makes me feel rich. No matter how straitened my circumstances, I can be part of services the church provides for the homeless, the impoverished elderly, and those living with AIDS. In other words, tithing reminds me that there are lots of people worse off than me who would love to have my so-called "problems." That's not to say that I wouldn't like to have more cash. But I have a roof over my head, food every day, family and friends, and occasionally even a ten-dollar student ticket to the symphony. Some days I feel like the luckiest person in the world. —*Mary Waltner, Chicago, Illinois*

● ● ● ● ● ● ● ● ● ● ● ● ● ●

Want to feel rich? Go to www.globalrichlist.com to find out where you stand on the global wealth ladder.

Is 10 percent enough? Studies show that few Christians give away 10 percent of their income. For nearly a decade, however, Sue and Victor Klassen have been giving away 30 percent of theirs. Victor is a researcher for Xerox, and Sue a full-time volunteer with a restorative justice program. They had been giving away 20 percent of their income until 1985, when the Vision '95 goals of the former Mennonite Church (which joined with the General Conference Mennonite Church to create Mennonite Church USA and Mennonite Church Canada) challenged Mennonites to increase their giving. For the next decade, Sue and Victor gradually upped their giving to 30 percent. For many years, Sue says, they hesitated to share their giving story publicly. "Scripture teaches us to not let the right hand know what the left hand is doing regarding donations," she says. "Furthermore, talking about money changes the way people think about each other—sometimes in unpredictable and uncomfortable ways. Yet we come back to how blessed we have been by people who have shared their stories—these have inspired and helped us on our journey." Sue adds that while giving more has meant sacrifices, it has not led to a sense of deprivation. "There's no asceticism here, but a deep watchfulness," she clarifies. "We observe ourselves having a lot more joy and a lot more financial security than many around us."

Is cheaper always better? Growing up, I was well schooled in the ways of being Mennonite. Frugality was next to godliness; isn't that what living more with less means? I had to step beyond my Mennonite world to learn why the cheapest purchase may not be the most ethical one. On a long drive home from a conference, a colleague patiently explained to me the value of buying "green" products, including organic produce. The conversation went something like this:

Fair trade is a market-based approach that empowers artisans in some of the most disadvantaged areas of the world by ensuring a fair wage for them and establishing a sustainable market for their products. Ten Thousand Villages is one of the world's largest and oldest fair-trade organizations.

"Bah," said I, "those things are just for wealthy yuppies. What are those who can't afford such organic purity supposed to do? Let them eat pesticides?"

"Ah, but remember the hidden costs," said he, "the costs that aren't included in the price of 'conventional' food."

"What hidden costs?" said I.

"Economists call them externalities," he said. "They are

the end products of conventional agriculture that no one pays for—at least not right away—but that cost us all: diminished topsoil, pesticides, and fertilizers in groundwater, fewer bees and other pollinators, fewer earthworms, fewer farmers, and weaker rural economies."

"Oh, those hidden costs. But if I spend less money by buying the cheapest items, I can live more simply and give more to charity."

"True, but by supporting the present economies with their hidden costs, you may be perpetuating the need for charities. Why not spend a little more up front? When you support a healthier and more enduring system by buying sustainably produced items, you are voting with your dollars for the world you want to live in."

• • • • • • • • • • • • • •

For each $100 (U.S.) spent in local businesses, $45 stay in the local economy, compared to $15 spent at nationally owned chains.[4]

"So what you're saying is, cheaper isn't always better?"

"That's right."

"Hmm. That idea will take some getting used to."

—*Dave Hockman-Wert, Corvallis, Oregon*

Don't scrimp on generosity. Those of us who try to live more with less sometimes need to be challenged to spend money. I think of my Japanese mother-in-law, who came home one time with roasted chestnuts from a street vendor. She didn't buy them for herself, as she doesn't really like them, but to help out the vendor. "He has to live too," she told me. That impressed me. What does our scrimping look like to our children and the unchurched? Maybe spending a dime on someone in front of us is sometimes just as important as saving a dime to send to an organization.—*Dora Kawate, Dillsburg, Pennsylvania*

The "monthly money." Dorothy and Orville Shenk gave our family wonderful more-with-less advice. With their encouragement, we began giving our children the money we were spending on their clothes, educational supplies, and school lunches. Then the children spent this money themselves. More: This glorious plan meant more autonomy for children learning both inde-

· ·

How can I shop responsibly?

- *When possible, buy locally.* I try to buy from stores that I can walk to, but since the downtown where I live has a limited number of businesses, I'm forced to drive at least a few miles to shop. I can usually buy food locally, and I also enjoy shopping at my local hardware store, which has excellent service along with competitive prices.

- *If you can't get it locally, try to get it from your economic region.* Within your region, give priority to businesses that are locally owned. This recycles money locally and avoids draining profits off to large corporations. I shop at a local building-supply store that has numerous stores within our area and have found that their prices often rival those of the large chains.

- *If you can't buy it within your region, give priority to businesses that are grounded in their own local economy or emphasize* environmental sustainability. For example, I like to buy out-of-print and used books, and I prefer to buy from independent bookstores that serve their local communities—even if they are in Oregon, which is far from my home in Pennsylvania. I do try to minimize distance and buy from the East, however, if possible.

- *If none of the above is possible, give priority to businesses and economies that emphasize fair trade and sustainability, whether local or international.* I love coffee, and I buy a lot. Coffee is largely an import to the United States, but I buy brands that are fair trade and shade grown, which emphasizes environmental stewardship and ensures that the producer is getting "fair" compensation for the product. While these criteria might not cover everything I buy, I know that every small effort is worth it.

—*Russ Eanes, Mennonite Publishing House*

pendence and money management. Less: Using this system, we fought less, spent less, and had almost no requests for money.

To begin the plan, I totaled the money we spent in each of these areas for the previous year and then divided it by family members. When they were in fourth grade, each child began receiving the money allotted at the beginning of the month. Initially we helped with the decision making, but very soon they were thrilled to be the masters of the "monthly money." They learned tricks such as packing their lunches to save money for school activities. We continued to help with large purchases, such as musical instruments.

Each month our family also set aside cash for groceries. We made decisions by committee at the grocery store as our children learned to make the funds stretch to the end of the month and to negotiate needs and wants. This system resulted in more headaches at the time, but our children arrived at their teens financially responsible and quite independent.—*Elaine Maust, Meridian, Mississippi*

Creative deprivation. When our children asked for something that we preferred not to purchase, I often told them we couldn't afford it. But then I realized I wasn't telling the truth. I began to tell them the real reason for not buying certain items so they could learn to be selective themselves.—*Loretta M. Leatherman, Akron, Pennsylvania* (1980)

Can you wear two pairs of shoes at once? "Where there is love, the skin from a flea covers five people." Growing up in Burundi, I heard these words constantly from my mother. One day I couldn't find my white dress and my matching shoes because my mother had given them to a young girl who needed nice clothes for her confirmation ceremony. When I objected, my mother asked me if I could wear two pair of shoes at one time. From this time on, my relationship to money and possessions changed. My mother taught me that true happiness comes from sharing, not from indulging.

• • • • • • • • • • • • •

"Here's a principle to remember: Even if prices run a bit higher, it's worth considering the small and local. . . . Any product raised, manufactured, and sold in its own locale saves everyone's energy supply. And the friendship you make with a druggist or woodworker humanizes your community."—*Doris Janzen Longacre*

After college I earned a very good income. Young, single, living far away from home, and not walking with Jesus, I constantly fell back on my mother's legacy of love, sharing, and simplicity. I used my money to provide housing and education for orphans back in Burundi. Then marriage came, with children, less income, and more obligations. Fortunately my family shares the same values and attitude toward money. We understand that the most valuable gift, our salvation, was given to us freely and through love, so we love others by helping them with God's money.

Many times we have had to send money to orphans who were in urgent need and to give offerings "out of our own needs." We make choices such as eating more at home, which saves money while keeping our family together. You can be certain: our children will pass on to their children my mama's words of wisdom, hopefully through action.—*Mukarabe Makinto-Inandava, Rancho Palos Verdes, California*

From two incomes to one and back. When John and I decided it was time for him to quit his "normal job" and put his energy into his passion of making art, we went from two stable paychecks to one. We put any major spending on hold unless it was absolutely necessary, we discussed purchases before they were made, and we had one credit card to be used only for emergencies. We survived that time so well that our son now says he didn't have a clue that our finances were so tight; he thought all families lived the way we did. Our lifestyle has not changed that much since those leaner days, and we stick to the same principles. Because of this, we can be generous to family members who are financially strapped and share with causes that speak to justice issues we are passionate about. Although we are preparing for the future, it's most important to us to live fully rather than to accumulate masses of money. It's a matter of money ethics to me.—*Phyllis Mishler, Goshen, Indiana*

Bartering. We have a small farm with a poultry operation. Recently a friend asked for some manure for his plot of ground. He has wood that we need for our fireplace, so we traded. This saved both of us money, gave us the opportunity to work together, and helped develop a beautiful and sharing friendship.—*Keith Lehman, Akron, Pennsylvania* (1980)

Bartering for goods and services occurs on an informal basis among friends and neighbors, but interest in Web-based bartering is growing among individuals and businesses. If you offer goods or services for barter, you don't need to accept something back immediately but can instead accept trade credits, which you can then use at a later time for obtaining something else. Bartering does not mean avoiding taxes; even though money has not exchanged hands, the market value of the good or service is considered taxable income.

Engage or divest? Communities in Canada and around the world are reporting that practices of some Canadian mining companies are contributing to their suffering. They remind us that we are part of the problem through our growing demand for mining products and our investments. In the fall of 2008, a Honduran Mennonite pastor and Mennonite Central Committee partner, who had long worked in researching the environmental impact of specific mines and advocating for stricter mining regulations, was granted political asylum in the United States. This partner had become aware that his name was on a hit list of human rights advocates and environmentalists. (A colleague had earlier escaped an assassination attempt.) His story points to a systematic attempt by powerful groups, including Canadian mining companies, to silence opposition and protect their interests. As Christians, we should consider how our investments and purchases link us to mining activity and whether these activities align with our faith and the teachings of Jesus.

I have tried to align my investments with my ethics, while hoping to realize a positive financial return. I hold a number of investments in "socially responsible" mutual funds, but in making an investment decision, I am often left living in uncertainty. Do you divest from a fund because a company doesn't line up with your values? Or do you attempt to improve a company by engaging it ("you can't change a company you don't own")? Are there other ways to direct investments for the common good? These are important questions to keep before oneself when considering how investments can contribute to a more just or less just world.—*Jon Nofziger, Abbotsford, British Columbia*

Save for retirement, invest in the poor. One of our stewardship goals has been to give as much as possible to programs that help people help themselves. In recent years we have found a way of having our savings for retirement greatly extend that kind of help. We do this through investing in self-directed individual retirement accounts (IRAs) designated for microlending programs around the world. These produce very low interest but have become our preferred way of saving for the future.

Low-interest microloans give enterprising families, farmers,

and other entrepreneurs some of the capital they need to get out of poverty. And the default rate on these loans is extremely low. In fact, while our mutual funds lost tons of value in the economic downturn of 2008, everything we had invested in IRAs designated for microlending remained secure. Were this to become the primary way that believers everywhere invested for their futures, it could revolutionize the way we reduce global poverty and offer aid to the poor—by giving them a hand up rather than simply a handout.
—*Harvey Yoder, Harrisonburg, Virginia*

> **Microlending is the practice of making small loans to entrepreneurs, often in the Global South, who don't have collateral or a credit history or who are outside the banking system.**

Plain, good stewardship. The problem with living more with less is that it is hard to know when you get there, or even when you are getting close. If living simply is defined by spending less money, what is the number at which you can say you have arrived? If it is measured by the amount of food you grow for yourself, at what amount of homegrown vegetables does "simple" begin? Much of what passes for living simply is a lot like what they say about being poor: "It's hard work and it takes all your time."

Linda and I are reasonably good at growing some of our own food, using the "things" of life until they wear out, and making do with what comes our way and what we already have. But we have found that it is important to be relaxed in the midst of trying to live more with less. Not worrying about life, as Christ commands in Matthew 6:25, is possible only by being clear about what life and the stuff of life means. As followers of Jesus who are not defined by what we own, we can then discern how much is "enough." Living more with less is not just a good idea or some ultimate goal that we're trying to reach; it is simply a result of plain, good stewardship.—*Lynn Miller, Bluffton, Ohio*

Bludgeon or invitation? To choose poverty means risking that others will interpret it as just another "consumer choice"—

a "lifestyle" rather than a commitment, calling, or, as Doris Janzen Longacre put it, a standard. If you consciously decide to live simply or below the poverty line—whether you do it for political or ethical reasons, or because you hear Christ calling—then you take on a moral burden. Unlike those who are involuntarily poor, you have the means not only to get money, but also to negotiate the challenges of poverty so that you can, as the title puts it, "live more." Whatever that "more" means to you, morally and otherwise, you get control over your life where others do not. Is that justice? If we're motivated by pride, then how simply we live becomes little more than a bludgeon with which to condemn others rather than a loving invitation to join in fellowship. Whether we count our wealth in dollars or time or friends or flowers or simplicity, do we gain more by hoarding or by giving?—*Kiko Denzer, Blodgett, Oregon*

• • • • • • • • • • • • • •

The Compact movement is made up of people committed to not buying anything new for an entire year. "Compacters," as they're called, agree to buy only a few necessities throughout the year and otherwise to borrow, barter, swap items online, shop at garage sales, or simply refrain from shopping.

Sabbath year. Every seven years, Sue and Victor Klassen get off the hamster wheel of consumption. During their Sabbath year, they refrain from buying anything nonessential. They're not legalistic about it, Sue says, and it's sometimes hard to determine what's "essential" and what's not. But the general practice reinforces the need to maintain and repair rather than upgrade and toss out. It's a "rest from more and better," Sue says. "It's so easy to just keep justifying more and more and more." The Klassens have done a Sabbath year twice so far, and they look forward to continuing this cycle of rest every seventh year. "It gives us a chance to reset our compass from the inexorable pull of the culture around us," Sue says, "and to reconnect with the power of 'enough.'"

• • • • • • • • • • • • • •

Find more stories, tips, and links to resources about money and stewardship at www.mpn.net/livingmorewithless.

11
Homes

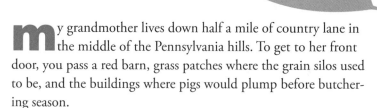

Renee Holsopple Glick

● ●

my grandmother lives down half a mile of country lane in the middle of the Pennsylvania hills. To get to her front door, you pass a red barn, grass patches where the grain silos used to be, and the buildings where pigs would plump before butchering season.

In Brooklyn, where I live, that same half-mile distance contains mostly restaurants, delis, brownstones, and apartment buildings. Instead of the murmur of a farmyard, the noise outside my fourth-floor apartment comes from car horns, neighbors on the stoops, and the rumblings of the subway.

We mark a trend in migration, my grandma and I, from the earlier agrarian roots of Mennonites in the United States and Canada to a more urban landscape, as families and individuals have relocated to city centers to work and study and settle. We find ourselves on vastly different ends of a spectrum as to the type of location we call home. But no matter where or in what type of shelter we live, we need to prioritize and tend to how we integrate ourselves into the earth's ecosystem. The messages we hear, from natural disasters to sermons to popular films with celebrity backing, make this clear: we need to consume less, reuse innovatively, and build sustainably.

In fact, "green building" is a term increasingly in vogue. The challenge we face is no longer convincing ourselves or others that our buildings should perform more efficiently to use fewer resources, both natural and financial. The challenge is ensuring that green ideals do not become a momentary, passing fad. We have to find healthy ways of constructing our homes—for example, knowing and choosing where our building materials come from. We also need to find healthy ways of deconstructing them—for example, utilizing the services of the increasing number of companies that salvage as much reusable material as possible.

The circumstances are different for each of us, with our particular environmental conditions (weather, climate, geography), economic conditions (our personal resources), and contextual conditions (from cityscape to wide open spaces). In all combinations, however, we are called to hold ourselves to high standards.

> "The dream itself—the dream for a perfect home—requires remodeling." —Doris Janzen Longacre

Demanding work

Truly educating ourselves on solutions that are relevant to our specific homes is demanding work. While it is well worth the effort, many sustainable building systems require investment of money or time or research. Geothermal conditioning (see page 115), which uses natural water sources to heat and cool spaces, can be highly cost-efficient in the long term but requires some upfront cost. Green roofs greatly reduce runoff and heat reflection, but they need the correct structural support (soil becomes quite heavy when wet) and drainage systems to prevent leaking. Solar panels, while rapidly improving in their usefulness, are still relatively cost-inefficient.

Yet instead of becoming overwhelmed with the statistics or investment required, we must recognize that the most important step toward healthier buildings is staying aware. Whether we live in a farmhouse among vast acreage, an apartment overlooking a highway, or a single-family house in a suburban neighborhood, we can strive for the following:

- *We can be cautious about what we accumulate.* Often the amount we own affects our expectations about how much living space we "need."

- *We can become aware of our assumptions about size and ownership.* Even though the average size of a new single-family house in the United States was slightly smaller in 2009 than 2008, it was still about 30 percent larger than the average house built in 1980, when *Living More with Less* was first published.[1] We can challenge cultural assumptions about how much space a household requires and find creative or communal solutions for our living spaces.

- *We can be wise about our building choices.* In new construction, the most important tool is how the building is situated on its site related to wind, sun, and landscaping. Similarly, in renovations or existing homes, the first step to improving energy efficiency is to focus on passive solutions, such as upper windows and skylights to let in maximum light and to cut down on electric light usage while letting in maximum heat in winter. Another passive solution is climate-appropriate cooling in the summer: closing all windows early in the morning, putting reflective, insulated

  Passive solar solutions convert sunlight into usable heat with little or no use of other energy sources.

  covers on windows to trap cool air late in the day, and opening windows at night to let in cool air. When possible, it's also best to choose materials that are local and require only minimal chemical upkeep.

- *We can be innovative about our waste.* Reusing or reappropriating materials when possible is an important part of healthy building habits.

My training as an architect means that I create space as a craft. Yet it's not only architectural training that cautions against a nonchalant approach to our built environment. As people of faith, we affirm that care for each other and the earth is central to our identity and mission.

Down her country lane, you can often find my grandma making dozens of cinnamon rolls as a way of caring for the people around her. Similarly, the ways we improve the performance of our homes show care for the earth around us. Including our buildings in our personal and communal understandings of stewardship provides a powerful chance to model our mission.

"Terrible" house. During Sunday dinner with friends, our hostess asked, "Did you have a nice house in India?" I hesitated. We were sitting in an L-shaped living/dining room furnished in coordinating colors. I wondered how to define *nice*. Before I had a chance to reply, our eight-year-old son, Douglas, said enthusiastically, "Oh yes, we had a real nice house in Calcutta." Actually, it was a terrible house. After living in it for six months, I was ready to write a manual on coping. This would include suggestions on how to respond to cockroaches, mice, and rats coming up drains, torn screens and broken window panes, bats flying through the dining room during mealtime, blown fuses, broken water pumps, and crumbling cement walls.

Then again, as a family we had our finest hours in our house in Calcutta. We played games or read. We talked, listened, learned, and sang. We had many guests. So yes, Douglas, we did have a nice house in Calcutta. In fact, it was a fantastic house. It was our home.—*Herta Janzen, London, Ontario* (1980)

Duplex living. Another family needed housing at the same time we did. Having several things in common—limited resources, concerns about lifestyles, and fairly good construction skills—we decided to build a duplex together. Because of our interests in sharing certain facilities, we have both outside and inside entrances into our basements and a door that allows us to move between units without going outside. We walled off a corner of our basement where we pool our tools. The shared freezer is in our neighbor's basement. Outside we share a lawnmower and picnic table and do some gardening together. It's great to have someone around for the job that takes an extra hand.—*Lowell Detweiler, Akron, Pennsylvania* (1980)

Three generations. One house. Helena and Patrick Cicero had long ago decided that Helena's parents could live with them when they got older. "Then one day my dad said, 'Why are we waiting?' and none of us had a good answer," says Helena. "It didn't make sense that we all had separate lawnmowers and appliances; plus living together while our kids were young would mean that their grandparents could be an active part of their lives." So three years ago the Ciceros and their two young children moved into the ranch house where Helena grew up.

Helena, Patrick, and Helena's parents, Amy and John Yeatts, who are all members of Harrisburg (Pa.) Brethren in Christ Church, share meals and food preparation, child care, housework, and yard work. Helena says that when people in her parents' generation hear of their multigenerational living arrangement, "they think it's the greatest thing—until they hear that my parents moved to the basement!" But her mother, Amy, says that the advantages outweigh any sacrifice in space or privacy. For one, she and John were able to travel to Zambia for a month and not worry about house or yard maintenance while they were gone. And Amy says that living with her children and grandchildren "keeps us in touch with young people in a way that we wouldn't be otherwise, which is a very good thing."

• • • • • • • • • • • • •

Buildings account for a significant portion of the greenhouse gas emissions that affect climate change. In the United States, buildings account for 38 percent of all carbon dioxide emissions.[2]

Privacy in small quarters. In central Vietnam, families are sometimes large and homes are often small. Beds are often curtained off for privacy. When we lived in Vietnam with our two small children, we rented a house with three small rooms. We used the front room as our office and living room. The middle room had a curtain down the center and served as a dining/sewing room, as well as a bedroom for the young Vietnamese woman living with us. The third room was also curtained off to make a bedroom for the four of us, leaving a walking corridor between the other two rooms and the kitchen—a small shed

built onto the side of the house. Our three children are still small enough to enjoy sharing the same bedroom. When they get a bit older and want more privacy, curtaining off their beds is an idea that seems practical in the United States as well.
—*Pat Hostetter Martin, Phoenixville, Pennsylvania* (1980)

Shingles into roads. When we needed to put on a new roof, we checked out as many options as we could. We decided that we would go with regular shingles, but we chose our contractor based on what the company planned to do with the old shingles. Rather than placing them in a landfill or burning them, the contractor we chose takes them to a recycling facility where they are ground up and used in road substrates, driveway asphalts, and other applications. Something simple, not profound, but it does make a difference.—*Larry Guengerich, East Petersburg, Pennsylvania*

Necessity breeds recycling. Mennonite Disaster Service (MDS) projects in Diamond, Louisiana, and Eagle, Alaska, are about as far apart as two U.S. projects can be, but they are connected by the common use of recycled building materials. In May 2009, the city of Eagle was flattened by an ice flood. Because Eagle is over eight hours from the closest large city, getting building materials was difficult. "If you came up short of a two-by-four, you couldn't just go to the lumberyard and get one," says Bill McCoy. He and his wife, Esther, were in charge of the project. So they reused wood and doors from the old houses to create outhouses, countertops, and cabinets, saving them time, money, and materials. "It was out of necessity; we didn't have the material," Bill says. "We were forced to do something that was pretty good."

The McCoys also headed up Katrina relief efforts in Diamond. They worked out an arrangement with the Federal Emergency Management Agency in which MDS could take the stairs from the front exterior of mobile homes once used for emergency housing. As it was all treated lumber, they could tear it apart to build what they needed. In some cases, they just connected the steps to a new home. "It was an excellent way

to reuse that lumber instead of having it burned," Esther says.
"We need to encourage each other to use what's available rather
than spending, spending, spending."—*Submitted by Paul Boers,
Goshen, Indiana*

ReStoring. After eight years as president of Habitat for Humanity in Ohio, Dean Horn opened the Habitat ReStore in
Bellefontaine, Ohio. Dean attends Bethel Mennonite Church
in West Liberty, Ohio, and opened the ReStore to create a
revenue stream for the Habitat
homes he builds with other
church members. The ReStore
receives most of its donations
from community members
and corporations. Dean sells
cabinets, doors, appliances,
paint, windows, lighting, and
furniture at the ReStore. "The
things that come from private

LEED (Leadership in Energy and Environmental Design) certification in
both Canada and the United States
provides verification that a building
or community was designed and
built in a way that improves energy savings, saves water, reduces
carbon dioxide emissions, improves
indoor environmental quality, and
stewards resources.

donors are usually things that people don't want to throw away
because they know they are still good," he says. Dean recently
saved three semi-truckloads of windows and doors from a ware-
house in Florida to sell at the ReStore. "If I hadn't taken them,
they would have gone in a landfill." As Dean stands behind the
counter at the ReStore, finishing off his volunteer hours, he
says, "We are all God's servants, and I am fortunate to be able
to do this at a young age."—*Submitted by Esther Shank,
Harrisonburg, Virginia*

Utility bill sticker shock. When we moved back to the West
Coast from Goshen, Indiana, in 2000, little did we know that
the bottom would fall out of California's economy within the
next three years. We arrived in Bakersfield on June 8, 2000,
and our first bout with the changing economy came that July
when we received our first electric bill, which was over three
hundred dollars (U.S.).We reluctantly paid the bill but immediately began to devise strategies that would prevent that from
ever happening again.

First, we changed all our light bulbs to compact fluorescent light bulbs. Then we began to use our major appliances at night (dishwasher, washer, dryer, etc.). Next, whereas we had always burned our Christmas lights 24/7 starting in November, that year we started later in the season and put the lights on a two-hour timer that allowed them to burn for only two hours in the evening. Finally, we decided to use our air conditioner only during the hottest part of the day—from 2:00 to 6:00 p.m.

● ●

How can we heat and cool efficiently?[3]

- *Get an energy audit.* Local energy providers often provide energy audits at a minimal fee. They offer suggestions for heating and cooling more efficiently, as well as estimates of how much a particular upgrade would cost or save in the long run.

- *Set up an energy budget.* Just as you may do with your finances, set a goal of reducing your home's energy consumption. Monitor your usage monthly and make adjustments.

- *Turn your thermostat up or down.* Turning it up three degrees (F) in the summer and down three degrees in the winter can save up to two hundred dollars (U.S.) a year.

- *Close off unused rooms.* Why heat or cool space you're not using? Close the registers and baseboard heaters—and then close the door.

- *Open or close the windows based on the temperature outside.* A fan in a window (blowing outward) can draw cooler air into a house through other open windows.

- *Drapes, blinds, and shutters can help keep a house cool or warm.*

- *Use ceiling fans.* Ceiling fans use less energy than air conditioners and can be used in both hot and cold weather. In the summer, set ceiling fans to turn counterclockwise; in winter, switch it to clockwise and use the slowest rotation speed.

- *Install storm windows and doors.*

- *Lower the temperature on your water heater.* Reducing the temperature setting on your water heater can save energy—about 4 percent for every ten-degree (F) reduction in temperature.

- *Insulate your water heater.* Install an insulating blanket on your water heater and insulate the first several feet of hot water pipes with foam sleeves. (Alternatively, consider a solar water heater, which often pays for itself in three to five years.)

- *Caulk and weatherstrip around windows and doors to plug air leaks.*

- *Install a programmable thermostat.*

- *Consider geothermal and solar options.* Call your local energy provider to find out about its green power options. Find out about your province's or state's tax rebates or credits for installation of a solar energy system.

That worked so well that within a couple of months we had reduced the bill to under one hundred dollars. Yes, California is an expensive place to live, but it doesn't have to be. With planning and good stewardship, it works out fine.—*Brenda Isaacs, Bakersfield, California*

Retrofit. About twelve years ago, we bought a house that was built in the 1880s. It was extremely energy inefficient. With a little bit of research online, discussion with friends, and advice from a local home improvement center, we found that there are good options for retrofitting an old house to meet fairly high environmental standards. We upgraded windows and sealed cracks. We insulated exterior walls and ceilings with cellulose and reflective barrier material. We upgraded to a high-efficiency furnace/air conditioner. These steps cut our energy bills by 50 percent.

Last summer we added various types of insulation, including fiberglass, cellulose, open-cell foam, and reflective barrier material in the walls and ceilings of two newly remodeled main-floor rooms. We laid reflective barrier material in our main attic. We knew this would help, but were astonished to find that now we only need to run our air conditioner at night at about 72°F (22°C) to keep our house temperature right around 72°F all day—with the air shut off. This is the case even when the outside temperature reaches the low one-hundreds F (upper thirties C) during the day.—*Doug and Jude Krehbiel, Newton, Kansas*

Heart(h) of the family. Several years ago we purchased a wood-burning cook stove. We were aware of particulate emissions and dwindling forests, but we determined that our energy was to come from a resource that surrounded us. As a self-employed furniture-maker, my husband, Andy, has a constant supply of wood: wood scraps, fallen or felled trees he is asked to take away, and even the wood rejected on trash day.

The stove has become a treasured friend and workmate. Our children wake to the sound of kindling snapping and a warm glow spreading through the house. A water pipe runs through the firebox, the hot water naturally rising to an insulated tank we installed in the hallway above. The stove cooks our food, including beans forgotten on one corner and perfectly done by supper. Laundry or mittens that hang beside and above the stove dry quickly even in the winter months. Warmth draws us in from all corners of the house. Favorite chairs and rockers have found permanent homes surrounding the stove, drawing family and guests to a central gathering place, the hearth and heart of our family.—*Wendy Chappell-Dick, Bluffton, Ohio*

Tubular. Jim and Susan Jantzen of Newton, Kansas, may know what it feels like to live underwater, or at least what it might look like. In 1979, they bought and refurbished an old house and installed a passive solar energy structure of water-filled tubes. Three big windows cover the south wall of their home, and in front of the windows stand thirteen tubes filled with clear water. "Originally the tubes were eight feet tall, but we cut them down to five feet so we could see out the windows," says Jim.

These tubes hold several thousand pounds of water. The water absorbs heat from the sun as it comes through the window and releases that heat when the room temperature drops below the water temperature. Jim and Susan also use a woodstove to heat the house. Because the water is heated by sunlight, the consistency of the water heat depends directly on the weather. "In the winter, there is less sunlight, so we have to use the woodstove more, because the water tubes don't collect as much heat," says Jim.—*Submitted by Esther Shank, Harrisonburg, Virginia*

Light. Using light-colored shingles on a new roof can cut the amount of heat the house absorbs. Repainting in a light color, especially south- and west-facing exterior areas, helps as well. Upgraded insulation in the attic and double-paned windows all around, complete with tinting to reflect sunlight, are good ideas too. Install white window shades, drapes, or blinds to reflect heat away from the house. Close curtains on south- and west-facing windows during the day. Install awnings on south-facing windows. Because of the angle of the sun, trees, a trellis, or a fence will best shade west-facing

• • • • • • • • • • • • • •

Solar power could provide energy to over a billion people around the world by 2020 and provide 2.3 million full-time jobs.[4]

windows. Apply sun-control or other reflective films on south-facing windows.—*Mary Waltner, Chicago, Illinois*

Geothermal energy. Where I live, the winters are cold and the summers are hot. Heating a home with natural gas and cooling it with an air conditioner seemed wasteful. I knew it would be only a few short years before our heating and cooling system needed to be replaced, so I began my research in 2005. I had heard of geothermal systems before—they've been around in various forms since the 1980s. Ours was installed in 2008. The system essentially extracts energy in the form of heat from deep in the ground, which stays at essentially the same temperature year-round—about 7–9°C (44–48°F).

Inside the home, a special unit converts this energy to heat our house in winter and cool it in summer. Because it runs entirely on electricity and our electricity comes from hydro-generation stations, no fossil fuels are required and there are no harmful emissions. It is "clean energy" in the sense that it doesn't require coal or nuclear power; instead, huge dams on rivers in the north provide the reservoirs of water that power the generators. Unfortunately, my electrically powered geothermal system is not entirely guilt-free: these dams often flood lands that were formerly hunting grounds and traditional lands of Canada's Aboriginal people.—*Dan Dyck, Winnipeg, Manitoba*

House of straw. Kim and Mike Martin, along with Mike's brother, Linford, and his wife, Chloe Grasse, are building a straw-bale house in Greencastle, Pennsylvania. With a wood frame and sturdy cement floor, the house begins like any standard house. But for insulation, the Martins are using straw bales, which fit between the frames and are sealed in with plaster to prevent moisture and pests. These bales provide thick insulation, and the cement floors serve as a passive solar energy source to heat and cool the house.

After several years of working in Mexico with Mennonite Central Committee, "we wanted to live somewhere where we could have a garden and animals," says Kim. "So we bought a used trailer and have been living in that on the property while the house is being built." They hope the house will be completed by 2011. The two families will have much of their own living space but will share a garage and laundry room. Mike and his brother have recycled many materials for the house and used metal roofing, which will last longer than conventional

• • • • • • • • • • • • •

Straw-bale construction is a building method that uses bales of straw for insulation or as building elements or both. Advantages include the renewable nature of straw, cost, easy availability, and high insulation value.

shingles. "We reused beams and other lumber from a barn we tore down and have used other recycled lumber from donations," says Kim. "We are trying to make balanced, environmental choices." —*Submitted by Esther Shank, Harrisonburg, Virginia*

Humanure. The trees and shrubs on Audrey Hess and Fred Oberholtzer's property have been growing at an uncommonly fast clip. The secret? Their fertilizer: "humanure" from their composting toilet. "It's like gold," says Fred. "It's an excellent amendment to the soil."

Audrey and Fred, members of Fairfield (Pa.) Mennonite Church, used a composting toilet during their MCC term in El Salvador. When they bought their house in Gettysburg, Pennsylvania, and discovered an inadequate septic system, they decided to build one in a closet in their bathroom. Their two young sons have learned to scoop sawdust on top of the bucket every time they use the toilet, and every few days their parents empty the buckets onto the compost piles at the back of their property. Fred is careful to add that they do not use humanure on their vegetable garden or other edible plants, but notes that any harmful bacteria do die off during the lengthy decomposition process. "It makes no sense to me why we as humans defecate in clean water and then further contaminate that water with chlorine and other chemicals so that it once again becomes potable," he says.

• • • • • • • • • • • • •

Find more stories, tips, and links to resources about homes at www.mpn.net/livingmorewithless.

12
Homekeeping

Doris Janzen Longacre

• •

a neighbor who moved from England to our small Pennsylvania town said this about her adjustment: "The first few months I went out every day and washed or swept the front steps. Then one day I looked up and down the street and realized that nobody else bothered much with what in England is a real mark of a good housekeeper. So I quit cleaning my steps. But what is it that one has to do here?"

Every community and culture has its unspoken standards. In Indonesia you sweep the packed earth around your house at least once, if not twice, a day. Many years ago in Canada and the United States, the way you did the washing was important. Laundry was a real job, what with the bluing, starch, tubs, and wringer. To accomplish it properly required skill and dedication. If we can believe the stories, people watched to see who got the sheets fluttering on the line first on a sunny Monday morning and checked if they were white.

Maybe it's just as well that we don't check the neighbor's sheets anymore, because keeping tabs on each other isn't the point. People should feel free to set their own style of homekeeping. But it can't hurt for each of us to take a good look at ourselves. Keeping things livable still eats up a tidy share of our time and energy. Whoever makes such a sizable personal investment in one activity must occasionally ask the question "Is there some *meaning* to this whole business?"

More than that, we can't afford to act too independently in our homekeeping. As long as one house is connected to every other

house through power lines, water and sewer pipes, garbage trucks, and the incessant stream of products and services moving in and out, how we keep our homes is the affair of everyone.

So, what are some guidelines for today for doing ordinary tasks well? Entries to this chapter show people changing their priorities. Old questions warrant new answers.

Is it clean?

People in Canada and the United States generations ago didn't have hot running water, shelves of detergent, or antibiotics to take whenever they caught a germ. No wonder they came up with "cleanliness is next to godliness." Keeping things neat was honest work, deservedly filling much time. It's still important. A grease-splattered stove and grimy bathtub don't mean you're living simply or that you've done something more significant with your time than cleaning. It may even mean that you're sloppy about your environment and other important matters.

But the opposite approach has more potential for disaster. In contrast to people generations ago, most of us now have every chance for reasonably clean homes, clothing, and bodies—without undue effort. We ought to be delighted with this development and know where to stop, contented. Instead, we often believe the advertisers: somewhere there is a sanitary land of soaps, sprays, and cleaning machines featuring cleaner than clean, whiter than white, and no smells but nice ones. If our culture buried people with their favorite tools, some people in Canada and the United States would go to their final rest with a paper towel in one hand, an aerosol disinfectant in the other, and a stick of deodorant laid at their feet.

Is it pretty?

The word *decorate*, as applied to making a home attractive, smacks of the same mentality as *entertain* in reference to serving guests. We need to rearrange our thinking before we start moving furniture and sewing curtains. Where do you start in deciding how a home should look? With glossy women's magazines? With what's available in the furniture store? With what's "in" this year?

Lest I come off a hypocrite, I confess that arranging objects, colors, and designs in our house is an aspect of homekeeping I dearly love. It's a great creative adventure, one that I won't give up without a fuss. An attractive home buoys my spirits.

Everywhere in the world, people arrange for some beauty, some expression of their ability to invent interesting subjects for their eyes and fingertips. The plainest cooking area behind a hut in Somalia boasts an intricately carved stool or colorful basket. Cooks across Asia encourage their charcoal fires with attractively woven fans.

But starting with "What will make this place pretty?" only puts you at the mercy of the latest magazine spreads. Instead, ask first, "Who are we?" and "What will we do in this room?" Designers call that *form following function*.

After you figure that one out, other questions follow. Since new materials of practically every kind are scarce and expensive, what do you have now that's useful to the function you have in mind? Is someone else discarding what you can repair and use? If you must appropriate a new material or object, is it designed to last or is it just a fad? Does it have only one use or multiple uses?

Will the item eventually become a disposal problem? A wicker laundry basket can be composted, but not a plastic one. You can refinish a wood floor and scatter cotton and wool area rugs, or you can cover it with synthetic carpet, which is a petroleum product. And when it becomes worn and soiled, the earth has no good place for it. But natural fibers make good rugs, paper, or mulch. You can refinish the wood floor again and again.

Finally, demand meaning from anything nonfunctional that you bring into your home. Replace mass-produced art with your own child's drawing or your grandfather's portrait. This, as much as anything, makes the difference between a home and what is only a decorated living space.

Is it new and strong?

Every system has its idols. Advertisers know by now which gods the Canadian and U.S. householder will obey. One more-with-less principle for homekeeping is to recognize these on sight and refuse to worship.

The first is simply *new*. Flip through a magazine and see how many ads carry that word. But new is a high, a temporary glow that sputters out when edges fray and chip. Newness saturation produces a longing for roots, for the comfort and even the status of old things. Thus little antique shops flourish down the street from giant discount stores. Cooks who feel compelled to line their kitchen counters with new appliances scour flea markets for old graters to hang on the wall, although they no longer know how to dismantle a cabbage without a food processor.

The second idol is *strong*. "I need something *strong*," wails a coughing drugstore customer. Something to solve my problem quickly, efficiently, once and for all, becomes the unspoken message. Never mind side effects.

Where's the off-on switch?

Energy conservation cannot be confined to one section, because it belongs everywhere. Certainly it applies here, and may be the single most important aspect of keeping the home.

Enough times we've been told to turn off the lights. But even specific good habits don't apply broadly enough. For example, now we're told to buy energy-efficient appliances. And certain appliances like the slow cooker and microwave get billed that way. But what the electric company leaflet doesn't mention is that every new appliance requires energy to manufacture, market, and eventually receive a proper burial.

● ● ● ● ● ● ● ● ● ● ● ● ●

Appliances

Twenty percent of all energy use in the average U.S. home goes to appliances.[2]

To sort through all these angles, we need a conservation ethic that makes us think along many fronts.

Principles gleaned from testimonies on homekeeping include the following:

- *Set a reasonable standard for cleanliness,* and pare cleaning products to the basics.

- *Reduce purchase of all products and materials* that are either non-renewable or not biodegradable. Begin with small disposables like Styrofoam tableware and plastic wrap, then include larger items such as plastic containers and furniture, synthetic rugs, and fabrics.

- *Systematically recycle* glass, paper, and aluminum. Compost organic materials from the kitchen and yard.

- *Save energy supplies* by doing some chores the slow way and by hiring people to help rather than by buying more machines. Redeem menial tasks by sharing them. Use the time to think, pray, and identify with those who have less.

- *Let meaning and function determine* the look of objects, rooms, and yards. Plan around people, their needs, and activities.

- *Arrange your home to bring the people in it into closer fellowship.* Having only one bathroom teaches consideration for others. One warm room draws the family together on winter evenings. Children want to play near the place where their parents work. Highlight enjoying each other, not the things you own.

- *Don't let lack of space or facility keep you from doing what's important*—inviting guests for meals and lodging, expanding your household, enjoying various kinds of family fun, cooking from scratch. Make do.

Use what you've got. While living in the interior of Brazil, we simply had to adapt to new situations. There were no alternatives. We used the resources we had. This included little things like beating egg whites with a fork and learning to sleep in a hammock. I find it's a challenge to continue this attitude now that we're back in the United States. I mentally put myself in a position of limited resources and ask myself, "What do I have right now that can be used in this situation?" 1 Timothy 6:7-8 helps me keep things in perspective: "We brought nothing into the world, so that we can take nothing out of it; but if we have food and clothing, we will be content with these."
—*Annette Eisenbeis, Marion, South Dakota* (1980)

Cleaner now. We no longer buy any bathroom or household cleaners. Originally I simply didn't like the idea of bathing my young daughters in a bathtub that had harsh residues, but I soon came to see that cutting out all of the chemical cleaners for our bathtub, toilet, and floors made sense on so many levels: less money spent, less garbage produced, fewer headaches from the chemical fumes, healthier children, and a healthier environment. We use baking soda, vinegar, or a combination of the two for virtually all our household cleaning, and I'm convinced my house is as clean as ever—cleaner, in fact, because I no longer worry about any harsh residues.—*Kirsten Krymusa, Nairobi, Kenya*

● ● ● ● ● ● ● ● ● ● ● ● ● ●

Most household cleaning needs can be taken care of with soap, water, baking or washing soda, white vinegar, lemon juice, borax, and a good scrubbing sponge.

Wipe down. Soap scum in the bathroom shower can be very preventable. I suggest consistently wiping down your shower wall with a hand towel after each use. Using castile soaps rather than conventional soaps for bathing also helps reduce buildup. Depending on the mineral content of your water, the combination of these two preventive measures can greatly reduce the need for more toxic soap-scum cleaners.—*Amber Near, Goshen, Indiana*

Up in flames. Many dollars are wasted on bathroom deodorants. The flame from one or two matches will eliminate odors. This is better than adding other foreign gases to the air. Of course, special precautions must be taken where children are involved.—*Mary Kathryn Yoder, Garden City, Missouri* (1980)

All-purpose cleaner. We tend to associate clean with a strong, bleach-type smell. We need to retrain our sense of smell when it comes to cleaning; for example, a clean house can smell like your favorite essential oil. Following is a recipe for my all-purpose cleaner.

> **2 cups / 500 ml hot water**
> **1 tsp. / 5 ml washing soda (sodium bicarbonate, available in most grocery stores)**
> **2 tsp. / 10 ml borax**
> **1 tsp. / 5 ml antiseptic essential oil (such as sweet orange, cinnamon, lavender, or tea tree)**
> **1/2 tsp. / 2.5 ml liquid soap**

Heat water and stir in washing soda and borax until they dissolve. Add your favorite essential oil and soap. Pour into spray bottle. Spray on counters or the front of appliances.—*Amber Near, Goshen, Indiana*

• • • • • • • • • • • • • • •   • • • • • • • • • • • • •

Window cleaner: A half-and-half solution of white vinegar and water gets windows clean. If there is streaking, add a few drops of liquid castile soap.

Furniture polish: Three parts olive oil and one part white vinegar makes a good furniture polish.

Disposing of the disposal. By the time we could afford a garbage disposal, our priorities had changed. We began to ask, Why spend money on another appliance requiring electricity and water? Why add to the city's waste-disposal system? Why buy commercial fertilizer for our garden while sending potential compost down the drain?—*Rosemary Moyer, North Newton, Kansas* (1980)

• • • • • • • • • • • • • •

Daily domestic water use per person in Canada is estimated at 90 gallons (343 liters). The average person in the United States uses 101 gallons (382 liters) per day.[3]

Dehumidifier water. We save water from our dehumidifier in the basement. We use the water in the washer and toilet, to water plants, and to mop the floor. Our dog prefers this water to tap water! We save 7.5 gallons (about 28 liters) a day when the humidity is high.—*Sharon Williams, Norristown, Pennsylvania*

Greywater. Living in the desert, where the average yearly rainfall in inches is only in the mid-teens (33–43 centimeters), has made me very conscious of my water usage. For the past couple of years we have been using a greywater system in our home. Big plastic tubs in the kitchen sinks collect the water from hand- or dish-washing. When the tubs are full, we use the water to flush the toilet or to water the trees and plants outside. (If you use it to water trees or plants, it's important to use environmentally friendly or biodegradable soap.) There is also a hose hooked up to our washing machine, which is then directed to one of the trees in the backyard. So every time we do laundry, the tree gets watered. Greywater systems save water and are easy to use.—*Erin Flory Robertson, Tucson, Arizona*

• • • • • • • • • • • • • •

A greywater system is any system for collecting dish, shower, sink, or laundry water that can be reused for other purposes.

Good to the last drop. Conserving water was an integral part of life for my parents and grandparents. I remember this practice especially with the way the women did laundry. The same water was used for several loads of laundry, and Mom always washed our dirty farm clothes last. Today I am very aware of predictions that water may become the most critical resource in short supply in the world. Already in the Shenandoah Valley we have had several summer seasons when we were urged to reduce water usage.

To take this concern seriously, I installed a rain barrel behind our shed and reinstalled the shed's spouting to direct water into the barrel. By elevating the

• • • • • • • • • • • • • •

All toilets, urinals, faucets, and showerheads installed in the United States since 1997 have been required to meet federal water efficiency standards. By 2020, these efficiency standards are projected to save enough water per day to supply four to six cities the size of New York City.[4]

barrel three feet off the ground, I can use a hose to water the garden rather than running a hose from our city water supply. I also brought a bucket into our upstairs bathroom, which is a long way from the water heater in the basement. Now we use the bucket to catch the water in the shower or sink while we are waiting for hot water to arrive, and then we use that water to flush the toilet. Taking these steps helps me carry on my mother's tradition and reminds me to be grateful for every drop.—*Paul Longacre, Harrisonburg, Virginia*

Dishwashers: yea or nay? As I thought about why we still wash our dishes by hand—besides the inertia of not wanting to hack out a space for a dishwasher and plunk down the cash— all the reasons sounded idiosyncratic, even sentimental. Yet as a stay-at-home dad, I find that cleaning up the dishes after the morning rush of breakfast and getting our second-grader to school provides an opportunity to take stock of the day ahead. In the spring, the window above the kitchen sink frames our neighbor's blossoming cherry and dogwood trees. After supper,

• •

How can we start saving water?[5]

- *Put a "displacement device" in your toilet tank.* A narrow jug filled with pebbles works well and can save up to half a gallon (almost 2 liters) per flush. Make sure that the jug doesn't interfere with the flushing mechanism.

- *Consider installing a composting toilet or a low-flow, dual-flush toilet.*

- *Take shorter showers.* Each minute in the shower uses about 2.5 gallons (about 9.5 liters) of water, so shortening your shower by two minutes can save several thousand gallons of water a year.

- *Switch to a low-flow showerhead.* You can cut your water usage per minute in half.

- *Rig up a greywater system* for collecting water in a bucket under your bathroom sink. You can use it to flush the toilet, water plants, or for a variety of other uses.

- *Fix leaky faucets and toilets.* A dripping faucet can waste 20 gallons (about 76 liters) of water a day.

- *Wear clothes until they're dirty.* Rewearing clean clothes a second or third day can drastically reduce a household's laundry. Hanging them up after each use lets them air out naturally.

- *Wash and rinse dishes in tubs.* If washing dishes by hand, use a tub of soapy water and a rinse tub rather than running water continuously over dishes.

dishwashing is my time to listen to news or the Phillies game on the radio. For our chore-deprived children, washing, emptying the drying rack, and putting the dishes away provide opportunities to contribute to our household economy. I'm sure stacking the dishes in a dishwasher could meet many of the same aims. Then again, how would we keep our hands warm in our cold kitchen in the winter?—*Ken Beidler, Philadelphia, Pennsylvania*

Going nuts about laundry. I use soap nuts instead of laundry detergent to wash our clothes. Soap nuts, also called soap berries, are dried fruits that release a natural surfactant when they become damp. I put a few soap nuts in a small muslin bag, toss them in the washer with our dirty clothes, and then can reuse the nuts at least one more time. The result is quite satisfactory, and in some cases it's even better than regular detergent. I also prefer them because they are not perfumed and don't irritate delicate skin. I've found that the overall cost is about the same as if I were to use regular laundry detergent—about thirty dollars (U.S.) for a six- to nine-month supply. Soap nut trees grow in tropical climates (in Florida, for example), so shipping might not be necessary for everyone. I also make a soap nut "tea" and put it in a spray bottle as an all-purpose cleaner. It degreases stove messes and is a mild disinfectant for countertops. Another (perhaps less noteworthy) use is to delouse people and animals. I'm hoping never to have a need to try that!—*Julie Zook, Dillsburg, Pennsylvania*

• • • • • • • • • • • • •

To reduce junk mail if you live in Canada, go to www.reddotcampaign.ca. If you live in the United States, go to www.DirectMail.com/Junk_Mail.

Drying. In Hong Kong, none of my Chinese friends had clothes dryers. I learned to do as they did. To conserve space, we clipped socks and washcloths to the lower edge of other things on the line. We hung shirts, blouses, and dresses on hangers before putting them on the line. I became efficient at stringing underwear on a bamboo pole. Now that I'm back in the States, I still do the same. If it's not a good drying day,

I simply postpone the job. Remembering others who work much harder to do their laundry has become my regular prayer reminder for them. I can't help noticing how people spend money for labor-saving devices and then more money for exercisers. This is hard to explain to Asian friends.—*Margaret Metzler, Kokomo, Indiana* (1980)

Hung out to dry. When friends of ours, Deb and Terry Brensinger of Mechanicsburg, Pennsylvania, were threatened with legal action from their homeowners association for hanging laundry outside to dry ("we're trying to keep the place from looking junky," the president of the association told the local newspaper), I was appalled.

Air-drying clothes can reduce the average household's carbon emissions by about 2,400 pounds (1,089 kilograms) a year.[6]

When I learned that about half of the homeowners groups in the United States prohibit laundry lines, I was indignant . . . until I remembered that our own laundry line usually hung empty while our clothes dryer hummed away.

So it was out of solidarity with the Brensingers that we began doing what we had intended to do for a long time: regularly hanging our laundry to dry. I was surprised how little time it actually took; it had always loomed in my imagination as oodles more time consuming and labor intensive than using the dryer. While we still use our dryer sometimes and while we don't have any homeowners association to tell us to stop, I do hope that one more full laundry line helps to normalize a practice that, at least in some communities, seems increasingly endangered.—*Valerie Weaver-Zercher, Mechanicsburg, Pennsylvania*

Dispense with disposables. I seldom use disposable items anymore. On the floor in front of the back seat of my car I keep a canvas bag full of reusable grocery bags, handy to grab when I shop for food. I've stopped buying paper napkins, since my husband and I use only cloth. They are easily washable and dry within an hour when hung out to dry. For picnics or potlucks, I use washable plates and tableware. I've even found that mirrors and windows can be washed with newspaper or polyester washcloths or towels, thus avoiding the use of paper towels.—*Kathleen Springer, Saybrook, Illinois*

Bags. Grocery stores that recycle used plastic bags may also accept shrink wrap, dry-cleaner bags, and other sources of plastic. I also include the bags the newspaper comes in and any fairly clean plastic bags, such as those used for bread, fruits, and vegetables. I save ones that aren't very clean to use for garbage or dirty items so that I don't use up the recyclable bags.—*Lorene Byler Miller, Goshen, Indiana*

And more bags. So many bags arrive free—brown sugar, frozen veggies, bulk foods—and in many other ways. I have a plastic bag drier on the edge of my kitchen sink. With nine spokes on it, I can easily dry a day's worth of bags. The next day, I put those bags away and am ready to dry another day's worth. Other methods of drying are certainly possible. My mother used to hang her bags on her clothesline.—*Linda Miller, Harrisonburg, Virginia*

• •

How can we use appliances more efficiently?[7]

- *Switch to cold water when washing laundry.* Washing in cold water saves energy and, except when clothes have oily stains, clothes still get clean.
- *Wait for full loads of dishes and laundry.*
- *Air-dry dishes.* Stop the dishwasher and open the door after the final rinse cycle, or use the "air dry" setting instead of the "heat dry."
- *Air-dry laundry.* Electric clothes dryers can put up to 5 pounds (2.5 kilograms) of greenhouse gases into the atmosphere per cycle.
- *Turn your refrigerator and freezer to the warmest settings.*
- *Unplug appliances when you're not using them.* Phantom power, also called standby power or vampire power, is the electricity drawn by appliances even when they're turned off. About 75 percent of the power used by appliances and electronic devices is used while they are turned off.
- *Use a smart strip on your appliances.* Smart power strips monitor electricity use in each plug and shut off the ones that haven't been used for a period of time.

Rags. I've found that the local Goodwill accepts clothing in any condition to be processed and used for rags. I've been told that any type of fabric can be used. At home, I don't buy paper towels; using discarded sweatshirts, T-shirts, and socks works just as well.—*Lorene Byler Miller, Goshen, Indiana*

Location, location, location. When our recycling containers were kept only in an out-of-the-way part of the house, my wife and I found it hard to remember to recycle. Putting recycling and compost containers right beside our trash can made it just as easy to recycle or compost as to throw away. Now taking out the trash is a rare affair.—*Nicholas Detweiler-Stoddard, Harrisonburg, Virginia*

Video of energy savings. I made a video with my eleven-year-old daughter about all the energy-efficient things we've done to our home over the years. In front of the camera, she talked about each item in our home and how it saved energy: a fluorescent light bulb, our woodstove, double-pane windows, insulated water heater, skylight, water-reducing shower head, etc. She had a blast doing it, learned a lot, and kids and teachers at school really liked it and complimented her when it was shown there on a parent-student-teacher fun night.—*Sam Nickels, Harrisonburg, Virginia*

Compact fluorescent light bulbs (CFLs) use up to 75 percent less electricity than incandescent bulbs and last up to ten times longer. As CFLs contain a small amount of mercury, check with your area solid waste authority to identify local recycling options.

Find more stories, tips, and links to resources about homekeeping at www.mpn.net/livingmorewithless.

13
Gardens, Farms, and Markets

Greg Bowman

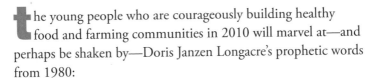

the young people who are courageously building healthy food and farming communities in 2010 will marvel at—and perhaps be shaken by—Doris Janzen Longacre's prophetic words from 1980:

> For our future we need a modern "organic technology." We need a blend between the peasant's ecological skill and our contemporary knowledge of what is possible. . . . Finding [this] blend means that we consciously choose to fit the way we live to the environment, not trying to reshape the environment to our whims. Sometimes this will cost more initially than the old system of using up, throwing away, and destroying. Certainly it will take more imagination. Above all, cherishing the natural order requires a willingness to live in God's image and live peacefully with the earth.

For citizens of the United States and Canada, thirty years seems like a long time. Yet it has taken that long for a broadly recognized new expression of agriculture, which loosely resembles what Longacre envisioned, to emerge. From Vancouver to Virginia, Sarasota to Saskatoon, farmers are starting to be rewarded for the quality of the food they produce and the care they give to their land, workers, families, and livestock. These new agriculturists, regardless of the size of their plot, farm with creation and their communities in mind and have found ways to connect with people who share these values.

These cultivators and livestock caregivers are collaborating with school food directors, grocers, chefs, and families. They all want to blend biology and farmer wisdom to produce authentic food in a transparent way. Eaters everywhere can better celebrate what grows within nature's limits by being more aware of seasons, farming processes, and creative recipe adaptation.

Blessed with real choices

Canadians and U.S. citizens are blessed with a growing crop of meaningful food choices for living more with less. More farmers are learning the intimate ways that living soil, plants, insects, and microorganisms interact positively when agricultural toxins are reduced or eliminated. Farmers and consumers now know of the growing evidence that even ultra-low levels of pesticides affect pregnant women and their offspring, making farms based on biodiversity our pioneers in producing food that is safe for nature and people.

There is a parallel cultural shift, visible in the statistics across income and ethnic/racial groups, toward two things that highly processed "industrial food" cannot supply: a yearning for some kind of meaningful human connection with food producers and a desire for food that is healthy in what it contains, in what it is free from, in how it was produced, and in what it represents as a force for good.

Many commodity farmers are in unprofitable situations due to high input costs and low prices for mass-produced milk, grain, and livestock. Some are transitioning to the new agriculture, which is also seeing a flood of young farmers from non-farming backgrounds, eco-entrepreneurs, corporate refugees, and second-career entrants.

The future starts here

New efforts by eaters, producers, and institutions include the following:

- *Buy fresh, buy local.* Fresh, local purchases are strengthening farm economies. This demand drives innovation by farmers to extend seasons and diversify crops. It entices cooks to explore new menus flavored by expanding lists of local options. Adding more value are combinations of local, sustainable, humane, and fair-trade attributes.

- *Producer-only farmers markets.* Usually held weekly at outdoor venues where farmers bring fresh or preserved foods from their own farms, producer-only farmers markets numbered more than 5,300 in the United States in 2009. Congregations, food advocacy nonprofits, and sustainable farming groups continue to explore ways to make this direct-marketing option more affordable and accessible to lower-income families while also upholding economic viability for farmers.

- *Community Supported Agriculture (CSA).* In exchange for early-season payment, CSA shareholders receive weekly amounts of fresh vegetables, herbs, flowers, and fruits. Distribution can be on-farm pickup, home delivery, or via drop-off sites. Multi-farm CSAs add stability, diversity, and convenience for eaters, increasing the range of food items available. Members usually receive weekly face time and/or newsletters from the farmers, with crop updates and recipes.

- *Grass-based meat and dairy.* What cows eat has a direct impact on their health and the nutritional makeup of their meat and milk. This solar-powered food system, which varies with season and geographic location, is finding success on farms where cows eat mostly grass, pasture, and forage.

- *Innovative regional marketing co-ops of rural organic farmers.* Many of these grow from Plain (culturally conservative Anabaptist) communities that work with non-Plain staff who provide sophisticated electronic systems. These tools coordinate production, marketing, real-time online inventory control, and distribution of fruits, vegetables, poultry, dairy, and livestock products. Enthusiastic buyers are often in urban regional markets several hours away.

- *Farm to institution.* School food directors are revolutionizing what students can expect on the menu. Many hospitals, retirement centers, and government-run agencies are also turning to farms to serve fresher food. This move circulates more dollars within the communities that support these institutions.

Shopping for shalom

There is a great hunger for food that nourishes our bodies and our communities. This quest allows people who are generally uncomfortable with religion to talk about their spiritual longings. It also lets Jesus-followers put words to our hope and our desire to care for creation. Farmers, eaters, and the people who weave them together are all important. These and others who help to carefully "till and keep" the global garden—in their work, eating choices, investments, and advocacy—serve as signs of the coming restoration of creation.

Feeding the soil. At Joshua Farm, an urban vegetable farm in Harrisburg, Pennsylvania, the end of the vegetable growing season doesn't mean the fields are left bare. In the fall, Kirsten Reinford, the farm's founder and manager and a member of Harrisburg Brethren in Christ Church, sows what are known as cover crops. "These crops aren't ones I'm planning to harvest or eat," says Kirsten of the winter rye, Austrian peas, and crimson clover she has planted. "Instead, I'm using them to feed the soil."

To produce the most nutritious crops, nutrients in the soil need to be replenished and renewed. This is often done with fertilizers, but since they can be washed away and affect wetland and marine ecosystems, feeding the soil is a more sustainable approach. Kirsten either lets the cover crops die back or cuts them down and allows them to enrich the soil. She notes that this is a method home gardeners can use on a smaller scale. While the environmental impacts are a key motivating factor, Kirsten recognizes that it comes down to basic systems, saying, "In essence, I'm trying to create humus, the stuff from which humans were formed in the biblical story and on which human life still depends."—*Submitted by Charity Grimes, Pittsburgh, Pennsylvania*

Yard equals garden. A seed of an idea began to grow after a trip to Europe in 2004 when I noticed that front yards don't have to be grass. *Let's raise food there—tomatoes, beans, beets, carrots, and all their cousins,* I thought. So for nearly five years I dreamed about no more mowing. Finally the dream became a reality. Starting in March 2009 I began making the soil to fill the raised beds that would grow our vegetables and herbs. Then my husband, Rich, built the cypress-wood, square-foot beds. It was a long and arduous process—creating the design for the beds, sifting the shale from the soil, and adding compost and manure to make a rich, friable medium in which to grow the transplants, seedlings, and seeds.

Sixty percent of the water used on the West Coast of the United States and 30 percent on the East Coast goes to watering lawns.[1]

Of course, all of this needed to be protected from the neighborhood rabbits, so we called on our friend and neighbor with carpentry skills to build us a lovely picket fence with a metal pest guard at the bottom. As the lush plants ramped up their growth, they began to spill out over the fence, inviting all to enjoy their beauty. What fun I had chatting with folks who walked by, curiously watching this unusual activity in someone's front yard.—*Jan Landes, Akron, Pennsylvania*

Buckets and boxes. In addition to the traditional backyard garden space, vegetables can be raised in unconventional ways and places. Tomatoes, peppers, carrots, and salad greens can be easily grown in five-gallon (18- or 20-liter) buckets or simple wooden boxes placed on a sunny patio or even a flat roof. Not only will you have the satisfaction of watching your crops mature from tiny seeds, but you will be able to enjoy fresh foods in season at the peak of flavor, just as God intended.—*Jonathan Fox, Scottdale, Pennsylvania*

Vermicompost. Worm composting turns fruit and vegetable scraps into rich fertilizer. It is simple, non-labor intensive, very odorless, can be done most anywhere (home, school, the office), and is very environmentally friendly. The voracious Red Wiggler composting worms can be purchased online or obtained from someone who does worm composting. Put them in a five-gallon (18- or 20-liter) bucket half full of shredded office paper, and bury your fruit and vegetable scraps under the paper. A pound (1/2 kilogram) of worms can handle three pounds (1.4 kilograms) of scraps a week.

Once or twice a year, we harvest the worm compost from

• •

How can we start to compost?[2]

• *Select your structure.* Compost bins come in different shapes and sizes. They're also relatively easy to make out of wood, wire, wood pallets, or other recycled materials. Compost can also be made in a simple pile or in a hole in the ground.

• *Know your colors.* All composting requires three basic ingredients: browns, which include dead leaves, branches, or twigs; greens, which include grass clippings, vegetable waste, fruit scraps, and coffee grounds; and water.

• *Choose a sunny spot for your bin or pile.* Warm compost decomposes faster.

• *Shred or chop coarse, dense, or large materials.* They'll decompose faster.

• *Turn the pile occasionally.* Using a pitchfork or shovel, "stir" your compost to aerate it and provide fresh food to the microorganisms. (This is not necessary if you have a tumbler, which you can simply spin.) Compost can be ready within a few months to a year, depending on how often you turn it and how warm it gets.

• *Things to compost:* fruit and vegetable scraps, egg shells, grass clippings, leaves, coffee grounds and coffee filters, pet and human hair, dryer lint, shredded paper, fireplace ashes, cereal boxes ripped into small pieces, and lots of other items. *Things not to compost:* meat scraps, dairy products, fatty food waste, bones, and dog and cat waste.

the bucket. I prefer the "compost tea" method: place all the contents of the bin into a large bucket of water and stir it up, then pour the "tea" through a colander or strainer into another bucket. The strainer catches the worms and uncomposted materials, which can then be placed back into the original bin (with more shredded paper to help the worms dry off). The liquid "compost tea" can be spread on gardens or house plants as a healthy plant food.—*Art Bucher, Philadelphia, Pennsylvania*

Compost with leaves. In the fall, make a large pile of leaves near your garden. Come early summer, after garden plants are established and the soil has warmed up, go to your now-flattened and soggy leaf pile. Under the loose leaves on top will be dense layers of matted leaves. Carefully peel off one-inch-thick (2.5-centimeters-thick) leaf mats, and lay them around the base of your garden plants and between rows. Aside from minimizing weeds and evaporation, the leaf mats help keep the root zone and soil surface cool, worm-friendly, and organically active. Every rain or watering produces "compost tea," and in the fall or spring the mulch can be turned into the soil.—*Mark Liechty, Oak Park, Illinois*

Fowling the yard. Our family has been enjoying organic, fresh eggs from free-range chickens for more than a decade. Besides being a source of excellent nutrition, our backyard flock has been an education for our four children about the source of some of their daily food. Doing the daily chores of feeding and providing fresh water for our hens has also helped to develop their work ethic. Another benefit of having hens is that we recycle most of our food scraps as chicken feed. Our friends also bring over their food scraps, and I even bring home my coworkers' food scraps from the lunchroom at work. It is our own little "food scraps to eggs" program.

My wife and I grew up in the suburbs. Raising our children with an experience of farm animals—chickens, ducks, sheep, and goats—has been a wonderful learning experience. The easiest place to start, and the source of organic, tasty eggs, is that backyard flock of hens. (You'll first want to check your local zoning ordinances and read a book or two about caring for chickens.)—*Michael Brennan, Scottsville, New York*

Know your meat. Our family decided to remove all animal products from our diet back in the summer of 1999. We lasted about six months, finding it difficult to eat in others' homes and to strictly avoid some of the foods we had formerly loved so much. We missed cheese, eggs, meat, and milk. Around the same time, I was beginning to shop at the weekly downtown farmers market and realized that I could buy meat and eggs from local farmers. This was a good fit for our food preferences without compromising my newfound desire not to buy commercial grocery-store varieties. Since then, the farmers whose grass-fed beef and pork and pastured chicken and eggs we eat have become our friends. We visit their farms and know their families. I have learned about the far-superior nutritional benefits of animal products grown on grass and have become convinced of the merits of buying in the local economy. And it tastes better too!—*Kris Shank Zehr, Harrisonburg, Virginia*

Livestock produced by factory farming are inefficient at converting grains and other resources into usable food. Beef requires 16 pounds (7.3 kilograms) of grain just to produce one pound (1/2 kilogram) of meat.[3]

Hunting. An often overlooked and sometimes shunned method of obtaining the meat you and your family eat is hunting. Wild animals may be at the pinnacle of free-range, organic, locally grown, hormone-free, lean, and sustainable sources of protein. Hunting for one's table fare is an alternative to agribusiness-supplied meat. Wild meat is typically very lean, and better for the heart due to extra Omega-3s and lower fat content.

Hunting requires you to be fit enough to pursue animals through the woods and over mountains. It gets you out to meet with farmers or ranchers in your community to talk about land access and wildlife impact. Stepping into a predator's shoes also brings you closer to the real nature of nature. God created everything to consume something else, from the mega-fauna on down to lettuce. Taking an active role in my omnivorous food chain gets me off the couch of passivity and into the tactile world of screeching, running, smelly life. On a spiritual level, I thank God for providing me this beautiful animal and its ability to sustain life for my family (something I rarely do for a beef and bean burrito from Safeway).—*Bryan Miller, Colorado Springs, Colorado*

Repelling deer. We live at the edge of Cuyahoga Valley National Park. While we love all the trails and park programs, keeping the white-tailed deer away from our trees and flowers is always a challenge. Instead of buying expensive deer repellent, we make our own:

> **½ cup / 125 ml milk**
> **½ tbsp. / 7 ml cooking oil**
> **½ tsp. / 2.5 ml granular dishwasher detergent**
> **2 tbsp. / 20 ml garlic powder**
> **1 egg**
> **Water (enough to make a gallon, or 3.8 liters, of this mixture)**

Mix in an old milk jug and let it sit outside for at least a day (the longer the better). In the spring, spray or pour on plants every few days or after each rain. After that, spray or pour on plants at least weekly or after each rain. As fall approaches, just give up and let the deer munch for winter.—*Amy Gingerich and Ryan Claassen, Hudson, Ohio*

Quiet mowing. I have mowed with a human-powered reel mower for the past twelve years. Although it becomes physically strenuous at times, especially in the lush spring season, I have never really regretted my decision. I get several benefits: I can combine aerobic and resistance exercise. I burn no fossil fuels (no choking exhaust fumes) and use no electricity. I can mow quietly; last time I mowed, two passersby, independently of each other, remarked on how quiet my mowing was. I also notice and appreciate the growing things in my path.—*Mary Janzen, State College, Pennsylvania*

How can we make our outdoor work greener?[4]

- *Compost your food scraps.* Work it into the soil in the spring. Compost provides a host of nutrients to plants, minimizes weeds, helps to prevent erosion, and helps maintain moisture.

- *Use a rain barrel.* By catching rainwater that would otherwise be lost to runoff and that can then be used for watering gardens and other purposes, a rain barrel will save most homeowners about 1,300 gallons (about 4,920 liters) during the summer months.

- *Use a manual lawnmower.* One gas-powered lawnmower emits the same amount of pollutants as eight new cars driving 55 miles per hour (about 88 kilometers per hour) for the same amount of time.

- *Plant native plants.* Native plants thrive in a range of conditions, require less maintenance and water, and preserve local biodiversity of wildlife.

- *Liberate your lawn.* Gradually plant biodiverse gardens, orchards, or native plantings that will yield food for wildlife or humans and/or require less fossil fuel to maintain.

- *Slow runoff.* Move soil to create shallow depressions along the sloping areas in lawns, fields, and pastures. Small humps built across unpaved, sloping driveways divert runoff in small doses to controlled receiving areas to prevent it from reaching damaging volumes that create gullies. Holding water longer in the area where it falls increases the amount that percolates downward to "recharge" precious groundwater reserves. Roofs, driveways, and parking lots made of porous materials reduce the excessive runoff of overdeveloped areas.

Food bank farm. I work with a food bank in Tucson that has a twelve-acre, pesticide-free farm that supplies several farmers markets with food. The farmers markets were started to supply food bank clients with food; clients receive vouchers from the food bank that can be exchanged for fresh produce. I started working with the farm as part of Mennonite Voluntary Service, and I am now on staff at the food bank, working five days a week at the farm growing vegetables for these farmers markets. I no longer buy vegetables from the supermarket but instead support the farmers markets and use produce that is in season.—*Maggie Barnes, Tucson, Arizona*

Corner corn. Where others saw just a weed-filled sand lot
in Albuquerque, New Mexico, Donna Detweiler and five of
the tenants in the apartment building she manages saw cherry
tomatoes, butternut squash, and Armenian cucumbers. With
a desire to grow their own plants but without the space to do
it, they got creative and decided to give a corner of the building's property a new life. The group started mapping out the
area one spring and set to spreading horse manure and compost, gathering trash cans to collect water runoff from the roof,
and planting veggies and herbs in planters and in the ground.
Despite the plot's exposure to the public right by the street,
their garden saw little vandalism and produced enough for the
gardeners to eat their fill and share with friends.

What once was a forgotten corner of land was successfully
turned into something beautiful and productive; there are even
plans to expand enough to sell at a growers market. "Often when
I came in the cool of the morning to check on our plant friends,
I would see nongardening residents just staring in admiration,"
Donna says. "They were appreciating the jumble of green life
that had miraculously taken root in a barren corner of their little
world."—*Submitted by Charity Grimes, Pittsburgh, Pennsylvania*

• • • • • • • • • • • • • •

**Community Supported Agriculture
(or Community Shared Agriculture) enables eaters to buy local,
seasonal produce directly from
farmers. CSA members typically
buy "shares" at the beginning of the
growing season and then pick up
a box of produce weekly. There are
about 1,600 CSA farms in 2010 in
the United States, with membership
ranging from less than twenty-five
into the thousands. Check out www.
localharvest.org to find a CSA farm
near you.**

The "God rule." When my five-
year-old son came skipping back
from the field, carrying ears of
corn and chatting with the farmer,
I was hooked. For us, belonging to
a CSA isn't just about eating delicious organic food or supporting
local agri-culture; it's about connecting our children to the people
who feed them. From gooseberry-
stained hands to eyes wide at the
sight of purple tomatoes, each
week held new adventures—at the farm and on our dinner
table. By the end of that first summer, we had developed the
"God rule" for food: "The best food on earth is created by God,

grown by people who care about God's earth, and prepared by the hands God gave us." Thank you, God, for CSAs.—*Joy Fasick, Gardners, Pennsylvania*

Gardening and prayer. Gardening is almost universal. Even in a world where so few people know where in particular their food comes from, we all know where food in general comes from, just as we all "know" where heaven is: the former, down; the latter, up. So whether I go out to the college's student-run garden, spreading dining-hall compost on the garlic and tomatoes, or to my grandparents' flower border, transplanting azaleas in the sandy New Hampshire soil, I connect down to the source of all our food. So does anyone else who ever gardened: from the people next door to the workers on industrial farms to the hunter-gatherer who decided that berries consolidated were easier to pick than berries scattered. So, too, when we connect to the source of our food, we connect to the source of life itself. God is down as well as up. When we garden, we remember that we are kneeling not only to plant, to uproot, or to harvest, but also to pray.—*Greg Albright, Allentown, Pennsylvania*

Farming Eden. For Tim Showalter Ehst, small-scale farming is both a professional passion and a faith conviction. When Tim and his wife, Krista, recently relocated to Atlanta, he hoped to find vegetable farming work in the city. His desire eventually led him to Berea Mennonite Church, which had property and "felt their land was a gift, but that perhaps they weren't using it to its potential," says Tim. Together, they developed a plan to run a CSA off the church's property.

Why turn a churchyard into a vegetable farm? Tim says their hope is that the farm will be one "that addresses food justice issues while providing a fun and healthy response to the surrounding community." His conviction runs deeper though, as Tim holds his faith and farming hand-in-hand. "We are called, in Genesis, to 'till and keep' the land," he says. "This is part of our call to reestablish Eden, to envision and enact the new earth, to realize the reign of God."—*Submitted by Charity Grimes, Pittsburgh, Pennsylvania*

Saturday market. Most Saturday mornings you'll find me at the local market nestled in the heart of downtown Kitchener. My morning ritual begins with making my grocery list, collecting cash and coins, grabbing my cart on wheels, and heading by foot to the market, which is about fifteen minutes from my home. At the market I can pick up most of the groceries I need for the week. Upstairs at the market I can grab a cup or a pound of fair-trade coffee and enjoy a breakfast burrito, waffle, Caribbean specialties, or my favorite: apple fritters smothered in sugar. The benefits of this weekly ritual are great: I get exercise and fresh air by walking, I often go with a friend who lives in the same building, I support local producers, and I am getting to know the vendors by name. As I put my groceries away, I'm already planning the homemade meals that I can enjoy all week long.—*Eleanor Snyder, Kitchener, Ontario*

Returning containers. I love going to the farmers market for all the wonderful produce. I take my own bag to minimize the bags I would get from vendors. However, for some things I do need to take a container. So I take them back: the berry boxes, the egg cartons, the paper bags the apples came in, the jars that held the jelly. Invariably the vendor is happy to have his or her containers back, and I send less to the landfill.—*Linda Miller, Harrisonburg, Virginia*

• • • • • • • • • • • • • •

Find more stories, tips, and links to resources about gardens, farms, and markets at www.mpn.net/livingmorewithless.

14
Cooking and Eating

Mary Beth Lind

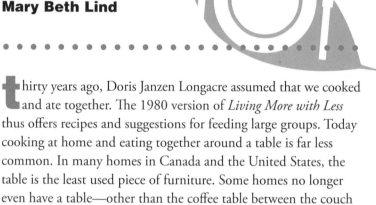

● ●

thirty years ago, Doris Janzen Longacre assumed that we cooked
and ate together. The 1980 version of *Living More with Less*
thus offers recipes and suggestions for feeding large groups. Today
cooking at home and eating together around a table is far less
common. In many homes in Canada and the United States, the
table is the least used piece of furniture. Some homes no longer
even have a table—other than the coffee table between the couch
and the television. Cooking for a large crowd has become a business: catering. And eating together, at the rare times when we do
it, often occurs in the car after visiting a drive-through.

So, what does living more with less in the twenty-first century
mean for cooking and eating? It means cooking and eating real foods
with real people in ways that nourish both the people and the planet.

While parts of our cooking and eating practices have changed
over the last thirty years, some things haven't changed. We still
express our values by how we cook and eat. Eating is more than
fulfilling a biological necessity. It is, in the words of Michael Pollan,
"about pleasure, about community, about family and spirituality,
about relationship to the natural world and about expressing our
identity."[1] It is an expression of our values. Recognizing eating as a
spiritual value, Longacre wrote, "We say as much about how well we
discern the Lord's body by the way we conduct potlucks, dinners,
and banquets as by how reverently we bow before the Eucharist."

Cooking communicates values

Longacre identified five life standards that continue to be relevant today: *do justice, learn from the world community, nurture people, cherish the natural order,* and *nonconform freely.* Our expression of these standards, or values, may change over time and under different circumstances, but our ways of cooking and eating communicate our values whether we acknowledge it or not.

These life standards can inform our selection, care, preparation, and consumption of food.

- *Selection: We can choose local, seasonal foods, whether from our own gardens, a local farmers market, or a CSA.* We delight in foods from different cultures. We choose real foods—"foods that rot," as Michael Pollan calls them—rather than food products with excessive additives and preservatives. Our selection of food expresses our values.

- *Care: We express our values by how we care for the foods once we have grown or purchased them.* Real foods, especially fresh fruits and vegetables, are perishable and should be handled with care. Knowing the correct temperature for storage (usually chilled) and limiting oxidation-tissue breakdown by storing in airtight containers are examples of this. It's also important to maintain correct moisture—too much and the food rots, not enough and the food wilts.

- *Preparation 1: We can nurture people by making the preparation of food a family or community project.* Children tend to eat better if they have been involved in the preparation. Seniors and singles eat better when they share the food and preparation. Hosting a canning party is a wonderful way to share this process.

- *Preparation 2: We can honor food by paying attention to the manner in which we prepare it. Body Talk* author Ingrid F. Moser, in her rules for everyday eating (paraphrasing the Leviticus dietary laws), states, "Food should be washed, chopped, . . . and baked with a grateful attitude and with tender loving care." *Washing:* Gone are the days of washing vegetables under running water. Water conservation requires that we wash vegetables in a pan of water in the order of cleanliness—washing the cleanest first and the dirtiest last. The dirty water can be used to water plants, thus putting the soil back where it came from. *Chopping:* The smaller that vegetables are chopped, the quicker they cook, thus saving energy. Cooking these smaller chopped foods in water results in greater leaching out of their nutrients, however, so use small amounts of water and save this nutrient-rich water for soups, gravies, and bread making. *Baking:* An oven uses lots of energy, so it is crucial to make wise use of it. Try to prepare more than one thing in the oven. For example, make the whole meal in the oven—casserole, muffins, and dessert. Keep the oven door shut to keep the heat in. An oven loses 20 percent of its heat every time the door is opened. Better yet, try a fireless cooker (see page 150.)

> "I want to meet more church administrators like the one I know who routinely skips one meal a day when board meetings make him dependent on high-priced restaurant meals. He takes apples and dried fruit in his suitcase and claims that this disciplined light eating cuts costs and clears his head for the Lord's business."—*Doris Janzen Longacre*

- *Consumption: We can eat in a conscious way that respects the food and our bodies.* Eating is a biological and social event, so eat with others as much as possible. Most importantly, eating should be done at a table. A table represents the center of a gathering of people around food in a way that honors both the food and the people.

This honoring of both food and people lies at the core of what living more with less means when applied to cooking and eating. Honoring both food and people is what continues to nourish us in body and spirit.

Senior salads. Every Wednesday at 8:00 a.m., eight senior citizens meet at the local senior center to make salads. We take turns purchasing the produce and bringing it to the center, where we share the produce and the costs. Based on suggestions from a nutritionist, we purchase the following: romaine lettuce, spinach, broccoli, cauliflower, red and green peppers, carrots, celery, and little green onions. Then we clean, chop, and divide the vegetables into bags. Each person gets a bag of vegetables to take home to use in salads, pot roasts, or whatever we wish. For people who live alone, this is an excellent way to provide a balanced meal.—*Viola King, Hesston, Kansas*

Salsa for all. One afternoon this past summer we held a salsa-making and canning gathering with our small group from Shalom Mennonite Church in Harrisonburg, Virginia. We all contributed what we had from our gardens or the farmers market, and we spent hours chopping and chatting. There was plenty of laughter and fresh salsa for all. Something about preparing and preserving food side by side creates powerful memories and a sense of community.—*Janelle and Jason Myers-Benner, Keezletown, Virginia*

Real fast food. Every Tuesday evening Douglas and Valerie Ehst of Akron, Pennsylvania, have fast food delivered to their doorstep—for free. And every Thursday evening they deliver. Once again—for free. The food is often organic and local and always nutritious and homemade. How is this possible? The Ehsts and another family have created their own meal-sharing initiative in which the two families take turns making a meal for the other. Although they do not eat together, the meal sharing has strengthened the connection between the families. Sharing meals relieves one family of meal preparation for an evening, exposes both families to new recipes, heightens their nutrition awareness, and enhances their conversation about food. "[Meal sharing] is a neat way of having a night where you don't prepare anything and are exposed to other people's recipes and their fun with cooking," says Douglas. "It's super-fast, and it's easy to get tasty, healthy food."—*Submitted by Karina Kreider, Akron, Pennsylvania*

• • • • • • • • • • • • • •
In 1970, people in the United States spent 26 percent of their food budgets eating away from home. By 2002, that number had jumped to 46 percent.[2]

Kitchen co-op. Several of us in Bluffton, Ohio, wanted to make more things at home rather than buying them. So we formed a co-op and listed the items we were good at making. Whenever we wanted something, we would look at the list and order it from that person. Each item was worth so many "co-op bucks," which could be exchanged with anyone else in the group for something she or he might want. Carmen made tortillas, Bobbie made salad dressing and bread, Becky made bagels, Wendy made granola, and so on. I offered my solar oven to other co-op members to use for baking casseroles and then delivered the casseroles after they were baked. Babysitting was also included in our list.—*Victoria Woods-Yee, Bluffton, Ohio*

Supper club. We are part of a monthly supper club with three other families. Each of us hosts the group every four months and provides the space to gather and the main dish. The rest bring side dishes. I'm always amazed how often the meal goes together so well, with little or no planning. The conversation is always lively. As we are all attempting to live out our values of stewardship and sustainability, I often find myself picking up great tips and ideas, along with the great food.—*Jason Myers-Benner, Keezletown, Virginia*

Standard guest meal. I determined to find a satisfactory way of serving meals so that they would not be so burdensome. We want to live out what we believe about the importance of hospitality. The answer was a standard menu that is nutritious, simple almost to the point of being symbolic, and economical in both time and money. Since then, every guest who eats around our table probably has the same meal as any other—stew or hearty soup, crusty bread, and fresh fruit—and absolutely no trimmings or additions except occasionally a pot of fresh garden mint tea.

For those who have great gifts in the area of cooking, such a plan may be unsatisfactory. For me, it is right. It multiplies our capacity for "having people in" or responding with joy when they drop by. I no longer wonder if someone will like this or that; I just serve it. Preparing the table is a task I thoroughly

enjoy. After all, making a standard or simple meal does not pre-
clude serving it with beauty and even elegance.—*Miriam Lind,
Goshen, Indiana* (1980)

Tea: three minutes. While living in Indonesia, I was often
invited to sit down and drink a glass of *strop* (a cold, sweet
fruit drink) or a cup of Javanese coffee before delivering my
brief message or conducting a business transaction. Because
of poor or nonexistent telephone service, personal visits were
frequent; because of the socializing ritual, they consumed much
more time than in the United States. This greatly reduced the
number of errands I could accomplish in a day but enhanced
communication and socialization. The slower pace and liquid
refreshment also made the heat and humidity bearable.

Since returning to the United States, we've tried to institute
more tea-drinking opportunities with friends who drop by our
house. We buy tea inexpensively in bulk rather than in tea bags.
With an assortment of herb teas next to the teapot, we're usually able to make good on our invitation. "Sit down. Tea will be
ready in three minutes."—*Paul Longacre, Akron, Pennsylvania*
(1980)

At-home eating. Entertaining by going to commercial eating
places is costly. By inviting people to our home to share a meal
and receiving return invitations, we gain three benefits: the food
we eat is more nutritious than many commercial meals, overall
cost is considerably less, and family friendships developed in this
way are invaluable.—*Bill Wiebe, Hillsboro, Kansas* (1980)

Floor meals. Inviting many people to eat with you may be
a problem if you intend to seat them all at a table. Try a floor
arrangement, as do millions in our world. Spread a sheet in the
center as the tablecloth. "Set the table" as you would on a table,
according to the number expected. Give only one spoon to save
on dishwashing. Take off shoes when ready to eat, and sit cross-
legged in front of your plate, holding it on your lap if you wish.
Children especially love this arrangement.—*Marie M. Moyer,
Telford, Pennsylvania* (1980)

This isn't supper! One day recently I heated and served some soup for my six-year-old daughter's supper while I scurried around, finishing up some cooking and baking projects. Between mouthfuls she asked, "When are we having supper?" Seeing my confusion, she clarified: "This isn't supper because we aren't eating together!" I quickly dished up a bowl of soup for myself and sat down beside her. *Now* it was supper!—*Janelle Myers-Benner, Keezletown, Virginia*

• • • • • • • • • • • • • •

The number of U.S. adolescents who report eating meals with their families most nights increased 23 percent from 1998 to 2005.[3]

Playing with food. Rebecca Thatcher of Akron, Pennsylvania, has taught her children to play with food. She has created a weekly food game, indirectly inspired by her late Colombian husband, that she plays with her two sons. At the beginning of each week, they cook one pound (1/2 kilogram) of beans, which they then try to make last as long as possible. The beans transform weekly from rice and beans to tacos and burgers. Eating, when approached creatively, "raises awareness about scarcity and teaches resourcefulness," says Rebecca, who also suggests donating the money saved by not eating meat to a local food bank. This final action maximizes the impact of her game.—*Submitted by Karina Kreider, Akron, Pennsylvania*

Weekly poverty meal. We lived in Samaru, Nigeria, for eleven years. When we moved to Kansas, we were concerned that our children be brought up feeling close to the problems faced by people in other countries. As a result, once a week our family has one supper that excludes meat, fish, milk, and dessert. Our meal may be a starch and a vegetable, rice with a little egg, or broth with bread. After about two hours, we may have a cup of coffee or tea. We each put forty cents into a globe bank, accumulating this for a nutrition project to alleviate malnourishment among the world's poor.—*David and Linda Norman, Manhattan, Kansas* (1980)

Homemade snacks. I'm still trying to figure out how to make snacks more convenient without falling prey to the ease of the prepackaged treat, grabbed as I dash a pack of hungry, grumpy children to piano lessons. Often, coming up with a quick idea is the biggest hurdle. One trick is to have a list of alternatives, many of which take only a minute or two to prepare:

- tortillas rolled up with hummus and spinach or cream cheese and jam
- popcorn
- leftover pancakes or waffles
- cheese with apple slices or crackers
- whole washed apples, oranges, or other fruits
- homemade trail mix (raisins, dried cranberries, nuts or seeds, and a sprinkling of chocolate chips)
- homemade muffins, cookies, brownies
- boiled eggs
- tortilla chips or homemade pita chips with yogurt dip or bean dip
- cut-up veggies with or without dip
- dried apple slices or other dried fruits
- yogurt with pear sauce or applesauce
- summer sausage
- granola
- pickles

—*Carrie Snyder, Waterloo, Ontario*

Fireless cooker. We use a simple cardboard box to help us cook. Inside, we put a circular piece of cardboard to fit the outside of a pot. The rest of the box is packed with shredded old sheets (or any kind of insulating filling). If you are cooking beans or rice or making stock, bring your pot to a boil on the stove and then put it inside the box. Close it up and then allow the food to continue cooking inside the box. It does a great job of keeping the heat trapped and therefore cooking your food without the use of fuel or electricity. We've used it to make beans, rice, stock, and other foods.—*Courtney and Steve Byers, Ephrata, Pennsylvania*

How can I save energy when cooking?

- *Use pans with tight-fitting lids. It speeds cooking time.*

- *Use pans that are the same size as the burner to absorb the energy and reduce heat loss.*

- *Properly clean and maintain appliances. They will use energy more efficiently and last longer.*

- *Use glass or ceramic pans in your oven. You can turn down the temperature about 25°F (about 14°C), thus saving energy.*

- *Cook large quantities of food at one time, and share or freeze extra. This is energy-efficient and community-building.*

- *Consider alternative cooking methods. Use a fireless cooker or consider buying or making a solar oven (instructions available on various Internet sites).*

Office lunches. I often prepare food on the weekend and take enough to the office on Monday for lunches throughout the week. If someone doesn't have a lunch or guests drop by, I share. Usually I take rice, beans, and tortillas, plus raw vegetables and fruit. Rice and beans are easy to prepare in quantity, and they are a good reminder of the basic meals eaten daily in Central America. While variety in our food throughout the day is important for good nutrition, fewer choices at a time help us not to overeat. I also appreciate not needing to plan for lunch every day.—*Linda Shelly, Newton, Kansas*

Restaurant leftovers. Recently we have started bringing reusable containers from home when we go out to eat at a restaurant. It reminds us that most of the portion sizes in Canadian and U.S. restaurants are far larger than the average person needs to eat, and we eat less with the intention to take the rest home with us for the next day. It also means that we don't need to use the disposable Styrofoam or plastic containers that restaurants offer. The first time we did this, I wondered what our server would say. She didn't even blink an eye.—*Wendy Janzen, Kitchener, Ontario*

Meat compromises. When we were engaged, we were happy to discover that neither of us likes to eat much meat. But for one of us, that meant eating meat once a week; for the other, it meant once a day. Although the carnivore still likes to eat more meat than the almost-vegetarian would like him to, we've mostly achieved equilibrium in our family. We are aware of how much good food is generally required to feed the animals that are killed for our food, especially beef. We try to alternate meat meals with non-meat meals. When we have meat, we tend to avoid steaks, roasts, and other mostly meat dishes. When we do roast a big chunk of meat, we enjoy one feast meal to appease the carnivore, but then the leftovers go into casseroles or other dishes in which only a little meat is used. We also try to buy meat from local producers who raise the animals in humane and sustainable ways. The chickens are free-range, not factory-farmed, and the beef is grass-fed. We also buy pickerel from nearby Lake Winnipeg.—*Byron and Melita Rempel-Burkholder, Winnipeg, Manitoba*

Vegetarianism and reverence for life. I've been a vegetarian for years. Actually, I am a lacto-ovo-vegetarian: I do drink milk and eat cheese and eggs. Sometimes our dinner guests wonder whether they are eating veal or beef or another kind of meat. It's always interesting to see their faces and hear the comments when they discover that the casserole is basically soybeans, with no meat at all. Of course, I can't resist the temptation to say that it contains as much protein as meat and that if more of us would abstain from beef, there would be more food available for the hungry people of the world.

• • • • • • • • • • • • •

Nearly 10 billion animals are slaughtered for food each year in the United States. That's about one-third more than the number of humans on the entire planet.[4]

The deeper motivation for being a vegetarian has to do with my worldview and philosophy of life, my concept of creation and redemption. It has to do with reverence for life—all life. In a sense, it is simply an extension of the pacifist or nonresistant principle. My wife, Elfrieda, isn't committed to the vegetarian principle and occasionally will prepare a separate dish for herself. It may be a bit more work, but it has never been an occasion for tension. We've never argued over either diet, but thank the good Lord for both.—*Peter J. Dyck, Akron, Pennsylvania* (1980)

Vegetarianism and poverty. Ten years ago, I was a volunteer with Mennonite Voluntary Service in Harlingen, Texas. My assignment involved assisting detained immigrants who had entered the United States without proper documentation. Though they came from diverse locations and backgrounds, a common trait shared by nearly all the immigrants I encountered was poverty. In an attempt to respond tangibly on a personal level to the extreme inequity I observed in my work, I stopped eating meat. I maintain a vegetarian diet today because I continue to seek ways to remind myself of disproportionate resource allocations worldwide and also because I think a meat-free diet makes sense from a health perspective. I aspire to incorporate other practices—like eating locally and in season—to promote justice through other food decisions my family and I make.—*Lisa Koop, Chicago, Illinois*

Sweet life, less sugar. I've always had a sweet tooth, so moving away from conventional refined sugar is an ongoing process for me. Increasingly I buy organic sugar and alternative granular sweeteners that are more environmentally friendly. Their higher price motivates me to use less, saving money and calories that I don't need. (Local honey is also a great substitute in many recipes.) Chocolate works the same way: I buy fairtrade chocolate and eat one fabulous square at lunch instead of a whole cheap candy bar. Organic chocolate chips go into occasional special treats, while I look to fruit more often for dessert choices.—*Cathleen Hockman-Wert, Corvallis, Oregon*

Homemade food for thought. I sometimes wonder whether my growing obsession with nonpackaged, home-produced food is head-in-the-sand behavior—as if, by removing plastic from my life, I will somehow right the innumerable wrongs that continue to be committed in the name of consuming, convenience, and self-contentment. I still drive a vehicle that burns gasoline. I still use a computer that runs on electricity, much of which comes from a coal-fired plant. Did you see the footage of oil gushing into the blue, blue waters of the Gulf of Mexico? I am culpable. I've been wondering whether my desire to control what we eat is a simplistic attempt at atonement, at optimism, a desire to do something, anything, to stem the flow—an act against hopelessness, or stasis. Well, if it is, so be it. I would rather do something out of hope than do nothing out of despair.—*Carrie Snyder, Waterloo, Ontario*

• • • • • • • • • • • • •

Processed food in the United States travels over 1,300 miles before being eaten; fresh produce generally travels over 1,500 miles.[5]

Fast from fast food. I attempt to eat as much organic and local food as possible, while avoiding conventional and processed food. I think it is better to spend more money on quality food but then eat less of it. At times when I cannot afford it or am out with friends who want to eat fast food, I will just fast from the fast food and not eat anything.—*Brett Little, Muskegon, Michigan*

Worth the hunger pangs. For years, the peace and social awareness committee at Canadian Mennonite University in Winnipeg, Manitoba, has put on a campus-wide event known as the Week of Solidarity. For five days, students gather with their "family groups" in the apartments of on-campus students twice a day for a tiny meal of rice and lentils, supplemented with limited bread and unlimited tea. The event is meant to make participants more aware of the hunger and weakness that millions experience every day. But it has also opened my eyes to a number of other things, such as the ways my body tricks itself into feeling hungry when it's not; the importance of a full and balanced diet for basic functioning; the delicate flavors of simple, staple foods; and the sweetness of a meal enjoyed with friends and fellowship. Over prayer, devotions, and conversation, my family group this year agreed that the experience was well worth the hunger pangs.
—*Erin Weaver, Red Lake, Ontario*

• • • • • • • • • • • • •

Find more stories, tips, and links to resources about cooking and eating at www.mpn.net/livingmorewithless.

15
Clothes and Bodies

Doris Janzen Longacre

• •

We wear clothes to keep us comfortable in varying temperatures and to provide the degree of modesty a culture expects. There you have the basics. After that, we branch out to *protection* (the construction worker's hard hat and steel-toed shoes), *convenience* (pockets for a pen, hammer, or stethoscope), and *visual interest* (a scarf).

All are legitimate. But enter plenty of buying power, technology that takes the toiling and spinning out of clothing production, and a modern fashion industry for which a spokesperson said, "It is our job to make women [add men and children!] unhappy with what they have." The result? Five-foot closets, seen as necessities in every singly inhabited bedroom. These replace the hooks on the wall and an occasional wooden wardrobe that, several generations ago, served large families.

Five-foot closet?

The average size of a closet in a master bedroom of a new house is now 6-by-8 feet (1.8-by-2.4 meters). According to census data, U.S. citizens bought about 75 percent more clothes in 2005 than they had ten years earlier. [1]

The result is also a lively thrift-shop movement in support of church agencies and other good causes. I support these shops. Any attempt to recycle instead of buying new is a foot on the brake instead of the accelerator. But we must realize that communities that can stock one thrift shop after another are rich, wasteful communities. To organize a thrift shop or buy there is blessed, but to live so that you have little to donate is an equally high calling.

Clothing connects to standards

Clothing connects with several standards of more with less:

Do justice. Why are we able to afford so much? Not only because production is efficient, but also because the mass production of cloth and clothing has long been the dull, repetitive factory work of poor people paid low wages. Today much of the inexpensive clothing on discount house and bargain basement racks comes from the sweatshops of Korea, Hong Kong, Taiwan, the Philippines, or Singapore. Young women, especially, provide cheap labor, often standing to work at monotonous tasks ten or more hours a day, six days a week.

At least they have jobs, we reason. At least they eat. And how can we know if it helps for us to buy more of this clothing or less? Although the lines that connect them with us are tangled, I believe Christians can never justify closets bulging with the products of another's exploitation.

Nurture people. The work of creatively restoring a garment to full use enriches the sewer along with the wearer. Many older people have developed mending into a careful art that they report enjoying more than sewing new clothes. My mother-in-law was such a mending expert. She could recover the most baffling rips with know-how and firm stitches. She often worked on the spot when a problem occurred, to keep clothing in circulation and avoid the discouragement of a large mending pile.

Cherish the natural order. Although the percentage of energy used to produce textiles is low, fabric production does deplete resources. Cotton is about twice as energy-efficient to produce as synthetics derived from petroleum and natural gas, including energy inputs for raising the cotton. Wool is even more energy-efficient than cotton. While synthetics are long-wearing and require no cropland for production, they are produced from nonrenewable resources and are not biodegradable.

Twenty-one percent of the energy used in U.S. households goes for changing indoor temperature. Therefore, the most important consideration connecting clothing choice and energy conservation is whether garments keep us cool in summer and warm in winter. Synthetics may come off well in climates that face no extremes. But they give free steam baths in hot weather and are cold and clammy in winter.

Synthetics cannot match wool for winter warmth. Wool is a scaly, stretchy fiber abounding with microscopic air spaces for trapping body heat. Although it is harder to

Current figure

In 2001, 26 percent of energy used in U.S. households went for changing indoor temperature. [2]

clean than most fibers, wool has an amazing capacity to shed dirt and wrinkles, and it needs less care than most fibers. Wool is long-wearing and biodegradable. If you don't like the rough texture of some wools next to your skin, try it over a layer of cotton for winter comfort. Layering can also reduce cleaning costs. For centuries, wool has been raised on the rocky hills of marginal terrain and requires the barest energy input to produce.

Fabric decisions do not need to be cast solely in terms of a natural-versus-synthetic fibers debate. Technology also provides us with combination fabrics. Washable, wrinkle-free materials that are mostly cotton or wool may be the most energy-efficient and inexpensive in the long run.

Nonconform freely. For most people, energy use in choosing clothing is scarcely a consideration. Style is what counts.

The Amish, one contemporary religious group descended from sixteenth-century Anabaptists, stopped the clock of style centuries ago. Their clothing expresses obedience to the *Ordnung*, or rules of the congregation, and to the suppression of *Hochmut*, or pride. *Hochmut* is a term formerly used in the Kansas Mennonite congregation in which I grew up. It means any way in which you try to put yourself above other people, and it carries the connotation of stuffiness, putting on airs, the upturned nose. *Hochmut* is a balloon waiting for a pin.

Where is *Hochmut* in the clothing practices of Canadian and U.S. churches today? Does it lie in not being able to wear the same dress or suit three Sundays in a row? In buying jewelry to complement each outfit? In the subtle desire to be respected as Christians?

Even in thinking that only those who wear jeans to church live simply?

Rules are no answer. Living more with less suggests freedom from legalism, recognizing that it comes in more than one form. Requiring so many pleats in the head covering or "jeans only" is one form. Being enslaved to the new and fashionable is another. Entries for this chapter exemplify these principles:

- *Dress for comfort according to the weather.* Failure to do so means energy waste in heating and cooling.

- *Buy or make high-quality clothing of timeless, classic cut.* Wear clothing until it wears out, mending carefully and creatively to keep a neat appearance.

- *Recycle unused clothing* for further wear or alternate use, being willing to be the recipient as well as the donor.

- *Express your personality through dress,* but do not regularly allow clothing to become an answer to boredom or a substitute for inner resources of self-assurance.

- *Respect your sexuality* and that of others with modest, becoming clothes.

- *If you wear a certain type of clothing to fit in, be aware of that and evaluate how it squares with the message of Christ's kingdom in a world of poverty.*

- *Heavy investment of time, money, or concern with what you wear is always a danger signal.* Remember Jesus' words, "Do not worry about . . . what you will wear. For life is more than food, and the body more than clothing" (Luke 12:22-23).

Bodies

Related to our approach to clothing is our care for our bodies.[3] With medical costs soaring, what more-with-less standards related to our bodies should we observe? Seven rules that couldn't be cheaper to implement are getting increasing attention in preventive health care. Dr. Nedra Belloc studied the relationship between living patterns and life expectancy. She centered on these seven habits: three meals a day, avoiding snacks, breakfast every day, moderate exercise two or three times a week, seven or eight hours of sleep at night, no smoking, moderate weight, and no alcohol (or only in moderation).

Belloc found that a forty-five-year-old man with six or seven of these habits could expect to live eleven years longer than one with only two or three. A study by Belloc and Dr. Lester Breslow indicated that a man who had six or seven of these habits was as healthy as a man thirty years younger who had only one or two. The significance of this finding jumps into focus when you consider that between 1900 and 1970, life expectancy for white, forty-year-old men increased by only half a year, despite all medical advances of that period.

● ● ● ● ● ● ● ● ● ● ● ● ● ●

Current figures

The *American Journal of Medicine* reported in 2006 that adherence to five healthy lifestyle habits—eating a prudent diet, doing regular physical activity, maintaining a healthy weight, limiting alcohol consumption, and not smoking—decreases the chance of a heart attack and lengthens lifespan. Studies have documented the effectiveness of such habits in reducing ill health and increasing capacity and function at the end of life.[4]

In other words, doctors and pills don't work the big miracles. It's the way we live that counts.

Could she have a pair of yours? While living in Calcutta, I was daily aware of the disparity between rich and poor. One day a mother came to our apartment to tell me that her daughter would be working in the mountains during the winter and needed a pair of warm slacks. "Could she have a pair of yours?" she asked. I knew I could not explain that I had only two pairs—a bare minimum in Canada and the United States. She would think that absurd. Were the Bible passages to be taken literally? After deciding which pair of slacks to give, I added the matching top as well. I'm embarrassed to admit now that I never missed that outfit. The remaining pair of slacks saw me through two winters.—*Herta Janzen, London, Ontario* (1980)

A layered dilemma. When shopping for clothes, Melinda Weaver of Baltimore, Maryland, has created for herself several guidelines for simplicity and modesty. When she goes clothes shopping, she begins by knowing exactly what she has in her closet and what she is looking for. She has been spared many items by simply knowing what is already in her closet. Melinda also avoids buying items that can't be worn alone. If she knows an item needs to be layered with another piece of clothing, she immediately knows that item crosses her modesty boundaries and she will not purchase it. Her policies cut down on the sheer quantity of clothes she collects and therefore save money, but also force her to keep a modest wardrobe that she feels comfortable wearing anywhere.—*Submitted by Karina Kreider, Akron, Pennsylvania*

Walking billboards. While many Americans tout brand-name clothing, Eric and Hilary Sauder of Ephrata, Pennsylvania, have chosen to advertise a more worthy, less worldly cause. The majority of the shirts they own from Charity Water and Light Gives Heat are produced by fairly paid adults in Africa and have the name of the organization displayed on them. "It [the clothing] is a walking billboard for global awareness, and wearing it not only makes others aware but also helps remind me of what I believe," says Hilary.—*Submitted by Karina Kreider, Akron, Pennsylvania*

Clothing exchange. After sharing children's clothes informally for a time, our Sunday-school class set up a systematic way of exchanging them. Twice a year, everyone brings clothing that is no longer needed to someone's home. We sort and spread them out. After each of us finds what we can use, we sort for the next exchange or send the rest to a thrift shop.—*Lois Beck, West Liberty, Ohio* (1980)

Thrift stores spoil you. Start the concept of shopping at thrift shops with your children early in their lives. The thing about thrift-shop purchases is that they are usually durable, classic, well-made clothing that people have gotten bored of, rather than worn into rags. So you end up paying a pittance for brands known for quality. Plus, thrift shops spoil you for mall shopping: who wants to buy a blouse when there are seventeen others just like it hanging there and twenty dozen in similar stores in the mall? Who wants that when you can get a one-of-a-kind find for pennies?—*Janice MacDonald, Edmonton, Alberta*

Prom dress: twenty bucks. B. Lani Prunés of Philadelphia has shopped for clothes at thrift stores for years. So when prom time rolled around, she thought, *Why go anywhere else?* First she looked up regular prom dress prices—"I felt they were ridiculous for a one-night party," she says. So she went to her favorite thrift store and found a prom dress for twenty dollars—a dress someone probably wore once or twice and that she says is "both cheap and elegant." Lani, now a student at Eastern Mennonite University, was proud of her reused prom dress: "I am never embarrassed about telling people, but rather I seem to brag too much about it! My friends are never too surprised that I would reuse a dress, but it makes them think about how logical it is." Lani says that buying her prom dress at a thrift store is part and parcel of her faith: "Shopping at thrift stores makes me appreciate the things God has given me."

Color correlation. Rarely, if ever, do Darren and Espri Bender-Beauregard of Paoli, Indiana, have to dig through their closets looking for that perfect shirt to match their pants. Their solution to the age-old question of whether their clothes "go with" each other is simple: they have hewn their wardrobes down to muted earth tones, which naturally match. "I concern myself less and less [with how I dress]; it's more functional and less for looks," remarks Darren on not worrying about specific outfits—another perk of keeping such a selective range of attire.—*Submitted by Karina Kreider, Akron, Pennsylvania*

Clothing as functional art. I enjoy making my own clothing by following patterns or designing my own by experimenting with fabrics and fibers. I like wearing a garment that expresses my individuality and personal style. Confidence and beauty come from within, but for me clothing adds to this in a good way. I've come to see that clothing, especially clothing designed and made by artistic and thoughtful people, is functional art—much like a beautiful ceramic pot.

I enjoy purchasing clothing from people who made it themselves or else taking the time to make it myself. I spin yarn from all sorts of fibers, but soon I'll be taking this enterprise a bit closer to the source: along with some of my friends, I will soon own a flock of sheep for their fiber. I anticipate that the process of knowing exactly where my wool/yarn/garment came from—down to the very follicle—will bring an even deeper appreciation of clothing and the labor and resources required to create it. Keeping clothing close to the source and the creator also ensures that its making is not destructive to people or the environment. While I don't purchase or make all my clothing in this manner, this approach inevitably means that I have fewer clothes than many. But they are of a quality and aesthetic that I truly appreciate.—*Jessica King, Lancaster, Pennsylvania*

Reusable cleaner bags. My husband takes his shirts to the laundry (I know, not sustainable, but it adds sanity to our lives). Each week he used to take his clothes in a different bag, which he would then dispose of after delivering his clothes to the cleaner. He suggested to the cleaner that, since she is also a tailor, she sew or design a bag with a drawstring that is reusable for each regular customer. She took the suggestion, and now he has two bags, nicely done with grommets for the string. He doesn't need to wait on the clerk, because his name and phone number are on the plastic tag on his bag; he can just drop it on the counter and leave. When he picks up, he has another bag on his hangers to take home and fill with shirts. He also periodically returns the slim metal hangers for reuse.—*Jill Landes, Souderton, Pennsylvania*

Diapers. With the arrival of our first child, my husband and I decided to use cloth diapers. We see cloth diapering as a way to practice good stewardship and simplicity: we can keep our

household waste to a minimum, and we can reuse what we have. Not only will we be able to reuse the diapers for our first child over the next few years, but these diapers will also diaper any future children that might come our way. Plus they can double as burp cloths. I also made my own cloth wipes for diaper changing by cutting up old T-shirts or fabric. When we travel, I simply wet a few cloths, put them in a sealed bag, and bring them along.
—*Courtney Byers, Ephrata, Pennsylvania*

• • • • • • • • • • • • • •

Over 4 million disposable diapers are discarded in Canada every day.[5]

Gray hair liberation. Like the ad says, I was "too young to look old." At age twenty-five I found my gray hair depressing, but going to Zambia for a teaching assignment meant goodbye to my hairdresser. Coloring my hair was not only impossible there; it was totally unnecessary. As I became interested in my new environment and acquainted with the reality of living in a less wealthy country, I saw aging and health care in a new perspective. I realized I had been acculturated to believe that hair color was important to the quality of life. This new awareness brought on my personal version of liberation.—*Barbara Weaver, New Holland, Pennsylvania* (1980)

Menstruation. Instead of using disposal items for menstruation, I use a reusable, flexible, rubber cup. This sanitary device is good for me (not a chemically doused, hyper-absorbent, whitewashed plug) and good for the environment (not using tons of pads and toilet paper that pile up in landfills). The cup has lasted five years so far, is easy to wash out, and saves me a lot of money. It also helps me reevaluate the belief that menstrual blood is dirty or bad.—*Sarah Thompson, Elkhart, Indiana*

No shampoo. Our family has decided to stop using shampoos and hair conditioners. In doing so, we've been able to cut out the expense, the plastic garbage, and the countless chemicals that we know are unhealthy for our bodies and the earth. Instead, we wash our hair less often, and when we do, we use baking soda and apple cider vinegar. After a few weeks of adjusting (this usually means a little greasiness), our hair finds its natural balance and is softer and healthier than it ever was when we used shampoo.

For shampoo, dilute 1 tbsp. (15 ml) baking soda in 1 cup (250 ml) water. This should be necessary only every few days at the most. With my baby and toddler, I rarely use anything besides warm water, and their hair is always clean. For a conditioning and detangling rinse, dilute 1 or 2 tbsp. (15 to 30 ml) apple cider vinegar with 1 cup / 250 ml water, apply to hair, leave for one minute, then rinse. This only needs to be done every few washes and is a better detangler than any conditioner I've used.—*Kirsten Krymusa, Nairobi, Kenya*

Caring for the temple. I grew up among Mennonite churches of Puerto Rico in the 1960s and 1970s, and Bible study was an important part of my church upbringing. One verse that stood out for me as a youth was 1 Corinthians 3:16: "Do you not know that you are God's temple and that God's Spirit dwells in you?" At the time, I understood that to mean that I should stay away from alcohol, cigarettes, and drugs. Now that I'm in middle age, this verse has a different meaning for me. Caring for the body is much more than abstaining from substances that harm the body. It involves understanding my body, how it functions, and what makes for its good care.

In the last few years I have learned that high cholesterol levels are an inherited trait in my family. I cannot change this, but I can manage it. At first, I thought I could eat less meat and more vegetables, but this alone did not help. Over two years ago, I began running. Combined with a healthy diet, exercise is working well for me. I run one hour a day as often as I can. Vegetables are a constant staple on my plate, and I monitor my weight. Often when I run, I become aware of God's presence. I think about who I am as a follower of Jesus. I also reflect and pray for others. Caring for my body is a spiritual discipline, since the Spirit dwells in my body.—*Rolando Santiago, Lancaster, Pennsylvania*

How can we obtain more quality at less cost in health care?

- *Decrease the number of tests.* It is estimated that 30 percent of diagnostic tests do not contribute to the quality of health care. Some of these tests are ordered because of the fear of a lawsuit. Open communication with your doctor will build mutual trust and allay the doctor's fear. There is also economic incentive for ordering some tests. When your doctor requests an expensive or arduous test, ask questions like, What are we looking for? What do we do if the test is negative? What if it is positive? What percent of the time is the test falsely positive or falsely negative?

- *Carry a medical summary with you.* If you arrive in the emergency room, a medical summary may prevent the need for a whole battery of expensive tests. If a summary of your records is available, one in seven lab tests will be unnecessary and one in twenty hospitalizations can be prevented. A listing of your drug allergies may prevent a severe allergic reaction and may save your life.

- *Take proper care of your chronic disease.* Chronic diseases like high blood pressure and diabetes have well-established guidelines for good control. Proper control of chronic diseases will decrease your need for hospitalization and prevent or delay disability. Establish a collaborative relationship in which both you and the doctor take responsibility for the best care for your disease.

—*Dr. Glen Miller, author of* Empowering the Patient: How to Reduce the Cost of Healthcare and Improve Its Quality

Lunch hour. Because I work in a sedentary occupation, I examined the "three square meals a day" rule. I don't need that much food. By adding calories that my body can't burn, I merely add weight to my frame. I decided to substitute exercise for eating at least once a day. For a time I used my lunch hour to clean out a large vacant lot in our neighborhood. It was satisfying to see the amount of constructive exercise I could get during this daily period. It also made a difference in the safety and beauty of the neighborhood.—*Mark Cerbone, Philadelphia, Pennsylvania* (1980)

Family planning. I come from a family of seven children. Years ago I wanted to have four of my own. But because ours is a different world from that of our parents, my wife and I decided to stop at two. We want to use the world's resources wisely. What does the size of our families have to do with this? Plenty. When God told Adam and Eve to be fruitful and multiply, he also commanded them to be stewards of the earth. Some people argue that they can have as many children as they want as long as they can support them. They advocate controlling population in countries like India. But every North American baby born claims a much higher percentage of the world's resources than a baby born in India. Since our Christian ideals call us to share equally, our decisions concerning the size of our families are important.—*Ray Martin, Accra, Ghana* (1980)

• • • • • • • • • • • • • •

Find more stories, tips, and links to resources about clothes and bodies at www.mpn.net/livingmorewithless.

16

Transportation and Travel

Nancy and Robb Davis

• •

The best energy saver may be staying at home." These are the words of Doris Janzen Longacre in her introduction to the chapter on transportation in the 1980 release of *Living More with Less*. In the three decades since then, it is clear that those living in Canada and the United States are doing anything but staying at home. It appears that, with regard to transportation, we are trying to live more with more.

The chart on the next page shows the trend in travel by different modes of transportation in the United States through 2007 since *Living More with Less* came out.[1] The automobile, which was the focus of this section in 1980, continues to have a privileged place in terms of total miles traveled. Many factors have led to the increase in vehicle miles traveled, including where we live, the size and structure of our households, workforce participation, and income growth, writes transportation specialist Steven E. Polzin.

The bottom line, however, is that in the period he studied (1977–2001), people in the United States were taking more trips by car, those trips were longer, and more of us were taking them. In addition, we were walking less—much less. And we barely used public transit at all—using it at about the same level in 2007 as we were in 1980. (Canadian rates of public transit use are higher, but

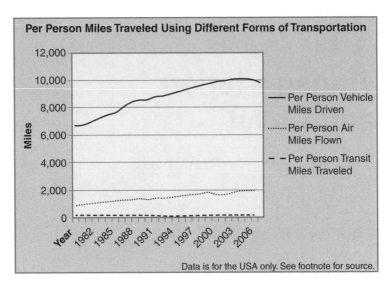

Per Person Miles Traveled Using Different Forms of Transportation

Data is for the USA only. See footnote for source.

car ownership trends are similar.) Polzin suggests that the growth trends might be slowing. Growth will most likely continue, however, despite the most recent declines from the 2007 economic slowdown.[2]

The sacredness of our relationship with cars has not changed. In fact, we have enriched this relationship with all manner of gadgetry, so that cars have essentially become rolling entertainment centers that almost seem to drive themselves. In addition, we routinely move thousands—in some cases tens of thousands—of miles to vacation in places our parents and grandparents could only read about or see on television. Airplane travel has actually grown much more rapidly over the period than automobile travel. Even though the per-person miles of air travel are much lower, over the entire period, per-person car travel increased by 45 percent while per-person air travel increased by 109 percent.

So the evidence is clear: we are still a restless people in need of . . . change? Entertainment? Experiences? Excitement? Whatever it is that we seek, we now know that this restlessness has costs in terms of pollution, overuse of increasingly scarce resources, carbon emissions, dislocation, stress, and fatigue.

Living in the "nearby"

What, then, would it mean for us to live more with less—less air travel, less car travel, fewer trips, shorter distances? Do we even think it is possible to live a good life by "staying home"? What would that look like? Is it enough to think we can really change things by maintaining our cars better, buying more fuel-efficient ones, or planning our trips better? Probably not. We first need to examine our prior commitments to traveling and ask why we are so enamored with lifestyles of ever-increasing mobility. We need to examine what living *more* looks like when we commit to traveling *less*. This means making decisions to live closer to home; to be part of our communities; to commit to life in the "nearby"; and to spend most of our time being present in places we know well.

Behavior change like this is never easy, so we want to suggest a few experiments that can help us try out the idea of living more fully in the nearby. See these experiments as first steps in a longer-term process of weaning ourselves away from the need to move.

- *Seek opportunities to serve, work, play, and rest in the "nearby."* Start keeping a journal of all the opportunities to do these things within twenty-five, fifty, or one hundred miles of home. Make it your goal to discover life in the nearby. Try this for six months. Discuss it with your faith community and your family, helping each other to focus on the advantages of living closer to home.

- *Take a sabbatical from air travel.* Try it for six months or a year. While this may not be possible for some people due to work obligations, at least commit to this kind of sabbatical for personal travel. Keep track of how the sabbatical changes the way you think about your life.

- *Take weekly (or more frequent) sabbaticals from using your car.* In fact, try to make these sabbaticals the norm. If you can't do this (for work or whatever reason), consider and write down all the factors that make it impossible. Discuss with others what it would take to remove these impediments.

- *Start a voluntary gas tax group to tax yourself for every gallon of gas purchased (see page 226).* Use the money to organize a group to talk to your local elected officials about how to make your community more bike- or pedestrian-friendly.

How much does gas really cost? Go to www.voluntarygastax.org to learn how to start a voluntary gas tax group.

Several of these steps share the idea of a sabbatical or rest. The restlessness embodied in the statistics about transportation tells the story of a people deeply in need of just that: a time to rest. Living more with less travel means trusting that rest itself is the best antidote to restlessness and that staying put has rewards that constant mobility cannot match.

The "cycling church." Several years ago, our family of four decided to give up driving the three kilometers (almost two miles) to church. We were among the first in our congregation, Home Street Mennonite Church in Winnipeg, Manitoba, to begin cycling to worship during the summer. At first, we cyclists would carry our bikes downstairs and leave them in a storage area. Eventually a retired church member built a bike rack and put it beside the sidewalk near the entrance. The rack was full in no time, and another rack appeared beside it, encouraging more people to cycle. Now both racks are full from late spring to early fall. We have even been called the "cycling church."

From late fall to early spring, our family walks to church. It takes a shade over half an hour each way—less when the Assiniboine River is frozen and we can walk across—but it has become important talk time (or if we're alone, think time). Getting to church is a kind of benchmark for other transportation decisions involving our car. Unless the weather is really bad or we need to run other errands, we will not drive if we can get to our destination in less than a half-hour by bike or foot.—*Byron and Melita Rempel-Burkholder, Winnipeg, Manitoba*

Pastor on a bike. A trip to Colombia is what got Dan Kehler on a bike. Pastor of Altona (Man.) Bergthaler Mennonite Church, Dan committed to driving less and biking more after a 2007 learning tour to Colombia with some members of his congregation. "One of the things that struck us was no one in the church had a car," he says. This was in stark contrast to their own church, which "looks like a car dealership" on Sunday mornings. That got him thinking about the global effects of using less gas. "I see a close connection between the economy of oil and the violence of the world," he says. "If I can be involved less in the economy of oil, I can be involved less in the economy of war." Not only that, his commitment to biking brings a personal peace: "The rhythm and cadence of the stroke—there's something centering about it."—*Submitted by Paul Boers, Goshen, Indiana*

All you need is two wheels . . . or one. I commute to my teaching job by bicycle on fair-weather days and by public bus and unicycle on cold, rainy, or snowy days. The unicycle fits easily on the bus for part of the trip, and braking on slippery surfaces is easier because the unicycle can't go as fast as a bike. Plus, I can hold an umbrella when I'm riding the unicycle so I don't get as wet. The trip provides a space in my day for exercise, a time to think and memorize poetry, a time to see the seasons change, and a place to meet people outside my regular sphere. The recent addition of a bike path alongside a river for part of the route has both lengthened the trip and increased my enjoyment.—*Darrell Yoder, Lancaster, Pennsylvania*

Drive less, reduce stress. After moving to Davis, California—known as the biking capital of the United States—my husband and I started biking to work and nearly everywhere else. We were amazed at how much less stress we felt simply because we drove less. It felt like a weight I'd been carrying for years was lifted from my shoulders. I never realized how stressful driving was until I lived in a community where I needed to drive only infrequently. In our two subsequent moves to Washington and Pennsylvania, living within biking distance of work has been a top priority in deciding where to live. Being able to walk or bike to work and downtown immeasurably enhances my quality of life, especially by reducing the stress and frustration of driving.—*Esther Prins, State College, Pennsylvania*

Meals on (bike) wheels. For many years I have been using my bike to run errands, shop for groceries, go to the post office and library, and get to meetings. While I was teaching at local public schools, I frequently commuted there on my bike. After a quick shower and change of clothes, I was ready to face my classes. I averaged six hundred to seven hundred miles of bicycling per year during my teaching years. Now in retirement I do about four hundred to five hundred miles a year.

Over a year ago I started volunteering for Meals on Wheels in areas close to my house, and after a few weeks I saw the opportunity to do the deliveries on my bike. So I rigged up a cooler on the back of my bike, and it has worked out fine, although I have to carry extra boxed meals in my backpack. I have not eliminated a car in our household, but I have saved many barrels of oil from being refined and have made a token reduction in air pollutants over the years.—*Steve Herbold, Cincinnati, Ohio*

No more "mom taxi"! American families seem to expect Mom to chauffeur her children everywhere—to music lessons, scout meetings, church or school activities, shopping, or friends' homes. Being a parent of six children and living in the country, I wasn't willing to become a taxi service. We gave our children bicycles as soon as they could handle them, around four or five years old. When they were capable of riding on main roads, we went with them on short excursions. Under our supervision, they began to watch for stop signs or cars. By seven or eight years of age, they could be trusted to go short distances on their own. After an eight-day bicycle trip one summer, four miles to music lessons seem easy. Our older children strap their violins to their backs—although we haven't solved the problem of an eight-year-old taking off with a cello.—*Kathy Histand, Sellersville, Pennsylvania* (1980)

Biking with bundles. The more we cycle, the more we discover how many options that mode of transportation opens for us. For example, we bungee-cord a shopping crate to the carrier and transport a lot of things, including groceries, sports equipment, gallons of paint, and casseroles for church potlucks. We have also cycled to the park, carrying folding lawn chairs, a Bocce ball game, and picnic fixings.—*Byron and Melita Rempel-Burkholder, Winnipeg, Manitoba*

Family errands on foot. My husband, our one-year-old daughter, and I live about a fifteen-minute walk from the nearest grocery store, a trip that typically takes five to ten minutes by car, depending on traffic lights. At least once a week, one or all three of us combine a trip to the grocery store with a forty-five- to fifty-minute walk. If all of us go, I carry an empty backpack while my husband carries our baby in a front carrier. After a full day of work for both of us, it's a great way to spend time with each other and our daughter, to buy what we need at the store, and to exercise—all without ever stepping into the car.—*Esther Prins, State College, Pennsylvania*

Walking as prayer. I started walking to work years after we chose a home that was within walking distance of the school where I teach. My schedule had always seemed too hectic and too complex to take the time for a twenty-five minute trek to the office. A time came when I fell into depression about what we humans are doing to God's creation and each other. As part of an effort to reach beyond this depression, I began walking to work one day a week. Soon this practice expanded into an everyday routine.

The United States is home to one-quarter of the world's cars. Most households own two or more vehicles, and there are more private cars than there are licensed drivers.[3]

The walk began to create a needed space between home and classroom. I practiced alertness to hear the arrival of the chimney swifts in April, to watch the shifting summer clouds and feel the sun's heat, to smell the dry musk of fallen autumn leaves, and occasionally to take a hard fall on winter ice. As I

walk, I pray for the welfare of the earth and all its inhabitants
and cling to God's promise of the New Jerusalem that will de-
scend to earth, bringing with it the river of life and trees whose
leaves are for "the healing of the nations" (Rev 22:2). Now that
our family is down to one car, I often walk to work because I
have to, but walking as a choice and a prayer has strengthened
my heart and motivated me to other acts of creation care.
—*Nancy R. Heisey, Harrisonburg, Virginia*

Share a car with strangers. If you live in almost any big city,
and even in many smaller ones, you may not need a car—you
can share one instead. You pay a membership fee, plus an
hourly rental fee. The cars are parked all over the city; you book
a car online, then stroll over and
pick it up, unlocking it with your
membership card. There's a small
mileage charge for longer trips,
but maintenance, parking, insurance, and even gas are included.

• • • • • • • • • • • •

Car-sharing programs are now available in more than 550 communities
in eight European countries and in
more than forty U.S. cities.[4]

Unless you use your car constantly, sharing a car is almost guar-
anteed to save you big bucks. And because it cuts way down on
the number of cars on the road, car-sharing is also a big boost
for the environment.—*Mary Waltner, Chicago, Illinois*

Share a car with a friend. When I came to Hesston College
to teach, I moved into an apartment with a friend. We decided
to share my car, thus lowering our transportation expenses
for gasoline and maintenance. Two years later, when the car
was in need of major repairs, Shirley bought a car. We traded
mine in, and I lent her some money, interest-free. Again we
shared maintenance and gasoline expenses. Learning to work
together and compromise enriched our relationship. We cut
out unnecessary trips, since the car wasn't always accessible. We
spent time going to and from places discussing our spiritual,
emotional, physical, and social growth. Working on many of
these areas jointly was exciting.—*Korrene Thiessen, Manhattan,
Kansas* (1980)

Thanks, thief. Darin and Julie Prey-Harbaugh got a little help
going green from an unexpected source: a car thief. When their car
was stolen in 1998, instead of replacing it, they lived without a vehicle for eleven years. The couple lives in Philadelphia where they
were able to use public transportation, borrow cars from friends,
and participate in car-share programs. This worked for a time,
until kids came. Having toddlers meant they had to carry two car
seats every time they used a car. Eventually, the couple decided
to buy a used Toyota Prius, but Julie would just as soon not own
a car. She says she makes more "stupid little trips," spends more
money, and is less likely to plan ahead now that they're car owners.
Her family's time without a car highlighted how often cars go
unused. "It's just sitting there, me owning it," she says. "When the
kids get big enough to carry their own booster seats, we'll probably
sell the car." —*Submitted by Paul Boers, Goshen, Indiana*

Recycled oil. My husband changes the oil in our vehicles,
collecting it in a container made for that purpose. We've found
two local car repair businesses that will use it to heat their
buildings.—*Lorene Byler Miller, Goshen, Indiana*

High school conversion. Switching to alternative energy
is entirely possible, according to Don Dyck Steinmann. He
supervises a group of twelfth-grade students who are converting a Chevy S10 pickup truck to run on electric power. The
project, called Rockway Tech's Zero Emission Vehicle, is part
of an alternative technologies course at Rockway Mennonite
Collegiate. "It's a great opportunity to learn and tangibly make
a difference," says Don, technology department head at the
Kitchener, Ontario, school.

The truck will run on twenty-four deep-cycle batteries—the
kind used in golf carts—that have to be set in metal boxes and
welded to the frame. That will give it enough capacity to go
30–40 miles (48–64 kilometers) on an eight-hour charge from
a standard household outlet. While those batteries won't last
forever, they are 98-percent recyclable.

Twelfth-grade student Cameron Penny started the project
with some trepidation because he had never taken a shop class

before; within a few months, he was welding with the best of them. Cameron says he especially values the project for its focus on reducing dependence on oil, a limited resource. "It's not going to be here forever," Cameron says. "It's important to find alternative sources of energy." Don says that he and the students have been impressed with the simplicity of this project. "It's something that they [high school students] can do," he says. "Why can't the car companies do something similar?"
—*Submitted by Paul Boers, Goshen, Indiana*

Fritter-mobile. The plan? To cross the United States in about sixty hours. The fuel? Leftover vegetable oil from the fritter booth at the West Coast Mennonite Central Committee Relief Sale. The reason? To "promote the fact that it is indeed possible to drive an ordinary car without using fossil fuels," says Ken Marten Friesen.

Ken and his friend Steve Friesen, both of Fresno, California, did the "Friesen Fritter-Fired Fossil Fuel-Free Drive Across America" on May 26–29, 2006. With the forty gallons of vegetable oil they collected from the relief sale and about thirty gallons of used soybean oil from a Japanese restaurant, Ken and Steve made the 2,950 miles (about 4,750 kilometers) from San Francisco to Rehoboth Beach, Delaware, in a Volkswagen Jetta TDI with an engine that Ken had converted to run on vegetable oil. They raised about $15,000, which supported environmental projects of MCC. Ken has converted about fifteen Jettas to use vegetable oil. These days, when he isn't biking to work, he still drives using the oil he collects from local Chinese and Vietnamese restaurants.

Making travel meaningful. We do what we can to reduce the impact of our travel by biking to school, walking to work, choosing housing with transportation in mind, and taking the bus. Yet we also travel long distances by car and plane, so we try to make that travel as meaningful as possible. We travel to visit relatives, and we travel to maintain the relationships that will sustain us all our lives. When we spend time in new places with people we know, we see the places in a much different way than if we were anonymous tourists. We have never regretted the memories we have created through spending time with family and friends, often sleeping in cramped or interesting spaces and joining in with their daily lives.—*Jeanne Zimmerly Jantzi, Salatiga, Central Java, Indonesia*

Family reunions and carbon. My wife and I live in Indiana. We are grateful that our three adult children have chosen educational opportunities and living places that help them use their gifts well. Currently they live in Oregon, Alabama, and California. Our challenge is to find ways to stay in touch without a huge carbon footprint. Now that there are three grandchildren, our desire for face-to-face time has increased. We have the goal of seeing each other twice a year, but each household also takes very seriously the importance of reducing our carbon usage and tries to be mindful of how the transportation required to get to our gatherings requires that we reduce our use of fossil fuels in other areas. We regularly use the phone, email, Skype, and Internet posting of photos to keep the personal connections strong between times that we're together.—*Luke Gascho, Goshen, Indiana*

● ● ● ● ● ● ● ● ● ● ● ● ●

Find more stories, tips, and links to resources about transportation and travel at www.mpn.net/livingmorewithless.

17
Recreation and Schedules

Doris Janzen Longacre

• •

a funny thing happened this morning on the way to writing this chapter about fun. I left home at 7:45 and walked five blocks to the office with my brain already busily sorting ideas on recreation. On arrival, I used my right hand to set my brown-bag lunch behind the desk as usual. Only then did I notice that my left hand held our fifth-grade daughter's Snoopy lunch pail. I had been oblivious to it bumping against my side for half a mile.

Fifteen minutes later, Snoopy was at the elementary school. I lost a bit of time, but took the whole thing as a last-minute reminder that ordinary days are peppered with crazy surprises.

If we turn down speed and noise enough to notice, life is ready with free thrills and gifts of beauty. Yesterday, on a walk through one of Akron's wooded areas, I stumbled upon a large natural garden of lavender and white phlox—right after I complained to someone that I had seen all the spring wildflowers in our area and was tired of hiking there.

A week earlier on another walk, a teenaged friend and I came upon an aeronautics show. Just as we passed a grove of maple trees, those windy gusts that precede a rainstorm hit. Within moments the air spun with thousands of two-inch helicopters—winged maple seeds whirligigging around us in nature's wild tree-planting frenzy. Choosing favorites and shouting through the wind, we watched some of them sail above the houses for blocks.

New ways of seeing

More-with-less standards for living never imply that we should stop the fun. Certainly these are grave days. Still, living more with less does not mean a somber lifestyle that preaches only responsibility and condemns beauty, excitement, and humor. It doesn't even mean rejecting the new. Although I shudder every time another advertisement shrills forth, "It's new!" in another way, newness is what we need. For it is in the very hope of a new kingdom, brought about by the eternal re-creative Spirit of God, that we may dare to laugh every day.

Recreation is the saving chuckle of the soul. It happens when we see a new thing or discover a new way of seeing. It is making a new thing and being remade, hearing a new sound and singing it. Nothing could be more in keeping with the nature of God.

In the apostle John's vision of the order to come, newness is a strong theme. At last God finds a dwelling place with us. The older order passes away. Then the One who sits on the throne cries, "See, I am making all things new" (Rev 21:5). That's at the end of the Bible, not the beginning. The God who made heaven and earth, who created us and is redeeming us, is not finished yet! Creation and re-creation never stop.

Leisure without rest

The process of re-creation requires leisure and rest. People in the Western world have leisure. Most of us do not need to slave every minute in order to eat. But only a few appear to have rest. Cheap energy supplies have allowed running to and fro at speeds and with a frequency never before possible. Profit-making work has begun to swallow Sundays and holidays. No wonder everyone has been getting so tired.

Are you busy?

The proportion of U.S. citizens who say they "always feel rushed" rose by more than half from the mid-1960s to the mid-1990s.[1]

Obviously, much of this fatigue takes place in the name of making more money, even though the pantry is already stocked. After all, by burning a little more gas and working one more evening a week, it is possible to chase down one more account, open another store, or farm another field. But it may not be possible to love a spouse, children, or the poor at the same time.

Others wear themselves out proving they are indeed worthwhile people. Get those new drapes up and the spring cleaning finished before Aunt Matilda arrives. Publish three articles a year or perish professionally. Fertilize the lawn. Support every bake sale. Keep that schedule untangled and keep those children on the run—soccer practice, violin lessons, art class, library day.

• • • • • • • • • • • • • •

The freedom of childhood . . . or not

In 1981, 40 percent of the average child's day was free time—the hours left over after sleeping, eating, school, and afterschool activities. By 1997, the average child had only 25 percent left for free time.[2]

A third way to justify exhausting yourself is to say you're "busy saving souls, for the night is coming" or "It's the Lord's work." This excuse is the one for which children and spouses are supposed to have no answer. But Jesus himself sometimes deliberately avoided crowds who waited for him to speak. He proposed a downright nasty end for those who offend children and made it clear that little ones had a right to his time (see Mark 9:35–42). He retreated to hills and private rooms to pray. His center was as much the garden as the throng.

Saying no

The best recreation may still turn out to be staying home and fine-tuning our senses. This isn't suggesting that we cut out all travel, meetings on important issues, vacation, or trips to visit relatives. It does suggest living by rhythms and priorities. Claim the freedom to say no both to good causes and to frantic, counterproductive efforts to have fun.

Happily, persons who choose to conserve energy supplies, save money, and nurture their spirits and relationships normally don't have problems finding recreation. Rarely in a discussion on simple living have I heard the question "But what can we do for fun?" The more critical danger is that those who allow themselves everything they want become unable to enjoy it. Less with more flies home to roost.

Testimonies on recreation offer these principles:

- *Beware of living in a way that allows no free time.* Do not feel guilty for taking regular periods to muse, meditate, or be silent or unoccupied. You'll do more praying.

- *Blur the distinction between work and recreation.* Invent ways to make dull work enjoyable. Redeem menial tasks by working together. Leisure activities might teach a skill, improve your home, augment your food supply, or serve others' needs.

- *Choose activities carefully.* For any form of recreation, ask a positive question: "Does this strengthen my own spirit and my relationships with others?" and a negative one: "Is it expensive in terms of money, energy supplies, or the natural environment?" Since so many activities are available that answer yes to the first and no to the second, don't accept many trade-offs.

- *Live* now *the way you would like to live.* "We'll take more time together when we've made enough to retire or when I get off all these church boards" can trail into "but then he had that heart attack." "I'll spend evenings with the children after these night classes are over" might end "but the children aren't home evenings anymore."

- *Use some recreation time for physical exercise.* Exercise is great preventive medicine and a more-with-less remedy for depression and being overweight.

- *A frequent desire to "get away from it all" signals other needs.* Look for the real problem. Make home a place in which you and your family enjoy staying.

Homemade toys. Living far away from the convenience of toy stores has forced me to create my own toys for my one-year-old and three-year-old, an inconvenience for which I'm truly grateful. Although I'm not a skilled builder or seamstress, I've made many toys for my children and have discovered what was true for generations before me: homemade toys are usually more durable, or at least repairable, than most bought plastic toys; they often cost less; they are free from advertising and brand-name marketing; and they foster a bond of love and creativity between parent and child. Some of our recent favorites have been a homemade felt board (with new pieces being added as imaginations grow), cloth blocks stuffed with leftover quilt batting, and a memory game made from close-up photos of faraway relatives. We've also written and illustrated simple storybooks and nursery rhymes about our children, which we laminate for durability and return to again and again.—*Kirsten Krymusa, Nairobi, Kenya*

Hot dogs not required. Growing up on a farm, we often carried meals to the field to eat together as a family even in the midst of a busy season. Any meal can be a picnic; hot dogs, hamburgers, and paper plates are not required. We keep picnic materials within easy reach so that we can have spur-of-the-moment picnics—a tablecloth as well as unbreakable plates, cups, and silverware. Dirty dishes can be piled into a bag and brought home to wash later. A laundry basket or a backpack can carry the meal. Hot food stays hot if placed in a thermal envelope or a soft-sided soda cooler, or wrapped in a blanket or towel. Cold food stays cold if wrapped in a towel with a reusable ice pack or placed in a small cooler. Eating outdoors in any season lifts the spirits and adds a little adventure to life. —*Jeanne Zimmerly Jantzi, Salatiga, Central Java, Indonesia*

Stargazing. We find stargazing a challenging and enjoyable family activity. All you need to begin is a guidebook to the stars—a star map is even better—a flashlight, and a place to go that is beyond the reach of streetlights. It takes ten minutes for eyes to readjust to night darkness, so we dim the flashlight with a cloth and rubber band. Even small children can find the Milky Way and the Big and Little Dippers. We find that the more we learn about the sky, the greater grows our wonder at God's creation.—*Becky Horst, Lederach, Pennsylvania* (1980)

Set up camp. One of the reasons I like to go camping is that it keeps me in touch with the basics in life. When you need to walk to fetch water for drinking and washing up, and when you need to walk a distance to the toilet, it makes you appreciate the comforts of home. When you need to be very careful with your garbage so that raccoons or bears are not attracted to it, you pay close attention to what you throw out. When backpacking or canoeing, you need to carry everything over the portage or along the trail, so you are very discriminating about what you take with you. A yearly camping trip reminds me of what is important and reminds me to live simply.—*Barb Draper, Elmira, Ontario*

Storytime: not just for kids. Almost nightly for the last twelve years, we have taken turns reading to each other. Generally our read-aloud lasts for about thirty minutes, and sometimes longer on weekends. Mostly we read fiction, but occasionally we delve into nonfiction or memoir.

Reading aloud each day helps us stay connected, and we often stop to interrupt each other with anecdotes from the day or to share memories sparked by something in a book. It also helps us unwind from the day and keeps us tuned in to each other rather than the television, the Internet, or countless other projects that might demand our attention.—*Amy Gingerich and Ryan Claassen, Hudson, Ohio*

Small group. On wheels. Every Saturday at 7:00 a.m., the Glen Riders meet to bicycle through the winding roads of Bucks County and Montgomery County, Pennsylvania. The Glen Riders was started as an outreach program from Blooming Glen Mennonite Church in Perkasie fourteen years ago. The group contains a mix of church members and people from the local community. According to Ken Hochstetler, a member of Blooming Glen and a regular Glen Rider, the group can consist of anywhere from four to forty members during the biking season, April to October. Ken likens the group to a church small group on wheels. "It's amazing the kinds of conversations you can have after being on a bicycle for three hours with a group of people," he says.—*Submitted by Alysha Bergey Landis, Harleysville, Pennsylvania*

Gang's all here. As expensive cable TV and home theaters become commonplace, we risk losing the fun of shared entertainment. In our town, a sports-loving couple that subscribes to cable bucks the trend by issuing a standing invitation for friends to come watch games with them. Often a dozen people will squeeze into their small living room, and the collective cheers, groans, and colorful commentary are half the experience.

My husband, Dave, loves soccer, and we've had memorable experiences watching World Cup games in public settings; one of my favorites is the rec center of our local university, where crowds of international students gather. In a society that cultivates isolation, group-oriented recreation is worth seeking out. I also like to "go local" with my entertainment choices. Community theaters, college choirs, and alternative movie theaters are to be cherished!—*Cathleen Hockman-Wert, Corvallis, Oregon*

Music nights. We invite other families to our house one evening a month for a potluck. After supper we make music together. Particular skills and talents determine the kind of music we choose. Music making is not just for professionals. Even young children sense the pleasure and value of music by actively participating.—*Shirley King, Newton, Kansas* (1980)

Family nights. For almost ten years, Jeff and Tonja Stern-Gilbert of Elkhart, Indiana, have been having weekly family nights. Their children get to choose an activity to do as a family. Jeff says, "There have been times when we weren't as faithful about doing family night and our kids have been the ones to say, 'When are we going to do family night again?' They enjoy planning an activity and being in charge of it."
—*Submitted by Alysha Bergey Landis, Harleysville, Pennsylvania*

Sustainable schedules. I don't always feel comfortable with our schedules, but here are a few things that contribute to what is usually a less hectic lifestyle, with more time to be together as a family: (1) We are unschoolers, or life learners. The girls (ages twelve and seven) and I are home together during the day, pursuing activities of our own choosing. (2) We have one car, which my husband, Kirk, uses for his job. Without a car, our daytime activities are naturally limited to home or nearby biking. (3) Our girls are involved in weekly dance class and choir during the school year, but both are located within five minutes of our home. (4) We don't travel much for extended trips, recreation, or even shopping. We have great local concerts and plays, a thrift store just down the road, a growing farmers market, and a burgeoning downtown economy. (5) When considering whether to take on something new, we talk together about what we need to give up to make space for the new, rather than just trying to cram it in and hoping we'll be fine. (6) We eat supper together almost every day.—*Kris Shank Zehr, Harrisonburg, Virginia*

Spiritual renewal. Amid busy schedules and heavy workloads, our Nigerian friends fasted regularly. They spoke highly of its value in strengthening their spiritual lives. We were attracted, but weren't quite able to discipline ourselves. But finally the pressure of work and responsibilities seemed overwhelming.

• •

How can we balance kids' sports time with family time?

- *Establish your limits* before *the season begins, and communicate with the coach.* Review the schedule with your child and inform the coach of dates you will not be there and why, giving priority to family and church events.

- *Realize that watching your child's game is* not *family time.* Schedule other activities that involve the personal interaction of all family members.

- *Don't attend every practice and game.* Give your child space, and have coffee with your spouse. Remember: it is your child's event, not yours.

- *Take a break.* Skip one season and schedule your family to serve at the local soup kitchen.

- *Find (or create) alternative programs*—ones without scoreboards, standings, travel, all-star teams, and uniforms with professional team names.

- *Replace organized play with free play.* Get the children in your neighborhood or church together in your backyard for pick-up games.

- *Count the cost.* Before registering, calculate the impact on your family's finances.

- *Remember that more isn't always better.* You wouldn't let your child eat the whole jar of peanut butter, so why let them play every sport every season? You can have more with less.

—*David King, director of athletics, Eastern Mennonite University*

We began rising at 5:00 a.m., to begin our day with two hours of prayer and Bible study. This period of renewal soon became a fixed habit. We hadn't yet set aside a time for fasting, but we had begun to fast on certain occasions for special reasons, especially during crisis experiences.

Then we came home to America to retire. Pressures were no less than in Africa. We had to adjust to a new way of life. More than ever we enjoyed our two-hour period alone with God early every morning. It was at this point that we began fasting regularly. On Friday, our fast day, we exclude all solid foods. Without being legalistic, we enjoy Fridays. We have more time for prayer and are convinced that, for us, fasting belongs with Bible study and prayer.—*Ed and Irene Weaver, Hesston, Kansas* (1980)

Mental memory album. While traveling from one place to the next on a trip, we enjoy reinforcing memories and reliving details with this game. Directions: (1) We establish a context for the guessing, such as "any place we stopped yesterday" or a particular point of interest just visited. (2) The person who is "it" thinks of an object everyone noticed and gives a clue concerning its size: large (buildings, trees, mountains), medium (restaurant table, picture in an art gallery, rowboat), or small (ice cream cone, chipmunk, quarter found on the ground). (3) Other players ask questions that may be answered with yes or no. For example: "Was it inside the national park?" "Is it something we all touched?" (4) Whoever guesses the object becomes "it" for the next round.—*Doris Janzen Longacre, Akron, Pennsylvania* (1980)

• • • • • • • • • • • • • •

Find more stories, tips, and links to resources about recreations and schedules at www.mpn.net/livingmorewithless.

18
Celebrations and Life Passages

Rebecca Seiling

• •

as a young boy, my Grandpa Horst eagerly anticipated Christmas morning. He would wake up and quietly slip down the stairs to find a dinner plate full of goodies set out on the kitchen table: two Brazil nuts, two walnuts, a few chocolates, hard candies, and one enormous, perfect orange. One particular highlight was the caramel-covered coconut candy ball. There would be ten plates, one for each of the children in his family.

For my daughter's fifth birthday, her five invited guests were asked to bring soap in lieu of gifts. At the end of the party, she was thrilled to have collected seventy-seven bars of soap to be donated to Mennonite Central Committee's overseas relief projects.

Simple celebrations. Good food, meaningful gift giving, laughter, the company of family and friends, relaxed merrymaking. Sound too good to be true? Many people find that harried planning, splurging, list making, and a flurry of shopping and stressing about details mean that holidays and celebrations exhaust rather than enliven. In the United States, landfills feel the current weight of the holiday season, with about one million extra tons (907,185 metric tons) of trash per week generated between Thanksgiving and Christmas.[1] Many people yearn for the simplicity of a bygone age, when people focused on family, faith, and friends instead of on the commercialized trimmings, trappings, and wastefulness of the season.

At their best, celebrations give us something to look forward to and something to remember. They have the potential to lift us out of the mire of day-to-day details. Simple celebrations can be joyful and rich events, focusing on relationships, faith, and time spent together rather than on gifts, matching decor, spotless floors, and elegant foods.

Quiet, small acts

Each new day gives us possibilities for celebration. Even a quiet, small act like lighting an evening candle is a way of showing thanks for the gifts of that particular day. By pausing to reflect, we show our gratitude for life's mundane yet beautiful gifts.

Sometimes I feel caught in the "innovation trap," wanting to celebrate in new and different ways each year. Yet I have come to greatly value ongoing traditions. Creating meaningful traditions around liturgical events such as Advent, Christmas, Lent, and Easter helps the whole family to focus on the stories and significance behind these holidays.

I have been amazed at how children can be the "carriers" of traditions. One year our family hosted others for a Seder supper during Holy Week. We celebrated this Passover meal, remembering that this was what Jesus did at the Last Supper with his disciples. Without knowing it, that year we had created a tradition. Four years later, our children ask, "Who are we celebrating the Seder with this year?" This has become a very meaningful part of our Easter season simply because our children assumed we would continue it.

• • • • • • • • • • • • • •

"By God's grace we can make both holy and merry the unique events that mark our years."—*Doris Janzen Longacre*

Is there such a thing as too much celebrating? If we celebrate everything, there is a danger that nothing will seem special anymore. In the *More-with-Less Cookbook*, Doris Janzen Longacre notes that because "in North America we tend to feast nonstop [this] can dull our festive joy." Saving certain foods and events for holidays or important milestones makes them extra-special. When our family lived in France, we enjoyed *merveilles*, crispy fried pastries topped with icing and sugar, which were available only for one month during Lent. Although we were sad to see them leave the store shelves, it made us appreciate them more than if we had eaten them all year.

Longacre gave several helpful suggestions to guide our simple celebrations:

- *Celebrate the meaning of life* at births, birthdays, marriages, deaths, various anniversaries, and special times. Living more with less does not mean abolishing commemorations and festivals.

- *Celebrations should nurture people and strengthen faith.* They are more than entertainment.

- *Separate celebrations from commercial interests.* Sometimes paid services are useful, but their availability must not dictate how we celebrate.

- *Spend money well and carefully on celebrations.* Overspending is the greatest temptation. Look for moderation and simplicity.

- *Cherish the natural world by saving energy and avoiding excess and waste.* Even at celebrative times, it's important to avoid products that litter and pollute.

- *Consider alternatives to giving gifts.* A gift of time, personal expression, or another innovation may best accomplish the purpose of gift giving—to serve the recipient's genuine needs and to reflect the giver's desire to show love.

- *Celebrations belong to families, churches, and communities.* Consider the involvement of others when planning events.

- *Remember that celebrations are not only for today.* Celebrations become our history. For once-in-a-lifetime events, like weddings and funerals, handle tradition sensitively. Make room for new ideas, but weed out what is cheap and frivolous.

Simple yet special celebrations are still an ideal that I strive for. I struggle not to get caught up in the details of hosting and to pare back to what is "enough" to make the event meaningful, life-giving, and memorable for all involved (including myself).

I sometimes think back to my grandfather, who as a boy had been so thrilled with nuts and an orange and a few small pieces of candy. He grew into a farmer who loved his land, and as a man he would celebrate the coming of summer rain by sitting on the porch and playing his accordion. I remember the way his foot stomped out a percussive accompaniment to the rain, the way that he drummed out simple celebrations of the small and the beautiful.

Birth. When our child was born, we wrote a letter to friends instead of using typical birth announcements. We gave details of Ryan's birth but also focused on our dreams for the kind of world in which he and all other children will live. We wrote, "In this time of great joy and concern we are all challenged by the vision of a 'new earth' of peace, plenty, and justice spoken of in Isaiah 65. In this world there will be no weeping, no calling for help. Babies will no longer die in infancy and all people will live out their life-span. People will build houses and get to live in them—they will not be used by someone else. Wolves and lambs will eat together; lions will eat straw as cattle do." We concluded by suggesting that those who wanted to share our joy and concern write their government urging changed national priorities, or send a gift in Ryan's name to a church agency to further peace and development work around the world.—*Duane and Ramona Smith Moore, North Manchester, Indiana* (1980)

Baby blankets. When I was expecting our first child, I didn't want to spend a lot of money on receiving blankets. I bought one full-size white blanket and cut it up into five small ones. I sewed binding around the edges and added embroidery designs. While saving money, I had the satisfaction of creating something special for our baby.—*Bev Martin, Stevens, Pennsylvania* (1980)

No gifts, please. Around each child's sixth birthday, our family begins hosting "friend" parties in his or her honor. The birthday child chooses the theme, the menu, the guest list, and what the cake should look like. The party celebrates the child in every way, with one significant exception. Our invitations read, "No gifts, please. Cards welcome!" We've received occasional phone calls from baffled parents, but the request has always been respected.

Why no gifts? Our family is trying to live a less wasteful life: less packaging and less of what we don't really need. (The birthday child does receive gifts at a more casual family meal.) We've discovered that "no gifts" definitely does not equal "no fun." If anything, the party is enhanced by an absence of greed and social comparison. The focus changes from getting new stuff to having fun with friends. We also don't hand out giant loot bags afterward but send every guest home with something they've made or used at the party.

We know we are asking our children to be different from some of their friends. That can be a hard thing to ask of a child. It's critical that our children understand we are not making arbitrary choices, but choices based on beliefs. When the question "Could my friends bring presents this year?" arises—and it has—we try to place our family's privilege in a more global perspective. That question gives us the chance to reflect on the riches we already have and how we might share our wealth, rather than asking for more and more.—*Carrie Snyder, Waterloo, Ontario*

"Recycle bycle." I had just returned from an overseas trip when Gladys reminded me of our youngest child's upcoming birthday and her desire for a new bicycle. Still preoccupied with the poverty I had seen, I asked, "What about all the bikes we already have rusting away in the garage? For us to buy another bike would be a sin." "I know what you mean," Gladys responded, "but each of the other children got a new bike. She has her heart set on it."

It isn't right to ask an eight-year-old girl to bear the responsibility for world poverty, so I decided to talk to her to see if she could enter into a decision with us. Choosing the occasion and my words carefully, I explained that we knew she needed a different bike, that the other children had each owned a new one, and that on the basis of equality she could demand one too. Then I told her the reasons we didn't want to buy another new bicycle just now. I made a suggestion: "Let's get a can of paint and refinish Susan's old twenty-six-incher. We can buy some decals and make it look good. And then let's send a check for seventy-five dollars to our mission board." I could tell immediately that this was a winner.

We did the work together: sanding, painting, adjusting, and straightening the old wheel. We called it her "recycle bycle." Every time she rode it she seemed to have a private, inner satisfaction. Today she cherishes the memory of a beautiful experience that helped teach her self-denial and concern for others.
—*Edgar Stoesz, Akron, Pennsylvania* (1980)

Graduation quilts. For several years I have been making denim quilts as graduation gifts. It takes a good bit of planning ahead, since the gift can't be bought at the last minute. My local thrift store sells denim jeans that come in with rips and tears. I use pockets, embroidery, and other special items to add to the quilt. I make the quilts big enough to use on a twin bed, for a football or soccer game, or for a picnic. I watch for suitable fabric for the back at local thrift stores.—*Linda Miller, Harrisonburg, Virginia*

Prayer shawls. Turning eighteen years of age is a significant milestone in the lives of our young adults. This often means leaving home as they pursue further education and develop their gifts and abilities. To celebrate this milestone, we have a time of blessing for them in our worship service at St. Jacobs (Ont.) Mennonite Church. They share about their future plans, and the parents reflect on their hopes for their child. The young adults are then presented with a prayer shawl, which has been knit by a congregation member. This is lovingly wrapped around them by the knitter during a prayer, followed by a congregational response. We want them to know that whatever their future holds, God will be with them, we will be supporting them with our prayers, and they will continue to be a part of our church community.—*Sue Shantz, St. Jacobs, Ontario*

Rings that bind. Our wedding rings are symbolic and personal. While visiting Peter's family, we enlisted his brother, William, to straighten with pliers the chosen raw material—paper clips. I held the clip strands as Peter and William braided: two bronze-colored clips to represent our lives, and one silver clip to represent the kingdom woven throughout. A friend loaned us his soldering gun to close the metal braid. The rings are sturdy and don't discolor our fingers. We do anticipate possible breakdowns. This reminds us that marriage cannot be taken for granted but requires care and sometimes repair. The strands have all turned silver—a parable of the all-pervasive and mysterious growth of the kingdom.—*Mary Sprunger-Froese, Saskatoon, Saskatchewan* (1980)

Green wedding? Sure. When our August 2006 wedding was written up in our local paper as a "green" wedding, we were somewhat bemused. Yes, our guests were invited to spend the weekend in A-frame cabins at a Mennonite camp in the mountains of Washington, encouraged to purchase carbon offsets in lieu of gifts, and warned that they'd be sitting on blankets in the grass during the ceremony. The wedding was a celebration of our supportive and talented community: friends designed our invitations, crafted our recycled-gold wedding bands, arranged our farmers-market flowers, provided our photography and music, and made an abundance of delicious vegetarian salads for the reception. We wore sandals, sang hymns in front of a patch of sunflowers, planted a native tree, and pledged our love for each other in

• • • • • • • • • • • •

Carbon offsets are either purchases or donations to projects involving renewable energy, energy conservation, or reforestation that are calculated to equal the same amount of greenhouse gases burned in another area of life. Reducing carbon emissions should take priority over carbon offsetting, but offsets can be one part of a comprehensive strategy to reduce carbon emissions.

front of those who mean the most to us. Our wedding reflected our commitment to each other and our commitment to God, simplicity, sustainability, and community. And hey, if that makes us "green," all the better.—*Sarah Kraybill Burkhalter, Seattle, Washington*

Wedding gifts. When I receive a wedding invitation and see that the couple has registered at a big-box store, I go online to see what colors they have chosen. Then I go to my favorite fair-trade store and buy them a gift in that color scheme. That way I know it will be something that will blend with their other gifts but will be something unique that also helps Third World artisans.—*Linda Miller, Harrisonburg, Virginia*

• • • • • • • • • • • • •

The average wedding in Canada in 2010 cost $20,129 (Can.).[2]

Into the ground. Simple wooden caskets are the centerpiece of Rick Zerbe Cornelsen's business in Winnipeg, Manitoba. By selling directly to families rather than through the conventional funeral home system, Rick says that he is attempting to "bring the death process back into the local community." Most of his business until recently has been local, although his design of an entirely biodegradable casket made of fast-growing soft woods is increasing the geographic reach of his business.

Rick says that some of his caskets are "fairly rugged looking, compared to what you see in funeral home showrooms." Buying a simple casket for a family member, he says, requires that "people be willing to show their love and respect for their loved one in ways other than through an ostentatious, fancy casket. I can often sense that people who buy my caskets don't think they need to impress everyone else with how much they loved the person. They know they did."

Ashes to ashes. Several years before my parents died, they mentioned that rather than the traditional burial, they would like to be cremated. I was somewhat surprised, because cremation was not common among people of their generation. Yet I understood their choice, for they lived close to the earth and their lives revolved around the turning of the seasons—the planting, the harvesting, and the resting. They expressed concern about the encroachment of the city on choice farmland and considered it best to use less land for their burial. They said that cremation just "made sense." For my mother, we had a visitation and funeral before cremation. My father preferred cremation immediately, so we honored his wishes and then held a memorial visitation and service. Their remains are buried together in a single plot, with a stone monument to commemorate their lives.—*Jeanette Seiling, Elora, Ontario*

The "bitter" in bittersweet. For many people, chocolate is an expected part of celebrating Valentine's Day, Easter, and Halloween. At Beach Lake (Pa.) United Methodist Church, these holidays are ideal times to raise consciousness about the bitter side of this sweet treat: the link between conventional production of cacao, from which chocolate is made, and child slavery and trafficking in West Africa. Fair-trade chocolate, in contrast, is regulated to ensure that laborers aren't exploited.

During Halloween, Beach Lake UMC members give treat-or-treaters fair-trade chocolate bars with cards explaining how fair trade is reforming the chocolate industry. This outreach and the publicity it has gained have led community members

In Ivory Coast, the world's leading supplier of cocoa, more than 109,000 children work on cocoa plantations under what the U.S. Department of State calls "the worst forms of child labor." Of those, 10,000 are victims of human trafficking or enslavement.[3]

to start buying fair-trade chocolate, coffee, and tea from the church. "I can't think of anyone, Christian or not, who disagrees with the golden rule of treating others as we want to be treated ourselves," says Pastor Mark Terwilliger. "When we become aware of how we're benefiting from the mistreatment of others, we can make choices that put our values into action."
—*Submitted by Cathleen Hockman-Wert, Corvallis, Oregon*

Advent festival. On the first Sunday of Advent, our church, St. Jacobs (Ont.) Mennonite Church, held an intergenerational party to kick off the season of Advent. Several people were asked to teach simple crafts, such as Christmas ornaments or decorations. Christmas music played in the background, and people could view a display of a collection of nativity sets from around the world. There were board games, crokinole boards, and a comforter set up for people to knot and that would be sold to benefit MCC. We enjoyed a "festive finger foods" potluck meal for supper, then had a carol sing afterward. It was a wonderful mixing of the small and the tall, and a meaningful way to start the Christmas season.—*Rebecca Seiling, Waterloo, Ontario*

One-hundred-meter Christmas. Every year our family discusses new ways to celebrate Christmas and gift giving—finding ways that are sustainable in terms of energy, time, quality of connection, and support of our community. We discovered it created less stress and established continuing ties with our community and one another. Our choice to remain in a small house within walking distance of Waterloo's downtown makes our decision to only purchase gifts, foodstuffs, and entertainment within a one-hundred-meter (109-yard) radius an easy and simple one to implement—with a touch of creativity. It fosters family outings, less spending, and more fun.—*Deborah Black, Waterloo, Ontario*

Christmas adventures. For Nereida and José Babilonia-Prunés's four children, gifts under the tree have been replaced by Christmas adventures. Each family member gets to choose a place where the family will go for a day; recent adventures have included trips to an aquarium, Washington, D.C., and a roller-skating rink. They always take public transportation to get to the chosen destination, which Nereida says adds to the sense of adventure. "People on the subway or bus often ask the kids where we're going, because the excitement is contagious. We get to spread the word, and people often say that they might try this with their families too."

The Babilonia-Prunés family, members of Oxford Circle Mennonite Church in Philadelphia, say the Christmas adventures fit better with their Christian faith than accumulating

• •

How can we celebrate Christmas in a more-with-less way?

• *Find meaningful gift-giving options* such as enjoying unique experiences together as a family, making relief kits to send overseas, and exchanging handmade gifts, gifts of time, and fair-trade gifts.

• *Consider potluck meals* to simplify food preparation for large gatherings. Potlucks can be filled with wonderful treats, and guests and hosts can share the responsibility of preparing food.

• *Create traditions* that do not involve gifts, like watching a live nativity, volunteering, caroling, baking, or giving to others.

• *Print off "Gift Exemption Vouchers"* from the Simple Living Network website (www.simpleliving.net/ftp/gift-voucher.pdf) and give them to family members and friends.

• *Create a budget and stick to it.* Record Christmas purchases in a notebook or computer file to keep track of money spent. Money can be well spent on gifts, but often the debt from the Christmas season takes months to pay off.

• *Find alternative gift-giving ideas* at www.buynothingchristmas.org.

more things. "It was getting outrageous, the amount of stuff the kids have," says Nereida. "This way we're spending time together. Then, when we all go back to our routines of school or work, we often say to each other, 'Oh, remember that week when we had all those adventures!'"

A twist on tradition. My husband's family had always exchanged gifts at Christmas. Then two years ago, my husband and I suggested that we give the tradition a new twist by making donations to charity in place of our regular gift giving. In response, some family members gave to the Red Cross or to the Alzheimer's Society in memory of Mom and Dad, who had both passed away that year. We chose to support a development project through Mennonite Economic Development Associates.

It made sense for us to give in these ways, especially since we all had more than we needed. In fact, we wish we had been brave enough to suggest such a radical departure from long-standing tradition much earlier. Today we're still working out what this new form of gift giving means for us as a family. Now that our Christmas celebrations no longer revolve around

opening gifts and talking about the latest DVD or new sweater, we're also needing to relate to one another in a new way. Perhaps that's another part of the gift we can offer one another.
—*April Yamasaki, Abbotsford, British Columbia*

Gifts of a new year. How can we remove the consumerism from Christmas and still enjoy giving each other gifts? Matthew and I asked ourselves this in the first few years of being parents and decided that we'd remove gift giving from Christmas and put it on New Year's Day instead. It was too confusing for young children to be told the "true meaning" of Christmas and yet see and hear and feel the focus on the gifts. Both of our extended families agreed not to exchange gifts at Christmas (we save that for birthdays). Christmas is now so much fun, as we can focus on the joys of connecting with family and friends and thinking about the true meanings of the season. On New Year's Day morning, our nuclear family eagerly gives each other gifts and delights in a leisurely day of new toys, puzzles, and books.
—*Nina Bailey-Dick, Waterloo, Ontario*

• • • • • • • • • • • • • •

About 40 percent of all battery sales takes place during the holidays. If you buy an electronic gift, consider buying rechargeable batteries to go with it, as well as a battery charger.[4]

Let there be (just enough) light. I love the festivity of Christmas lights, but a little mindfulness can go a long way when deciding how to use them. (1) People seem to put up their lights earlier every year, but the number of days you use your lights will affect your electricity consumption. Consider waiting until after the first Sunday of Advent, and take them down right after New Year's. (2) Put your lights on a timer, rather than having them on all night. (3) Limit the number of lights you use. The popular style with five or more bulbs resembling an icicle exponentially increases energy use. (4) Consider switching to LED. While more expensive, LED lights use at least 80 percent less electricity than incandescent bulbs. LED lights also tend to last longer, and when one bulb goes out, it doesn't make the whole string go dark.—*Cathleen Hockman-Wert, Corvallis, Oregon*

An answer to buying parties. Each year I get invitations to buying parties. Although I enjoy the fun of being with friends, I'm bothered by the whole idea behind the parties. They encourage me to buy things I don't need and to schedule a party so my hostess and I can win lovely gifts. If I agree, the overbuying continues. So I designed a different kind of party to replace the buying kind. In October I invited friends for a craft party. We made small Christmas tree ornaments that we then gave to a thrift shop in our area. I supplied the materials and light refreshments. The fellowship of that evening easily equaled a buying party. Guests had the satisfaction of learning to make something and of helping a worthy cause. The thrift-shop manager was delighted to have seasonal, handmade items to sell. And I was able to play hostess with a clear conscience.—*Susan Hurst, New Holland, Pennsylvania* (1980)

Blessing basket. We celebrate housewarmings of neighbors and friends with a blessing basket. It includes a loaf of bread with a note that the home will be blessed with adequate food; a box of salt, that family life will be preserved and blessed; a jar of honey or jam, that they will be blessed by life's sweetness; a bar of soap, that they will be blessed with good health; and a candle, that the light of Christ would shine within their new home. If the home is distant, we pack a blessing box to send and substitute a bread mix instead of a loaf. In our troubled times, blessings are comforting and sustaining.—*Annie Lind, Portland, Oregon*

Wrap with scraps. Our children enjoy making their own wrapping paper by coloring, painting, or pasting pictures on plain newsprint or other scrap paper. We use scraps of cloth, felt, or yarn to make a bow. Real or artificial flowers, fall leaves, or evergreen branches sometimes decorate our gifts. We make tags from old greeting cards.
—*Mary Jane Hoober, Hesston, Kansas* (1980)

● ● ● ● ● ● ● ● ● ● ● ●

Find more stories, tips, and links to resources about celebrations and life passages at www.mpn.net/livingmorewithless.

19
Technology and Media

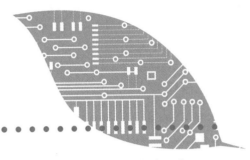

Isaac Villegas

●　●　●　●　●　●　●　●　●　●　●　●　●　●　●　●　●

What do I want? I asked myself as I lay in my bed and thought about the day. I stumbled out to the office in our house and turned on my laptop. With a cup of coffee in hand, I began my web-travels around the globe.

First I checked the news, read a few recent posts on the blogs I follow, then responded to a few emails and deleted several others. This would not be the last time that day that I checked the news or my email or browsed my favorite blogs. In fact, I probably repeated my news-blog-email travels twenty to thirty times during the day. Through these media technologies, I was connected to the world, to people and places miles away—across oceans and continents.

What do I want? I asked myself that day as I clicked and typed, roaming the world with my fingers, communing with people around the globe through networks of silicon. Perhaps my computerized wandering through the Internet taps into a desire deep within me for communion, for a human connection. Perhaps media technologies feed on dreams of companionship—primordial dreams like those remembered in the story of Adam and Eve, each belonging with the other, sharing the same flesh.

We are lonely people. So with the click of a mouse we try to convince ourselves that we are not alone: with an email, a blog entry, a tweet, a Facebook update, a glance at the news. The proliferation of news media and communication technologies supplies another story about another person in another country for my consuming pleasure—I can look them in the eyes and know that I am not alone. And the burgeoning market of social media via the Internet offers points of connection with a host of others around the globe: with my computer and smart phone I can constantly update my status on Twitter and Facebook just to convince myself that someone wants to know the minutiae of my life. I want to know that someone cares about my life and wants my companionship—or at least a status update.

The spirits of workers

But the companionship promised by the technological marketplace hides a lot of ghosts from my view. The computers and televisions and phones I use to wander the world are haunted by a multitude of laborers whose work I consume as I click and dial. The people who made the technological tools I enjoy are, for all practical reasons, dead to me. When I use technology, I access the human power that went into making that piece of technology, yet I do not want the people who assembled the apparatus to come along. I don't want to think about them and their work, and I certainly don't want their companionship. Indeed, a deep irony is hidden in our use of media technologies: we turn to them to satisfy our lonely boredom, yet we do not want any relationship with those who produce them.

The technologies I use do not bear any trace of the labor and resources that went into their production—except for the piece of paper that reads, "Inspected by 43672." "The point of having your own object world, and walls and muffled distance or relative silence all around you, is to forget about all those innumerable others for a while," writes cultural critic Fredric Jameson. "You don't want to have to think about Third World women every time you pull yourself up to your word processor, or all the other lower-class

● ● ● ● ● ● ● ● ● ● ● ● ●

Those "innumerable others"

Computers and especially monitors contain high levels of heavy metals such as lead, mercury, cadmium, and chromium, which pose health risks to production workers and environmental risks to water supplies near landfills where they are eventually dumped.[1]

people with their lower-class lives when you decide to use or consume your other luxury products: it would be like having voices in your head."[2]

While we are introduced to a new world of relationships through the Internet, we are also invited to do the impossible: to relate to every person at once, to browse every screen at once, to pay attention to every update at once, to shift instantaneously from one site or medium to another. Through such visual stimulation we begin to enter a dream world composed of bits and pieces of real people in real places, yet the images manufactured on our screens are emptied of flesh and blood—people ravaged into recyclable images for the never-ending loop of consumption called the Internet. We dream of companionship and intimacy, yet we seldom look beyond the plastics and silicon at our fingertips.

When we consider our use of technological devices, we can ask ourselves several questions:

- *How can we make sure technology serves our relationships rather than the other way around?* In what ways can all the bits of technology in our lives serve as invitations to form networks of caregiving? And in what ways can we be reminded of and connect with the workers whose handprints are on our computers?

- *What do our media habits reveal about our deepest desires?* As the ancient inscription at the temple of Apollo at Delphi says, "Know thyself." What is it that we are searching for when we endlessly browse and tweet and text? Relationship? Entertainment? Distraction?

- *What are we* not *doing when we are in front of a screen?* When we cozy up to our technological devices, whom are we ignoring and why? What practices or hobbies or relationships are we not cultivating?

So it is, with our attention divided between this screen and that one, we reach out for belonging, companionship, and union with others. And so it is that our technologies are haunted by the workers whose spirits reach out to us through the plastic keys we press and the screens at which we stare. The challenges of our technological age are these: to name our loneliness and to feel the multitude of people whose spirits now haunt our houses and offices. To paraphrase a passage from the book of Genesis: "Listen . . . the blood and sweat of your sisters and brothers are crying out from your computers" (Gen 4:10). They are our companions as well, whether we want them to be or not.

What's that in your cell phone?

Tantalum, tungsten, tin, and gold are used in virtually every electronic device: computers, cell phones, gaming devices, and digital cameras, among others. These minerals are also at the root of the violence in Congo. The Congolese armed groups that perpetuate the war, which is the deadliest conflict since World War II, earn hundreds of millions of dollars each year selling these "conflict minerals" to electronics manufacturers.[3]

Screen time, green time. Jewel Gingerich Longenecker of South Bend, Indiana, and her husband, Fred, are intentional about how much time their children—Jace, age twelve, and Jenae, age fourteen—spend in front of a television or computer or other screen-driven technology. They strive for a balance of activities that involve technology and ones that don't. Afternoon activities like television, movies, and computer games all fall under the category of screen time, which Jewel and Fred keep a close eye on. "We started at thirty minutes a day," says Jewel. "Part of what matters so much is that you don't focus on what you don't allow. I also think it's important what you do instead." The Gingerich Longeneckers continue to make sure their children are involved in activities like ceramics, cooking, and gardening, and other outdoor activities that involve hands-on creativity. "We talk about it, and we work at each challenge as it comes up," Jewel says.—*Submitted by Laura Schlabach, Goshen, Indiana*

Home free. We have tried to let our technology work for us (and not vice versa). We have decided that the computer and other technical equipment are only in our home office: at the end of the workday, the computer is turned off and isn't turned on again until the start of the next business day. All electronic devices (computers, printers, TVs, etc.) use power even when they are not "on" (this is called phantom power use), so you can plug your various devices into a power bar, which you switch off when not in use and thereby save energy.—*Jane Snyder, Waterloo, Ontario*

Setting limits. When eleven-year-old Benjamin Sommers wanted a handheld video game system, he paid for it with his own money. This was the condition set by his parents, Kendal and Robina Sommers, of Goshen, Indiana. "I think the main motivation was that we wanted him to realize that money doesn't grow on trees and you've got to work to earn things, learn their value, and take care of them," says Kendal. When Benjamin eventually upgraded to a system that included Internet features, Kendal and Robina required a few parental controls such as password access. The Sommers allow Benjamin and his sister, Priya, age eight, to access primarily websites aimed for children. "We have to log in and be there while they're doing it," Kendal says. Figuring out technology guidelines such as Internet limits is hard, he adds. "It's a constant tension of letting them explore things but protecting them too."—*Submitted by Laura Schlabach, Goshen, Indiana*

• • • • • • • • • • • • •

Kids between the ages of 8 and 18 are spending more than 7½ hours a day using electronic devices. And because they're often media multitasking, they generally cram 11 hours of screen time into those 7½ hours.[4]

No app(le)s. At the end of the first decade of the second millennium, few Canadians or U.S. citizens expect that a twenty-five-year-old would choose to live without Internet access or a TV in his home. Still, here I am. I will not make a bold prediction that it will never change. Yet for now I have learned that the less I watch TV, the longer my evenings feel; the fewer websites I surf, the later I tire. I cook. I host. I talk to people in person. I write. I read. And I have time left over.

I won't say I don't miss TV. I do watch it when I visit friends or family, and I certainly don't leave the room when that hypnotic blue glow comes on. I check my email at work and have a digital presence. Yet I long for a life in constant communion with God and God's creation. Backyard gardens and flower-themed wallpapers on computer desktops make for pretty poor substitutes. This time we don't need app(le)s to expel us from the garden. There may be no social network telling me if anyone is following, which is fine. When it comes to guidance, my preferred GPS created the North Star.—*Kevin Ressler, Lancaster, Pennsylvania*

Blogging. As we post comments on public websites and engage in online conversations, we should recognize that the Internet is a semi-permanent, searchable record of our words. Something you write or post in the spur of moment can be there for a long time. Your words online are easily ripped out of context and used as ammunition against you. I once wrote a blog post at work in the morning, and the next moment a prominent blog-

• •

How can I blog and comment on blogs responsibly?

- *Pay attention to your tone.* It is much harder to communicate your tone with written words than with embodied speech. Humor and sarcasm are incredibly difficult to communicate on a blog. You may think you are writing a cheerful response to a thought-provoking post, but to some it may come across as a challenge, a complaint, or even rude.

- *Resist the temptation to post comments or blog anonymously.* When you find yourself wanting to comment anonymously, it usually means that you want to state something you wouldn't say if you were in front of the person. It is important for Christians to have conviction behind our words, but it is more important that we claim them as our words.

- *Remember that online conversations are fast-paced and permanent.* When you begin blogging or commenting, you will notice how fast conversations shift and how suddenly the "hot" conversation of the moment has moved on to something else. But just as happens in regular conversation, we often say things we don't exactly mean. Try to view your interactions with blogs as a taped conversation. Even if it is something you wrote in the spur of the moment, there is a good chance it will remain on the Internet for years. Be mindful of your words, that you may engage in peaceful conversation.

—*Matt Shedden, associate pastor, Lebanon (Ore.) Mennonite Church*

ger had dissected my every word and made me look uninformed and ignorant. I tried to clarify my intentions through comments on his blog, but we were unable to reach any mutual understanding. While I deleted that blog post long ago, my words live on on the Web.—*Matthew Shedden, Lebanon, Oregon*

Facebook fast. Instead of giving up a sugary food or a favorite television series for Lent, Maya Kehr, 22, gave up Facebook. This is the second year Maya has given up Facebook for Lent. "The way I approach Lent is that you're giving up a behavior and hopefully replacing it with something that changes or redirects your focus," says Maya. But Lent doesn't only involve giving something up, she says; it also means adding something that increases one's focus on God and people.

"[Facebook was] leading to vanity and also preventing me from paying attention to people around me, working at relationships in person in a more direct way," Maya says. A graduate of Bethel College in North Newton, Kansas, Maya believes that Facebook can negatively affect social interactions in a college context, where there are plenty of opportunities for taking photos that eventually end up on Facebook. In addition to improving her efficiency in schoolwork, giving up Facebook led her to become more thoughtful about her interactions with friends and classmates, she says.
—*Submitted by Laura Schlabach, Goshen, Indiana*

• • • • • • • • • • • • • •

Adults in the United States who use the Internet spend more than 20 hours a week online.[5]

A little less crazy. Nekeisha Alexis-Baker's role as a graphic designer at Associated Mennonite Biblical Seminary in Elkhart, Indiana, means that she deals with technology daily. "One of the really odd things about my world is that I spend a significant portion of my day on the computer, yet I have an overall general unease with technology," Nekeisha says. Her personal struggle in simple living is to utilize the benefits of technology while also recognizing its limitations. "I sense that the promises technology makes are not really ones that it can deliver on, at least not in ways I find to be substantial," she says.

For this reason, Nekeisha and her husband have opted not to have a television in their home or to upgrade their cell phone plans to include texting and Internet access. "Even something like not having a television means we're not exposed to so many ads," she says. "We're trying to make regular life—or at least our home life—a little less crazy than it could be."—*Submitted by Laura Schlabach, Goshen, Indiana*

Cell a no-sell. I'm often asked why I don't own a cell phone—usually by friends who want quick access to my attention. Their arguments in defense of the cell include safety (If your car breaks down in the middle of nowhere, you could call for help); connection (I could text you); upgrading (You could get rid of that old land line); and efficiency (You could keep your calendar, emails, and addresses in one place). Yet my reasoning is quite simple: I think a cell phone would decrease my quality of life.

Wendell Berry's treatise "Why I Am Not Going to Buy a Computer," an earlier defense of a similar ilk, counters all but the first of those arguments. Berry scorns replacing an old tool with a new one unless the replacement meets nine criteria. These include that the new tool "should do work that is clearly and demonstrably better than the one it replaces" and that "it should not replace or disrupt anything good . . . and this includes family and community relationships." While Berry's

● ●

How can I use electronic devices responsibly?

- *Reduce the amount of electronic technology you use.* Do you really want to be reached twenty-four hours a day on a mobile phone? Set up guidelines as to the amount of time you want to use your electronic devices, and ask yourself, "What would happen if I didn't have _____ device?"

- *Reuse the technology you have.* Take good care of the electronic items you have, purchase a new piece of technology so that it can be flexible to include the inevitable upgrades later, or buy used technology. Perhaps you could rent a piece of equipment that you need only for a short time.

- *Recycle.* Find a reliable electronic waste recycler.

—*Jane Snyder, coordinator, Greening Sacred Spaces*

first statement justifies the fact that I don't need a cell, the latter is for me an especially compelling reason to avoid one: it should not disrupt anything good. I find goodness in being fully attentive to each embodied moment—a birdsong outside my window, the eyes of a friend in conversation, or the silence of evening. I've watched cell phones encourage disembodied living, splitting our minds between "here" and "there." Full attention is a spiritual practice.

I'm not a purist: my husband owns a cell phone that I borrow when I travel, and if I ever lose ready access to a land line, I might find I need a portable phone. Yet always I want technology to be my tool, at my service to enhance my quality of life. Until my circumstances create a need, I will live well with my email, my land line, and good old-fashioned conversation. —*Suzanne Ehst, Constantine, Michigan*

Mass media diet. Mass media (newspapers, radio, television, the Internet) play a major role in shaping our personality. They provide the user with news, entertainment, education, and even religious content. The amount of time an average person spends with mass media in her or his lifetime is enormous. As a source of education, mass media have a prevailing value: marketing. Ultimately they represent the values of financial gain for the automobile, banking, oil, and weapons industries. I strive to decrease my time as a blind mass media user. Instead, I seek out alternative sources of information that increase in me and my family Christ's core value: love for creation and for humanity as a whole.—*Rodolfo Jimenez, Plainfield, Illinois*

• • • • • • • • • • • • •

In 2009, watching TV accounted for about half of the leisure time of people in the United States ages 15 and over.[6]

• • • • • • • • • • • •   • • • • • • • • • • •

Find more stories, tips, and links to resources about technology and media at www.mpn.net/livingmorewithless.

Manufacturing a desktop computer and monitor requires 530 pounds (22 kilograms) of fossil fuels, 50 pounds (22 kilograms) of chemicals, and 3,330 pounds (1,500 kilograms) of water.[7]

20
Meetinghouses and Churches

Darren Kropf

● ●

We shape our buildings, and then our buildings shape us.
—*Winston Churchill*

as coordinator of Mennonite Central Committee's creation care work in Ontario, I visit many congregations advocating for energy conservation and solar energy. I often lead with the above quotation and then ask the congregation to share what values their building conveys about the people who built or inhabit it. Common responses include "We designed a large foyer to encourage fellowship after worship"; "Our large kitchen exemplifies our love of good food and good conversation"; and "The simple—some might say plain—interior decorating shows our commitment to simplicity and humility."

I smile and nod at the glowing responses. I confess to them, however, that their building tells me something a bit different. I ask what messages their congregation conveys to the community when every light in the building is on, though natural light would suffice in many cases; when the energy used to air-condition the building is contributing to climate change that negatively affects subsistence farmers in sub-Saharan Africa; and when the large parking lot and lack of bike rack encourages the burning of oil that spurs conflicts around the world.

The majority of congregations in Canada and the United States need to look long and hard at the buildings constructed in the name of Christ. Do we incorporate the radical values of justice and peace as taught to us by Jesus? The second part of Churchill's quote—"our buildings shape us"—reminds us that our natural and human-made environments affect us in deep and profound ways. Our meeting spaces are meant to foster the formation of the people of God. But what happens when the sacred relationship between the faith community and its Creator is compromised by poor stewardship choices?

Sacred spaces must be ethical

Commenting on his synagogue in Maryland, which received an Energy Star for Congregations award, Rabbi Fred Scherlinder Dobb remarked, "A space is only sacred if it's ethical. It's hard to feel we even have the right to build this without ensuring 'first do no harm.' And can a building even be called holy when not every step has been taken to ensure minimal effects?"

With some creativity, the spaces we gather in to worship, disciple, and serve can deepen Christian discipleship. They can build up relationships and be a visible witness to the community in which they are situated. Not only that, but they can teach positive stewardship values to their members. Certainly a community that chooses not to build is walking the more-with-less talk, but simply using resources more efficiently can also make a huge difference. According to the Energy Star program, if all religious worship buildings in the United States cut energy use and costs by 25 percent, they would prevent five million tons (4.5 metric tons) of carbon dioxide from going into the atmosphere and save five hundred million (U.S.) dollars. Just think of the ministry opportunities that could happen with that money!

• • • • • • • • • • • • •

"[The lack of biblical instructions regarding meetinghouses] may be a blessing. It forces us to concentrate on what is important—the quality of life of the believing community—rather than on the physical facilities. It helps us recognize that church is wherever God's people meet, be it a barn, a house, or a building with a steeple and a cross."—*Doris Janzen Longacre*

As your church community discerns the best way to make your gatherings embody the kingdom of God, consider the following ideas:

- *Cut the phrase "going to church" from your vocabulary.* Church happens at home, in the workplace, and anywhere disciples gather to do the work of God. It does not require a centralized location away from our homes and communities. Alternatives include "We participate at the community church" or "We go to worship on Sunday mornings."

- *Recognize the resources buildings require.* Besides the dedicated group of trustees, very few people in the church understand the true costs that go into constructing and maintaining a building. Educate the community on the building's energy bills so that everyone is eager to use energy and resources wisely. And by all means, never stop thanking the individuals who put in countless hours to keep the facility clean, welcoming, and well managed.

- *Consider attending the church in your community.* The great majority of Christians in my area drive past four or five churches on their way to worship. It might not make sense to switch churches in your current stage of life, but we do need to challenge a consumer approach in which people select the church with the best programs to meet their wants and needs. Alternatively, we can foster a culture in which arriving to worship by foot is celebrated for its low impact on the environment and for its ability to make church members present in the community.

- *Get outside.* Nearly everyone has a story of an intimate connection with God while experiencing God's beautiful creation. Then why do we always do church in buildings? Seek creative ways to bring church activities outdoors as much as possible.

- *Think behavior first, then technology.* When it comes to energy conservation, a common misconception is that technology is the key to energy efficiency. In reality, it is behavioral change that creates energy savings. Make a weekly schedule and track when your church building is in use. Who uses the building and when? What are the needs of each group using the building? Once you have determined your needs and sought ways to modify them appropriately, apply technology upgrades to maximize energy efficiency.

- *Reject the "if we build it, they will come" approach.* If you are thinking about building a new meetinghouse, design your building to be multipurpose and used by many groups throughout the week. Collaborate with community groups or social service agencies—before drawing up plans—to ensure your building will be used by more than just your own members. The last things most communities need are large church buildings with members spending hours brainstorming ways to get more people to come to it, rather than leveraging existing resources to meet human need.

- *Never stop praying and seeking God's direction for responsible use of the church's resources.* "Unless the Lord builds the house, those who build it labor in vain" (Ps 127:1).

One way or another, our meeting places will shape our community. Let's be sure these spaces shape us into the community God calls us to be.

Carbon donations. Following increased popular attention to climate issues in 2007, a group at Rockway Mennonite Church in Kitchener, Ontario, began searching for concrete ways to address ecological concerns. They decided to start a carbon offset program. Participants measured their carbon footprints and set aside thirty dollars for every ton of carbon they produce. The goal was primarily to help families make the connection between their lifestyles and the amount of pollutants they produce. Raising funds was secondary, says group member Lewis Brubacher.

In 2008, seventeen households donated $4,948 (Can.), and in 2009, eight households contributed $3,040. They used a portion of the money to do an energy audit of Zion United Church, where Rockway Mennonite meets. The results of the energy audit showed that increasing insulation above the sanctuary would greatly improve energy efficiency. The group is currently arranging to use carbon offset money to make this happen. As renters, Rockway Mennonite Church members won't see a direct financial benefit from reducing energy use. All the same, they say it's worth doing. "The church in the broadest sense will benefit, not to mention the environment," Lewis says.—*Submitted by Paul Boers, Goshen, Indiana*

Church-generated energy. Our congregation, Hillcrest Mennonite Church in New Hamburg, Ontario, has been very proactive in reducing our environmental footprint. In the fall of 2007 we completed an energy audit of our building, which helped us determine what to do to save the energy it was consuming. To date, we have found a savings of about 9 percent due to our energy-saving efforts, and most of these were relatively simple and inexpensive changes. This year we passed a proposal to install a solar photovoltaic system that will generate electricity and supply it to the grid under Ontario's Feed-In Tariff program. This was the next logical step for us after doing what we could to conserve energy.

Churches have saved between $8,000 and $17,000 (U.S.) per year by adopting sustainable building practices—anything from switching their light bulbs to adding solar panels.[1]

There are many reasons we want to conserve energy and generate renewable energy at our church. We are all getting quite concerned about climate change and are beginning to see the injustice of it as we learn that the people most affected by climate change—mostly people in the Global South who live near deserts and coastlines—have contributed the least to climate change. We also believe that as a church we need to be leaders to our own members, to the neighborhood, and to the broader church. Some people say that the church shouldn't get involved in large financial projects like this, but I say, If not the church, then who?—*Rob Yost, New Hamburg, Ontario*

Oil-free worship. Corvallis (Ore.) Mennonite Fellowship traces its origins to October 21, 1990: Oil-Free Sunday. Conflict was escalating in the Persian Gulf, and Christian Peacemaker Teams was urging congregations nationwide to forego driving for one day, in recognition of the role our oil consumption plays in the crisis. About a year before this, four families in Corvallis had begun meeting weekly for fellowship, but on Sundays they still traveled to Albany Mennonite Church (15 miles, or about 24 kilometers) or Prince of Peace Mennonite Church (8 miles, or about 13 kilometers).

They had talked about forming a church closer to home, but it wasn't until Oil-Free Sunday that they first met on a Sunday morning. In a hard rain, about twenty-five people walked and biked to one family's home. Crammed in the living room, with kids on the floor, they sang and shared. From this beginning, a church took root. After growing too large to meet in homes, the fellowship began renting its current space in a college campus ministry building within walking and biking distance of many families.—*Zanne Langstraat, Corvallis, Oregon*

Driving past churches—on the way to church. For Mennonites from Kitchener-Waterloo, Ontario, a region with at least a dozen Mennonite churches within reasonable driving distance, it is not unusual for Sunday worshippers to drive past several other Mennonite churches on the way to their chosen congregation. There's no question that burning fossil fuels is one of the main contributors to global warming. So several years ago, in a lead-up to Earth Day, the pastors from those Mennonite churches began to discuss what our churches could do to reduce our impact on the environment. One idea in particular emerged as a way to invite our congregants to live out environmental stewardship in a practical way.

On the Sunday closest to Earth Day, congregants were invited to travel to church by a more environmentally friendly means—by bus, bicycle, or foot—or to attend a church closer to their home. It may seem relatively insignificant for a couple of hundred Mennonites to park their cars for one Sunday morning out of the entire year, but sometimes a small idea can lead to big changes. Since that Earth Day initiative, it seems like more people are biking or walking more regularly to my church. They may have discovered that it's not as difficult as they had originally thought, and that it's actually a much more enjoyable way to travel on a Sunday morning. Several families have made the conscious decision to attend a church that is closer to their home. I wonder what other changes this Earth Day initiative may have inspired.—*Chip Bender, Kitchener, Ontario*

Daycare center sans rent. Throughout the week, Mag Richer Smith, pastor at First Mennonite Church of Iowa City, can hear the sounds of children laughing and playing. Her office sits above Home Ties Day Care, a free childcare program for refugee, homeless, and low-income families. The daycare has operated rent-free in the church since the program began in 1995. Though independent of the church, Home Ties has developed strong connections with the congregation over the years. Members regularly teach and volunteer with the program.

"This is like our daycare and not just a place that uses our space," Mag says. In fact, the congregation has recently completed a $250,000 (U.S.) building addition that will be used solely by the daycare; the church has no plans to use the room. For its part, the daycare allows parishioners to see firsthand the needs around them. "I think there's a growing awareness of the needs in the community," Mag says. "It gives us a face to that." —*Submitted by Paul Boers, Goshen, Indiana*

Tithing on new construction. Ten years ago, when my congregation built a new multipurpose room/gymnasium, we also agreed to tithe the cost of our new addition to support churches in other countries. Just as personal tithing means spending less on myself and giving more to others, so tithing as a church could work in a similar way. In this case, we spread the tithe over five years, working with existing denominational agencies to identify and send funds where needed. This included assisting churches in Congo, Indonesia, Macau, Thailand, Kenya, and Tanzania. The more-with-less benefit of learning about churches around the world continues even today, since even though that season of tithing has now been completed for some years, we still see ourselves very much a part of the global church.—*April Yamasaki, Abbotsford, British Columbia*

No mortgage. It might be easy to define The Table by what it doesn't have—no formal leadership, no building, and no week-to-week worship plan. But that's not how this Harrisonburg, Virginia, congregation sees it. Running their church without these elements creates space for creative, engaging worship to take place. Each week, a group of "worship hosts" meets and spends time with the lectionary text for that Sunday. These texts and the group's reading of them become the driving force behind the worship service. They often explore nontraditional means of working with Scripture, from drawing to monologues and from quilting to small-group discussions.

Since the congregation has no pastor to pay and no building to maintain (they rent space at Eastern Mennonite University),

• •

How can our congregation care for creation?

- *Find like-minded individuals,* and start meeting together for prayer and discussion of creation care in your congregation.

- *Consider adding creation care initiatives and values* to the job descriptions and agendas of your peace committee or group of trustees.

- *Evaluate how well your congregation cares for creation.* Download a congregational score sheet from the Mennonite Creation Care website and analyze how well your church cares for creation.

See also the resources at www.greeningsacredspaces.net or www.webofcreation.org.

- *Get an energy audit for your church building,* then consult with your pastor or elders team about the best way to utilize the score sheet or results of the energy audit in your congregation.

- *Join a network of churches* committed to environmental stewardship. Possibilities include Mennonite Creation Care Network's 100 Shades of Green and the National Council of Churches Eco-Justice Programs.

they can afford to be generous with all that they have. If someone brings up an organization or individual in need of financial help, the church gives. "There's never a question," says Laura Amstutz, worship host. "It's done."—*Submitted by Paul Boers, Goshen, Indiana*

Urban collective. In urban San Diego, Jason Evans and others have started a grassroots community to "build community, seek justice, promote sustainability, and interpret/embody the Way of Jesus" in the city. The community began when a group of pastors and church leaders, including Jason, established a group of house churches called Matthew's House. In 2003, Jason and his wife, Brooke, along with a few others, broke off of Matthew's House and began Ecclesia Collective. Jason describes the collective as a group of "post-church, no church, and Jesus followers of the 'Anabaptistic' type in all shapes and sizes."

Ecclesia Collective has evolved since 2003 and has hosted many projects in San Diego, including house concerts and art shows; Make Something Day, which encourages people to make presents for Christmas instead of shopping on Black Friday; and Justice Kitchen, a project to bring people closer to the origins of their food and to have a delicious meal and conversation.

"There are six communities right now," says Jason. "Two of those also have cohousing communities within their faith community. One of them has three living spaces on one property with nine people total." The collective not only consists of community living but emphasizes worship as well. "We are convinced that church is best understood as people, not a place or an event."—*Submitted by Esther Shank, Harrisonburg, Virginia*

Building share. Chicago Community Mennonite Church (CCMC) has been renting worship space for thirty years. For the last thirteen of those years, the church has been renting from First Church of the Brethren, a multiracial church on the west side of Chicago. They also share the building with Iglesia de Roca Esperanza, a Mennonite-related primarily Latino/a congregation. Several service agencies also use the building. "Sharing space is hard work," says Megan Ramer, pastor. Scheduling is often a challenge, maintaining communication between the groups can be difficult, and all groups have to compromise. On the other hand, the arrangement allows the churches to pool resources to accomplish tasks that would have been too much for any single one. For example, CCMC and First Church of the Brethren run a tutoring program that draws on the people, time, money, and energy of both congregations.

Sharing space also gives the church a chance to participate in greater diversity. "Renting gets us intimately connected with two congregations that look different from us demographically," says Megan, whose congregation is primarily white. The three congregations worship together at least three or four times a year. "It's a chaotic, lovely mix," she says. So while the idea of buying their own space "gets tossed around from time to time," Megan says that the benefits of renting and sharing outweigh the challenges. It's part of who they are and who they've always been.—*Submitted by Paul Boers, Goshen, Indiana*

Benediction, then tomatoes. After summer Sunday services at Berkey Avenue Mennonite Fellowship in Goshen, Indiana, you might find members strolling outside to check their tomatoes. When the congregation acquired some vacant land adjacent to their building, it was intended as a possible site for a future building addition. Until then, however, the congregation decided to create a garden. Today some of that land has been turned into a thriving community garden with almost thirty plots. The generosity of organizer Lowell Nafziger with his time and his tractor, the decision to let each gardener determine her or his own standards, and the sharing of minimal expenses all help to make this garden work.

The garden is full of plots of vegetables and flowers and is tended by people who don't have room at home for a garden, who wanted additional space, or who just wanted to give gardening a try. As neighbors take notice, it's also beginning to reach outside of the congregation: some have joined with plots of their own, and there are plans to extend the invitation to all neighbors next growing season. "All the gardeners have the opportunity to chat with each other while gardening," says David Heusinkveld, another organizer, "and often they exchange produce with themselves, the congregation, or neighbors." The garden has enriched the congregation's life and brought joy, David says. "Our garden has become a weekly and visible sign of generosity, community, hospitality, stewardship, and God's goodness."—*Submitted by Charity Grimes, Pittsburgh, Pennsylvania*

Nature paths. Our church, Harrisonburg (Va.) Mennonite Church, is located on a wonderful hilltop property. For years we mowed this property all around the church. Then one visionary soul thought about creating a path around the perimeter. We now have a committee of people all working to care for God's creation by creating this path. The path is almost a half-mile (0.8 kilometers) long. We have planted about fifteen native trees, with ten more going in soon. We have planted native bushes and native wildflowers, plus many daffodils. We have a sign marking the start of the path and twelve stations along the way. We have not one, not two, but four guides developed for the path. Our hope is that it will introduce our children to aspects of nature they might not have considered before. But we also want it to be a place for our church adults and our neighbors around the church to connect with God in nature.—*Linda Miller, Harrisonburg, Virginia*

Mailbox recycling. Tubs for recycling paper are placed close to the church mailboxes in our congregation, Ridgeview Mennonite Church in Gordonville, Pennsylvania, so people can discard papers they will not be using. Other paper for recycling is also placed in these tubs. The paper is taken to MCC's Material Resource Center, where it is sold for recycling, thereby generating income for MCC.—*Nelson Yoder, Gordonville, Pennsylvania*

● ● ● ● ● ● ● ● ● ● ● ● ●

Find more stories, tips, and links to resources about meetinghouses and churches at www.mpn.net/livingmorewithless.

21
Strengthening Each Other and Organizing Communities

Sheri Hostetler

● ●

this book has thus far detailed mostly individual, household-level, and congregational changes that help us live more with less. Necessary as those are, they aren't enough. We live in a fundamentally different world from the one in which *Living More with Less* was first published, and the changes needed now must also happen at communal and societal levels. In short, there are some changes we can only make *together*. And for that, we will need strengthened, robust, organized communities.

The game changer is global warming. Thirty years ago, when Doris Janzen Longacre wrote the first edition of *Living More with Less*, we hadn't even heard of it. It's not that the planet wasn't warming; humans had been pumping carbon dioxide into the atmosphere at an increasing rate for the previous two hundred years, ever since the beginning of the Industrial Revolution. But in 1980, not even climate scientists understood the effect this was having on the planet. Not until 1988, eight years after the book's publication, did we begin to understand that we were warming our planet and that this warming had begun long ago.

Still, at first we thought of climate change as a potential problem for our grandchildren. Scientists didn't really know what a safe amount of carbon dioxide in the atmosphere would be, nor did they know the level at which the doorway into a changed planet irrevocably opened. So they pegged that level, somewhat randomly, at 550 parts per million, double the 275 parts per million that had existed in the atmosphere for the ten thousand years prior to the Industrial Revolution. We were nowhere near that level and thought we had time to change our fossil fuel-burning ways.

Faster than we expected

But then glaciers and Arctic ice started melting at an alarmingly fast rate. Changes in rainfall patterns began causing drought in places like Australia and the American Southwest and an increase in hurricanes, cyclones, and flooding elsewhere. Ocean acidity rose by 30 percent, and coral reefs became threatened with permanent extinction. Whole island nations are being swallowed up by rising seas. One report estimated that three hundred thousand people each year, mostly from the Global South, are dying due to global warming.[1]

The planet is clearly changing must faster than expected. Climate scientists recalibrated as new data came in and as computer models got more sophisticated. And in 2007, Jim Hansen, the NASA scientist who first forecasted global warming in 1988, said that 350 parts per million was the new "safe" number for carbon dioxide levels, the number at which we could live on a planet much like the one we had been used to for the past ten thousand years. The problem is that we are already at 390 parts per million. The door has already opened.

The world we live in now, thirty years after the first *Living More with Less* was published, is a scarier one. The stakes are higher than we could have imagined in 1980. Back then, we were concerned with global poverty, inequitable distribution of wealth, the soul sickness of what we now call "affluenza," and the oil crisis of the 1970s. While those concerns must still inform our work, we now must also understand that we are fundamentally changing the operating system of the planet. Our burning of fossil fuels is warming, melting, drying, acidifying, and flooding the earth—so much so that one environmentalist has suggested we need to call Earth by a new name, since it is a fundamentally different planet than the one on which most of us grew up.[2]

Walking together over the threshold

We are at a threshold moment. We can continue on as before, in denial or disbelief, refusing to look through the door that has opened. We can hope that a technological big fix will slam the door shut, saving us at the last hour. Or we can begin to walk together into the new world that is coming, one no longer fueled by readily available, cheap oil.

But we will need to walk *together*. Household-level changes like those detailed in this book are important, but they will not add up to the big changes needed to keep the most catastrophic climate changes at bay. For that, we need to reshape our society, one community at a time. We will need to "relocalize" as we begin to wean ourselves off fossil fuels.

For example, in the United States, the average carrot travels 1,838 miles (2,958 kilometers) to our tables.[3] Only in a cheap-oil economy could such a carrot even be conceivable. In the world that is coming, we will need to grow our carrots locally. This movement toward local agriculture is already well underway as community gardens, farmers markets, and CSA farms grow like . . . well, carrots. In my former hometown of Oakland, California, a group of people came together to form City Slicker Farms in a low-income section of the city where few residents have access to food sources other than corner liquor stores. They now offer a Saturday farm stand (which also provides vegetable starts), community composting (drop off your kitchen scraps, pick up compost), gardening workshops, and assistance in creating backyard gardens. This is the level of community participation needed as we move forward into our future.

We also need local energy based on renewable sources. We're further behind the curve on this one, but initiatives like the Mennonite Initiative for Solar Energy (see pages 228–29) provide a model of what is possible on a community level. And, needless to say, we will need to drive less. To make that possible, our communities are going to need to lobby local governments to provide better public transit, higher building density, and even sidewalks where needed. We will need to bike, carpool, and car share.

As we walk together through this open door, we may find—as Longacre and many others said thirty years ago—that our quality of life will increase as we leave behind our rampant individualism and consumerism. The world that is coming doesn't look quite as bad if you value community, good food grown with others, and a more robust, participatory democracy.

As people of faith, we also recognize that our relationships in the coming world may look more like what God intended. It looks like a world in which we recognize our limits as creatures on a planet with finite resources. It looks like a world where the richest don't disproportionately use more of the world's resources. It looks like a world where we concretely care for the "least of these," since climate change most affects those living on the edges of economic security.

Humility, humus, and humor

Humility is a word that must characterize our relationship to the coming world. Humility means knowing our place in relationship to the Creator and creation. It also comes from the same root as the word *humus*, the rich organic matter from which healthy plant life emerges, and humor. We will need abundant amounts of all of the above—humility, humus, and humor—as we walk through this doorway together.

Here are some more things we can do together:

- *We need to act locally and also nationally.* Even more can be done to curtail climate change—and faster—if governments get on board. Find a group that lobbies the federal government to curb carbon emissions—like www.350.org, which has a special outreach effort to faith communities—and get involved.

- *We can educate ourselves and our faith communities about relocalization movements.* This includes movements like Transition Town (go to www.transitiontowns.org). A good place to start is with local agriculture. Educate your congregation about the 1,838-mile carrot, and pledge together to eat locally (as much as possible) for one month.

- *We can educate our children about the importance of living more with less.* A child in the United States uses seventy times the energy of a Bangladeshi child and consumes far more of the earth's other resources too. A U.S. child thus contributes much more to climate change than a child of the Global South.[4] Now, more than ever, it's time to change our and our children's consumption patterns.

- *We can talk to our elders and to recent immigrants.* People over age seventy and those who came more recently from countries in the Global South have experienced life in societies not based on cheap oil. Thus they have skills and stories about how to live more self-sufficiently, sustainably, and locally.

- *We can imagine a better future.* It's easy to become overwhelmed by the magnitude of the changes that need to happen. But instead of focusing on what we must give up, we need to talk about what we can gain from changing our way of life.

Skill shares. As many folks in our congregation at Living Water Community Church in Chicago became increasingly aware of how our lifestyles and eating habits are affecting creation, a number of us got together to talk about ways we could lessen our negative impact. Living in an urban environment, we face many challenges to growing our own food and minimizing our waste. We found, however, that among us we have many skills in living and eating more sustainably.

In the fall of 2009 we started monthly "skill shares" on topics related to food justice and sustainable eating. A member of our congregation who is a soil scientist led a skill share on composting and vermicomposting, and several members of the group showed their worm bins and shared tips on what has worked well for them. At another skill share, a full-time parent led the group in a few domestic activities in which she has become proficient: making yogurt, sprouting seeds, and brewing kombucha (fermented tea). We will meet to order seed packets together for our containers and community gardens, and in the spring we will learn to build a cold frame to extend our short Illinois growing season.

People in our group started out with varied levels of experience in living and eating sustainably, but as more people join our monthly meetings, we are finding that many of the resources for learning to live in a way that is easier on the earth are right here in our congregation.—*Annie Gill-Bloyer, Chicago, Illinois*

"Sharing" lists. Our Mennonite fellowship members each listed items we had to share with others and skills we had that we could teach or use for others. Items ranged from household appliances to car-repair tools. Skills included crocheting, knitting, typing, bicycle repair, and car maintenance. Now each summer there is a rush on my pressure canner. It's an expensive item, needed only a few weeks each year. With a little planning, we all have time to use it.—*Ruth Guengrich, Ann Arbor, Michigan* (1980)

Toilet paper trials. Our creation care group at Harrisonburg (Va.) Mennonite Church organized a "toilet paper trial" among ourselves. With so many brands now claiming green production and varying amounts of recycled and post-consumer content, we thought this might enable us to try a number of different kinds without having to buy lots of rolls apiece. It also gives us a chance to share some really bad jokes.—*Linda Miller, Harrisonburg, Virginia*

Barrels in church. Doug Ehst just wanted to make a rain barrel. He had heard of the benefits of collecting rainwater to use on gardens, so he began researching the best ways to make a strong, leak-proof barrel and looking for a suitable container. There's a food supplier down the road from Doug's house, and they had large food barrels he could buy used for only three dollars (U.S.) a pop. (It's important that these are food-grade barrels, he notes, so that they won't leach harmful chemicals into the water they collect.) Once he had a barrel, it was just a matter of drilling holes and then attaching a spigot and an overflow hose. All told, his barrel cost about $20 (U.S).

Doug brought his barrel to a retreat for his church, Blossom Hill Mennonite Church of Lancaster, Pennsylvania, to show people and give them instructions on how to make their own. Before he knew it, Doug was signed up to lead a workshop at church on building rain barrels. The congregation made fourteen barrels at the "rain barrel-making party" for use at their homes. He also put together another six for other members of the congregation. Now the fifth-grade teacher is considering selling barrels online during his summers.—*Submitted by Paul Boers, Goshen, Indiana*

Taxing the tank. They call it the "craziest tax you've ever heard of." The voluntary gas tax is exactly what it sounds like: a completely voluntary, self-imposed tax on fuel. Members of the voluntary gas tax group in Goshen, Indiana, charge themselves for every gallon of gas they buy. Most pay fifty cents per gallon, though it's not strict; members set their own tax rate. "It's not like the IRS code," quips Karl Shelly, a member of the group and co-pastor at Assembly Mennonite Church in Goshen.

The gas tax group meets a few times a year to report their taxation and decide how to use this money to support environmental initiatives. The group has bought trees for low-income neighborhoods, donated an energy-efficient washing machine to a local food pantry, and supported a Mennonite Central Committee environmental education fund, among others. All told, the twenty- to thirty-member group has collected and used approximately $8,000 (U.S.) in the two years since it began. They hope that this tax will help them change their gas-buying habits, support green organizations, and raise awareness that gas prices don't reflect the foreign policy and environmental costs of oil dependence.—*Submitted by Paul Boers, Goshen, Indiana*

Hosting those between homes. Selah House, an intentional community in Harrisonburg, Virginia, consists of Abigail Spurrier, Grace Schrock-Hurst, Matt Ropp, Chris Esch, and Lars Åkerson. They share a three-bedroom, two-bathroom "funky seventies-style house" and have lived together in community for two years. Matt and Lars graduated from Eastern Mennonite University a few years ago, and the other members graduated in 2010. Selah House residents eat dinner together Monday through Thursday, taking turns cooking. Everything with the house is shared: resources for food, rent, and utilities, and all belongings. They also meet every Wednesday to worship together.

"This has been a time to be honest with one another and provide support and encouragement," Abigail says. "None of us knew each other too well before we lived together, but we joined the community with the common desire to seek Christ and figure out what that means for us as a community." Selah House spends forty dollars a month on groceries, retrieving most of their food from Dumpsters; they say it's one way the community strives to live simply. "We all want to explore tangibly what it means to live as Christ calls us in Harrisonburg," Abigail says. Selah House also hosts many individuals who are between homes. "We don't like to label 'the homeless,'" says Abigail. "This is something we have only recently begun, but we usually have someone stay with us for one or two weeks out of a month."—*Submitted by Esther Shank, Harrisonburg, Virginia*

Homestead. In June 2002, my wife, Elizabeth, and I purchased a twenty-acre (about eight-hectare) farm with a house and barn built in the 1860s. Other families shared our vision of running the farm as a cooperative, and this group has now grown to eighteen families. We are beginning our eighth growing season. The farm produces a variety of vegetables, herbs, fruits, nuts, eggs, and meat. The vegetable garden is about a half-acre (a little less than a quarter of a hectare) and produces over fifty varieties of vegetables. We have our own breeding stock for goats, chickens, ducks, and geese, which produce

• • • • • • • • • • • •

Permaculture is an approach to designing human settlements and agriculture based on sustainable natural ecologies. Entire neighborhoods, such as Village Homes in Davis, California, have been modeled on its principles.

eggs and meat. We also buy feeder pigs and lambs in the spring to butcher in the fall. The vegetable garden does not simply provide us with fresh produce for the table, because we have planted various crops with long-term storage in mind.

We have had three primary goals: (1) to produce quality food for our families using organic practices, (2) to build community, and (3) to improve wildlife habitat. These goals grew out of our common Christian faith that living more simply leads to being better stewards of God's creation. Simple living is not easy. The *simple* in *simple living* describes the overall system of production for any activity or object. The fact that most of our food is produced on the farm and, therefore, requires little transportation other than walking it from the barn or garden to our kitchen is simpler in terms of the means of production, but not in terms of our labor. It would be much easier for us to buy everything at Wal-mart.

Of course, anyone who lives in our modern world must make certain compromises or accommodations, and Elizabeth and I certainly have our own faults in this regard. We are fortunate, however, to live in an area and to have developed a community in which living simply is a value shared by many of our friends.—*Raymond Person, Bluffton, Ohio*

Backbone of community power. Through the Mennonite Initiative for Solar Energy (MISE), MCC Ontario is assisting communities to begin their own energy generation. What started as a small effort to simply raise questions about energy use and its impacts on our global neighbors has ballooned into hundreds of individuals and churches getting involved in bringing more solar energy to our electrical grid. By working as a community, we have overcome many of the barriers that individuals often face when considering a solar energy system.

Basic education on the technology and incentives available is provided through online materials and information nights. Any advocacy needed can be done collectively. A "creation care loan" was even negotiated with the local Mennonite credit union. But perhaps most importantly, MISE has formed relationships, which are the backbone of community power. These relationships encourage us to hold each other accountable in responsible energy consumption and in ensuring that the benefits of energy generation are equally shared throughout the community. This program has also mobilized an often-overlooked segment of the church: tradespeople. These highly skilled and knowledgeable individuals do not always find their skills employed by the congregation, but they are invaluable leaders in putting our creation-care theology into action.

At the time of this writing, over a dozen homeowners have installed solar systems. Even more encouraging are the congregations that are actively pursuing solar energy. How many churches have roofs soaking in sunlight every day? The church community is ideally positioned to pool resources and become a leader in bringing clean, renewable energy back to communities.—*Darren Kropf, Kitchener, Ontario*

Gardening through hard times. The members of the Mennonite Voluntary Service (MVS) house in Elkhart, Indiana, owned by Prairie Street Mennonite Church, are using the property and several others to create community gardens. Working alongside the Elkhart Local Food Alliance, those in the MVS house wanted to make use of the many empty lots and fresh soil in Elkhart. Nicole Bauman, an MVS member in Elkhart, says they wanted to use urban gardening as a way to empower and build each other up during a time of high unemployment in Elkhart County. The group has held several neighborhood demonstrations and workshops (all free and open to the public), teaching low-impact gardening techniques. Nicole says that the hope is to teach skills that people can take and use either for paid work or for creating their own gardens.

Currently, the MVS garden has berry bushes and fruit trees among many other plants to create mini-ecosystems within the garden. The group is also focusing on vertical growing, making the best use of the space given. So far this year, it has started three gardens throughout Elkhart County and has been offered

many other empty lots. The produce has been shared with neighbors as well as with a number of local food banks.
—*Submitted by Alysha Bergey Landis, Harleysville, Pennsylvania*

Healthy kids, healthy planet. Rainbow Mennonite Church has had an active presence in the Rosedale neighborhood of Kansas City for fifty years. But that presence got even bigger when it joined the Healthy Kids Initiative, a local faith-based advocacy effort to reduce childhood obesity by promoting active living and healthy eating. Perhaps not surprisingly, the things that make for healthier children—local food and transportation not dependent on fossil fuels—also make for a healthier planet. The initiative has already started several community gardens in the Rosedale neighborhood and a farmers market that accepts food stamps. (Rosedale, an economically and ethnically diverse neighborhood in Kansas City's urban core, has no major grocery store.) Rainbow's members volunteer at the Healthy Kids Club, an afterschool program emphasizing exercise and outdoor play, and at an annual Healthy Kids Carnival that celebrates activities and food that promote healthy living.

Rachel Hostetler, the church's community service coordinator, has helped gather signatures for a petition asking the city to put sidewalks in the neighborhood that would make it more walking- and biking-friendly. The neighborhood has already received a grant to add a bike lane to a Rosedale thoroughfare. "Becoming involved with the Healthy Kids Initiative seemed like a natural thing for our church to do," says Rachel. "It was an opportunity to collaborate with others to better the community."—*Submitted by Sheri Hostetler, Alameda, California*

Transition your town. Communities interested in ending their dependence on oil now have a template for doing so. The Transition Town movement began in 2005, when Irish professor Rob Hopkins and his students created the first strategic design for a community to lessen dependence on fossil fuels; the "energy descent plan" focuses on the "relocalization of food, energy, economics, healthcare, transportation, water, and waste." Charletta Erb, a member of Living Water Community Church in Chicago, became involved in the movement after reading Brian McLaren's *Everything Must Change: When the World's Biggest Problems and Jesus' Good News Collide.* She joined a low-carbon diet group, sold her car, and became a part of the first Chicago-area Transition Town, in Rogers Park. More than 145 towns worldwide have become Transition Towns, including seventeen in the United States.

Charletta says Transition Town efforts include "community gardens and backyard vegetable plots, building materials like straw bale and cob, energy generation from solar and wind, and development of local currency and greywater systems. It means re-skilling ourselves in everything from farming to darning socks." Steering committees and working groups focus on building community resilience and reducing carbon footprints in the various areas of community life, based in local energy and skills. "This is a natural platform for raising issues of spirituality and the stories that define us," says Charletta, a graduate student in marriage and family therapy. "It provides an open door for Mennonites to speak into today's cultural awakening to earth care and the quest for meaning beyond individualism and consumerism."
—Submitted by Alysha Bergey Landis, Harleysville, Pennsylvania

A carbon footprint is an estimate of all emissions of carbon dioxide and other greenhouse gases induced by the activities of individuals or groups. Carbon footprint calculators abound online; one of the most comprehensive is at www.earthlab.com. Zero Footprint Youth Calculator (http://calc.zerofootprint.net/youth/) is a great one for kids.

Find more stories, tips, and links to resources about strengthening each other and organizing communities at www.mpn.net/livingmorewithless.

Afterword:
A Generous Orthopraxy

Brian McLaren

● ●

When Grace and I got married in 1979, somebody gave us a copy of the first edition of the *More-with-Less Cookbook*. It was our first introduction not only to some amazingly thrifty yet tasty recipes but to the whole subject of simple living. A few years later we came across *Living More with Less*, which built on that foundation.

To be honest, back then, when we were living on low teachers' salaries, the primary attraction wasn't what simple eating and simple living did for the poor or for the planet: rather, it saved us money. Saving money was our "gateway drug" into the simple-living movement. As radically committed twentysomethings, we lived in community, hosted a fledgling house church, had big debates about the virtue of going vegetarian and the vice of Styrofoam cups, and gained a deeper appreciation for the issues of poverty by living in a low-income neighborhood outside Washington, D.C. Eventually, we changed careers from teaching to ministry, serving in that same community for twenty-four years. Always that message of simple living hummed in the background of our lives like an unobtrusive theme song.

Nervous, edgy, and angry

But a few years ago, the song got a lot louder for me. When I wrote *Everything Must Change: When the World's Biggest Problems and Jesus' Good News Collide*, I began to realize more fully the radical import of the call to a simple, responsible, regenerative lifestyle. Since writing that book, I've seen all my behavior against the backdrop of four crises:

- *The planet crisis.* A "developed" way of life that takes resources faster than the earth can replenish them and that pumps in toxins faster than the earth can detoxify them.

- *The poverty crisis.* A global economic system that creates extravagant luxury for the few while withholding basic necessities from the many.

- *The peace crisis.* A political and military system that mass produces weapons—including weapons of mass destruction—in a self-defeating search for peace through violence.

- *The religious crisis.* Religious systems that embed adherents in suicidal narratives of fear, revenge, isolation, domination, elitism, victimization, dualism, and consumption—rather than in a healing narrative of reconciliation and the common good.

Once you start noticing these interwoven themes, they jump out at you from headlines and news broadcasts. You see them camouflaged in political speeches and sermons. You even see them in advertisements, TV shows, movie plots, and grocery store aisles. And if you're like me, you start to get nervous, edgy, and maybe even a little angry.

Generosity toward others and ourselves

In this situation, it's way too easy to become an ecological nag, a pain-in-the-neck for poverty, a peace provocateur. It's easy to get to the point where you can't be happy unless you're making somebody somewhere feel guilty for eating *that*, for buying *this*, for listening to *them*, or for living *there*. In other words, having overcome the temptation to be a mindless consumer, drifting along with the currents of a misguided, hell-bent culture, you become susceptible to another temptation: the temptation to become a critic of everyone who now is where you once were.

How do we thread the needle—when, on the one hand, we want to evangelize for simple, ethically responsible living, and on the other hand, we don't want to increase resistance to our ideas by wagging fingers at all our friends and relatives for failing to buy fair-trade coffee or compact fluorescent light bulbs? Three things, I think, can help us.

First is the realization that *if we've changed, others can too.* And if our change is ongoing, so will theirs be. We need to extend grace for others not to be on the same timetable or to make the exact same decisions, just as others have extended plenty of grace to us—and are in fact doing so now, since each of us has a long way to go when it comes to truly consistent ethical living.

Second is the realization that *the changes that matter most can't be made by individuals but must be made by society at large.* For example, if you manage to get off the fossil-fuel-based grid, congratulations. I hope to join you someday. But the fact remains that the grid goes on, and so our environmental future depends on converting the grid from stupid, dirty energy to smart, clean energy. For that to happen, we need to win friends to the big picture, not just nag them about the details. No question: details matter. It's in the details that commitments are turned into habits and habits into values. But the details that matter most to me might differ from those that matter most to you. Ultimately, what matters most to the cause is that all our habits and values synergize to create tipping points and large-scale movements for needed change.

Third is the realization that *Christian faith is at its best when it is about grace, not guilt.* Other faiths could sign on here too. Our orthodoxy—or "right belief"—must be a generous orthodoxy, a gracious orthodoxy. So must our orthopraxy—or "right action"— be a generous, gracious orthopraxy.

Grace begins, of course, when we look in the mirror; we won't extend it to others if we don't receive and enjoy it ourselves. And that's important to remember when reading a book like this one, because simplicity can become a tyrannical legalism if we let it. There's always another light to be turned off, another degree of heating or cooling to be sacrificed, another drive to be foregone. The good desire for simplicity can turn sour, like a hypervigilant guard dog mistaking its owner for an intruder. When that begins to happen, it's time to recall Jesus' words about his mission: he came that we might have life, life in abundance and fullness . . . not life in guilt, austerity, or neurosis. Simplicity "under law" and simplicity "under grace" are two very different ways of life indeed.

Grace is the best motivation for a more-with-less lifestyle. Having received grace ourselves, we want our neighbors in poverty to receive it too. Even our enemies need grace, we realize. So do the rivers and streams, the soil and wind; we don't want to stress them to their limits, but rather to treat them gently, graciously, generously. And the same goes for the birds of the air, the fish of the sea, the flowers and creatures of the field. We want all to be given all the grace they need to thrive and prosper. It is our joy to live with less so that others may have enough.

This is the more-with-less life: it is full of conviction and also full of grace. It is committed to practical action and also to expansive generosity. It is eager to do what's good and beautiful and also to do it in a good and beautiful spirit. It is confident that an abundant life is a simple life, and that one enjoys more by grasping less.

Contributors

 **Nekeisha Alexis-Baker** is a native of Trinidad and a former New York City resident. She received her bachelor's degree from New York University before relocating to Elkhart, Indiana, with her husband, Andy. There she graduated from Associated Mennonite Biblical Seminary, where she now serves as a graphic designer and does anti-racism work. She is a writer and speaker with interests in animal ethics, veganism, and creation care from a Christian perspective, anarchist politics, and radical Christian faith.

 **Malinda Elizabeth Berry** teaches theology and directs the MA program at Bethany Theological Seminary in Richmond, Indiana. She is a member of Mennonite Church USA and has contributed to denominational peace and justice work over the years. She is a graduate of Goshen College and Associated Mennonite Biblical Seminary and is completing a PhD in theology at Union Theological Seminary.

 **Greg Bowman** is an agricultural journalist specializing in organic farming and local food systems. He is engaged in several organic farming-as-ministry explorations in Pennsylvania and Ohio.

 **Nancy and Robb Davis** live in Northern California and have been "car-free" since early 2003 (this includes eighteen months living on the East Coast). Nancy advises undergraduate students in the department of electrical and computer engineering at UC-Davis, and Robb consults with agencies on maternal and child health issues and on monitoring and evaluating health programs. They have two grown children, neither of whom have car licenses, and a grandson. In 2010 Robb took a year's sabbatical from flying, which forced him to stay closer to home.

 **Leonard Dow** is pastor of Oxford Circle Mennonite Church in Philadelphia, serves on the bishop team of the Philadelphia District of Lancaster Conference, is chairperson of the Oxford Circle Christian Development Association, and is vice chairperson of the MCC U.S. board. He and his wife, Rosalie, have three children.

(Photo of Leonard Dow by Jon Styer/Eastern Mennonite University.)

 **Doris Dube** and her husband, Jethro, are currently service workers with MCC in Lesotho. Doris is a former teacher, a former associate editor of the Brethren in Christ magazine *Good Words*, former Africa editor for Courier, and former MCC co-country representative for Zimbabwe. She is a mother of three sons and twin daughters and a member of the Brethren in Christ Bulawayo Central Church.

 **Aiden Enns** is the founder and editor of *Geez* magazine. He was a regional editor for *Canadian Mennonite* and a managing editor of *Adbusters* magazine. He holds degrees in religion and journalism and is a member of Hope Mennonite Church in Winnipeg, Manitoba. He finally planted grapes this year and is committed to watching them grow into productive vines.

 **Renee Holsopple Glick** is an architectural designer living in Brooklyn. She likes exploring, language, and cooking with leftovers.

 Rachel Waltner Goossen is professor of history at Washburn University in Topeka, Kansas. She is the author of *Women Against the Good War: Conscientious Objection and Gender on the American Home Front, 1941–47.* She and her family attend Southern Hills Mennonite Church in Topeka.

 **Sheri Hostetler** is the pastor of First Mennonite Church of San Francisco and a backyard permaculturist. She gets help in the garden from her husband, Jerome, and son, Patrick, who thinks grubs are really gross.

 **Cara Longacre Hurst** is an artist and art teacher at Conestoga Valley High School in Lancaster, Pennsylvania. She lives in southern Lancaster County with her husband, Kevin, and their two daughters, Anika and Claire. They attend Community Mennonite Church of Lancaster.

 **Beryl Jantzi** serves as the stewardship education director for Everence (formerly Mennonite Mutual Aid) and lives in Harrisonburg, Virginia, with his wife, Margo Maust Jantzi. Prior to working for Everence, Beryl pastored in Pennsylvania and Virginia for over twenty years, most recently as lead pastor at Harrisonburg Mennonite Church in Virginia.

Arli Klassen is executive director of MCC and also served with MCC in Lesotho, in leadership of Africa and Connecting Peoples programming, and as leader of MCC Ontario. Arli has studied theology, sociology, and social work and enjoys reading, bicycling, canoeing, gardening, and travel. She and her spouse, Keith Regehr, have two daughters, Alison and Jennifer, and are members of East Chestnut Street Mennonite Church in Lancaster, Pennsylvania.

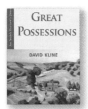

David Kline is an Amish minister and organic farmer in northern Ohio. He is author of *Great Possessions: An Amish Farmer's Journal* and *Scratching the Woodchuck: Nature on an Amish Farm.*

Darren Kropf lives in Kitchener, Ontario, and serves as creation care program coordinator at MCC Ontario and as a youth pastor at Breslau Mennonite Church. He enjoys cycling around town, camping with friends and family, and a good, competitive board game.

Mary Beth Lind, co-author of *Simply in Season*, is a registered dietitian, gardener, and writer. She resides and gardens in Philippi, West Virginia, where she attends the local Mennonite church.

Brian McLaren is an author, speaker, and leader in emergent church circles. His most recent book, *A New Kind of Christianity: Ten Questions that are Transforming the Faith*, was published by HarperOne in 2010.

Carol Penner lives in Vineland, Ontario, where she works as the pastor of First Mennonite Church. She is married to Eugene and has two young-adult children, Katie and Alex.

Hugo Saucedo is the director of Mennonite Voluntary Service. He lives in San Antonio with his wife, Danielle Miller, and two children, Gabriel and Isla. Hugo and his family are members of San Antonio (Tex.) Mennonite Church.

Bethany Spicher Schonberg and her husband, Micah, manage Plowshare Produce, a CSA farm in central Pennsylvania. They share land and a home with Bethany's parents and are members of University Mennonite Church in State College.

Rebecca Seiling lives in Waterloo, Ontario, with her husband and two daughters and attends St. Jacobs Mennonite Church. Rebecca has been a teacher at both the elementary and the high school level and is the author of *Plant a Seed of Peace* (Herald Press) and *Don't Be Afraid* (Faith and Life Resources). She also has worked as a writer and editor for the Gather 'Round curriculum.

Nancy Sleeth of Wilmore, Kentucky, co-directs the nonprofit Blessed Earth (www.blessedearth.org). She is author of *Go Green, Save Green: A Simple Guide to Saving Time, Money and God's Green Earth* and *The Year of Living Without: One Woman's Quest to Regain Peace and Quiet.*

Dorcas Smucker, a minister's wife and mother of six, lives in Harrisburg, Oregon. She is a columnist for the *Register-Guard* in Eugene, Oregon, and has written three books.

Isaac Villegas is the pastor of Chapel Hill (N.C.) Mennonite Fellowship. He is also the co-author of *Presence: Giving and Receiving God* (2010).

Mitsuko and Yorifumi Yaguchi are members of Yuai Mennonite Church in Sapporo, Japan. Mitsuko was a translator and editor of the Japanese version of *Living More with Less*, along with Toshiko Aratani. Yorifumi is a poet; *The Poetry of Yorifumi Yaguchi* and *The Wing-Beaten Air* were published by Good Books.

Acknowledgments

Valerie Weaver-Zercher

● ●

First thanks go to all the contributors of entries to this volume; sharing one's story can be intimidating, and I'm grateful for their willingness to slip the rest of us a glimpse of their private thoughts and household lives. Thanks also to the writers who contributed longer pieces to this project, all of whom went above and beyond the call of more-with-less duty by offering leads, contacts, and suggestions.

Thanks to Paul Boers, Charity Grimes, Karina Kreider, Alysha Bergey Landis, Laura Schlabach, and Esther Shank for serving as story collectors. Their tenacity and creativity in tracking down narratives for part 3 was immensely inspiring. None of these young adults was born when *Living More with Less* was published in 1980. All of them are answers to the question of who is prepared to lead us into the next three decades of more-with-less life.

My deep gratitude goes to Cathleen Hockman-Wert, who offered counsel and information at countless points along the way and whose comments on the manuscript were always pitch-perfect. Thanks also to Luke Gascho, Cheryl Zehr Walker, Nancy Adams, Dora Kawate, Mary Beth Lind, Erin Weaver, and Susan Nisly, all of whom reviewed the manuscript at various stages and made wise and informed comments on how to make it better.

Others who offered invaluable feedback and assistance include Jessica King, Kathleen Temple, Jennifer Halteman Schrock, Rolando Santiago, Dave Hockman-Wert, Andrea Geiser, Kim Dyer, Sara Wenger Shenk, Steve Kriss, Stacy Stoltzfus, Dave Weaver-Zercher, and members of the Slate Hill Sunday school class. And the steady stream of emails and phone calls that Amy Gingerich at Herald Press received from me are a testament to her impressive editorial intuition and skill at fitting details into a larger vision.

Thanks also go to Paul Longacre, Nancy Heisey, Cara Longacre Hurst, and Marta Longacre van Zanten for their gracious support of this project and encouragement along the way.

• •

*Find more stories, tips, and FREE leaders guides for small group and Christian education class discussions of **Living More with Less** at www.mpn.net/livingmorewithless.*

Notes

• •

Mennonite Central Committee Preface

1. United Nations Food and Agricultural Organization, "Hunger," www.fao-ectad-tunis.org/index.jsp?pIdLangueChoix=2&pArticleId=6074&pRubriqueId=3911.
2. United Nations World Health Organization, "Health through safe drinking water and basic sanitation," www.who.int/water_sanitation_health/mdg1/en/index.html.
3. "Overview: Understanding, Measuring, and Overcoming Poverty," World Bank, August 2008, http://web.worldbank.org/WBSITE/EXTERNAL/TOPICS/EXTPOVERTY/0,,contentMDK:20153855~menuPK:373757~pagePK:148956~piPK:216618~theSitePK:336992,00.html.

1: Living More with Less in Retrospect

1. Doris Janzen Longacre, "More-with-Less II Book Proposal," memo, February 23, 1978, "Living More with Less 1978–1980," IX-6-3, Box 155, Mennonite Church USA Archives—Goshen, Ind.
2. Longacre had similar contracts with MCC and Herald Press officials for both books. MCC provided a budget for research assistance and manuscript preparation and provided administrative support; Longacre had the use of an MCC office. She was not paid for her writing time but drew a part-time salary for speaking and engagement in broader hunger-related educational projects. Following receipt of $10,000 (U.S.) in royalties for each book, Doris (and later Paul) arranged for subsequent royalties to go to MCC. While working on the *Living More with Less* project, she noted: "While it is impossible to predict how well the book will sell (cookbooks do better than other books so the *More-with-Less* experience may not repeat itself) I am hopeful that royalties will at least reimburse MCC for expenses

and me for my time." Quotation from Doris Janzen Longacre memo to William Snyder, January 6, 1978, "Living More with Less 1978–1980," IX-6-3, Box 155, Mennonite Church USA Archives—Goshen; see also Paul Longacre memo to Reg Toews, August 22, 1980, "Publishing Agreement on *Living More with Less*," in folder "Living More with Less 1978–1980," IX-6-3, Box 155, Mennonite Church USA Archives—Goshen.

3. Charlotte Fardelmann, "Learning to Live More with Less," in *Living Simply*, eds. David Crean, Eric Ebbeson, Helen Ebbeson (New York: Seabury Press, 1981).

4. Anne Warkentin Dyck, "Memorial to Doris Janzen Longacre," MCC Annual Meeting, Kidron, Ohio, January 25, 1980, in folder "Living More with Less 1978–1980," IX-6-3, Box 155, Mennonite Church USA Archives—Goshen.

5. Paul Longacre, quoted in *Living More with Less* (Scottdale, Pa.: Herald Press, 1980), 12.

6. Quoted in Peggy Schmidt, "'Living More with Less' Sequel," *The Sunday News* (Lancaster, Pa.), November 2, 1980.

7. Edgar Stoesz to Doris Janzen Longacre, January 27, 1978, "Living More with Less 1978–1980," IX-6-3, Box 155, Mennonite Church USA Archives—Goshen.

8. Doris Janzen Longacre, attachment to memo to William Snyder, January 6, 1978, "Living More with Less 1978–1980," IX-6-3, Box 155, Mennonite Church USA Archives—Goshen.

9. Doris Janzen Longacre to Peter Stucky and Luis Correa, August 17, 1979, "Living More with Less 1978–1980," IX-6-3, Box 155, Mennonite Church USA Archives—Goshen.

10. Doris Janzen Longacre, "More-with-Less II Book Proposal," memo, February 23, 1978 "Living More with Less 1978–1980," IX-6-3, Box 155, Mennonite Church USA Archives—Goshen.

11. "More-with-Less Entries Called For," MCC press release, May 19, 1978, "Living More with Less 1978–1980," IX-6-3, Box 155, Mennonite Church USA Archives—Goshen.

12. Ultimately, the ideas of 310 contributors appeared in *Living More with Less*.

13. Review of *Living More with Less*, *Library Journal*, December 1980.

14. *MCC Workbook*, 1979 (Akron, Pa.: MCC), 1–2.

15. Another harbinger was the appearance of the first *Mennonite Your Way Directory* in 1976, which emphasized Mennonite frugality and encouraged overnight stays in homes on a donation basis. By 2010, the Mennonite Your Way website advertised listings for about 1,700 hosts in more than sixty countries. See http://www.mennoniteyourway.com/Myw/.

16. Mennonite Central Committee news release, October 17, 1980, "Living More with Less 1978–1980," IX-6-3, Box 155, Mennonite

Church USA Archives—Goshen. The review is David E. Anderson, "Tells How to Live Simply," in *The Herald-Telephone* (Bloomington, Ind.), September 27, 1980.

17. Suzanne Geissler, letter to the editor, *Christian Herald*, December 1980, in Herald Press "Living More with Less" review file, Scottdale, Pa.

18. Rudolf Dyck, review in *Festival Quarterly*, May/June/July 1980, 31.

19. Mitch Finley, review in *Visitor*, March 4, 1984, 8–9.

20. Mary Fox, "Book Encourages Philosophy of Life With Less," *Goshen News*, October 6, 1980, 2.

21. Editors, "20 for the 20th Century," *The Mennonite*, February 22, 2000, 6.

3: Introduction

1. Doris Janzen Longacre used the original submissions for the 1980 book to formulate the five life standards. Some of the 1980 individual entries are reprinted in this volume; these entries are indicated with "(1980)" at the end of the entries. Contributions to the thirtieth anniversary edition were obtained in a variety of ways: interviews by story collectors, word of mouth, invitation, and a call for submissions for *Simply Sustainable*, a project that was initiated as a companion volume to the *Simply in Season* cookbook but then not published.

2. Doris Janzen Longacre, *More-with-Less Cookbook* (Scottdale, Pa.: Herald Press, 1976), 12.

4: The Five Life Standards

1. Doris Janzen Longacre, *More-with-Less Cookbook* (Scottdale, Pa.: Herald Press, 1998), 6.

2. I have used standard transliterations from Koine Greek to English. An additional observation: the term *home economics* is redundant because *economics* already means "household." Perhaps this redundancy made it more acceptable for women to learn about economics. Perhaps, culturally speaking, this redundancy has been a way to depoliticize the private sphere of the home.

3. The Bible uses the words *tabernacle*, *mishkan*, and *Shekhinah* to describe God's dwelling and presence in the world.

5: Do Justice

1. The current figures come from the Stockholm International Peace Research Institute, http://www.sipri.org/yearbook/2009/05, and from the Congressional Research Service, "Conventional Arms Transfers to Developing Nations, 2001–2008," September 4, 2009, http://opencrs.com/document/R40796/2009-09-04/.

2. "Canada's Living Planet Report Launched," Global Footprint Network, http://www.footprintnetwork.org/en/index.php/blog/af/canadas_living_planet_report_launched; and One Planet DC, http://www.oneplanetdc.org/.
3. Nafziger's and Franz's suggestions included advocating for the following: (1) lowering tariff barriers against goods from poor countries; (2) giving stronger voice to poor nations in international agencies like the International Monetary Fund; (3) forming rules to govern multinational corporations and to ensure that poor countries benefit from their own resources; (4) addressing global unemployment; (5) establishing a world grain reserve and offering development assistance to poor nations; (6) retaining economic ties to poor countries that are not capitalist; (7) stopping arms sales to countries with poor human rights and economic development records; and (8) revising North American farm policies that would safeguard small family farms.

6: Learn from the World Community

1. Speech given by Romeo Maione at the MCC annual meeting in Kitchener, Ont., January 1978.
2. "Kaguya" is a moon probe launched by the Japanese Aerospace Exploration Agency in 2007.

7: Nurture People

1. Wendell Berry, *The Unsettling of America: Culture and Agriculture* (New York: Avon Books, 1978), 30.
2. "Labor-Saving Devices Are Killing Us," *USA Today*, March 2001.
3. Henry Fairlie, "America's Real Energy Crisis," *Washington Post*, June 24, 1979, G8.
4. Tara Parker-Pope, "A One-Eyed Invader in the Bedroom," *New York Times*, March 4, 2008, posted at http://www.nytimes.com/2008/03/04/health/04well.html.
5. MCC News Service, December 1, 1978.

8: Cherish the Natural Order

1. Wendell Berry, *The Unsettling of America: Culture and Agriculture* (New York: Avon Books, 1978), 30.
2. Mary Evelyn Jegen and Bruce U. Manno, eds., *The Earth Is the Lord's* (New York: Paulist Press, 1978), 22–43.
3. Wendell Berry, *A Timbered Choir: The Sabbath Poems 1979–1997* (New York: Counterpoint, 1999), 141.

9: Nonconform Freely

1. Willard Swartley, "Mennonite Higher Education Facing the 1980s," *Gospel Herald*, September 26, 1978, 726.

2. Sandra L. Calvert, "Children as Consumers: Advertising and Marketing," *The Future of Children*, 18:1 (Spring 2008), posted at http://www.princeton.edu/futureofchildren/publications/journals/article/index.xml?journalid=32&articleid=62.
3. "Geographic Mobility 2009," U.S. Census Bureau, 2009.

10: Money and Stewardship

1. "Facts and Figures," Coalition for Financial Security, http://www.coalitionforfinancialsecurity.org/facts.htm.
2. "General Statistics," Networks Financial Institute at Indiana State University, Networks Financial Institute, http://www.networksfinancialinstitute.org/Finance/facts-figures/Pages/default.aspx.
3. Nathan Dungan, *Share, Save, Spend: Financial Sanity Leaders Guide*, 2005, 1.
4. "'Buy local' movement picks up steam in Pittsburgh," *Pittsburgh Post-Gazette*, March 14, 2010, posted at http://postgazette.com/pg/10073/1042411-68.stm.

11: Homes

1. Chris Morran, "Shrink Ray Hits Size of New Single Family Homes," *The Consumerist*, June 18, 2010, posted at http://consumerist.com/2010/06/shrink-ray-hits-size-of-single-family-homes.html.
2. Tim McEnery, "Green Building Goes Global," U.S. Green Building Council, July 21, 2009, posted at http://www.usgbc.org/News/USGBCInTheNewsDetails.aspx?ID=4155.
3. Compiled from Nancy Conner, *Living Green: The Missing Manual* (Sebastopol, Calif.: O'Reilly Media, 2009); David Gershon, *Low Carbon Diet: A 30 Day Program to Lose 5000 Pounds* (Woodstock, NY: Empowerment Institute, 2006); and Michael Abbaté, *Gardening Eden* (Colorado Springs, Colo.: WaterBrook Press, 2009).
4. *Good Stuff? A Behind-the-Scenes Guide to the Things We Buy*, Worldwatch Institute, http://www.worldwatch.org/node/1488.

12: Homekeeping

1. "Municipal Waste Generation," The Conference Board of Canada, 2008, http://www.conferenceboard.ca/hcp/details/environment/municipal-waste-generation.aspx#top.
2. "Appliances and Home Electronics," U.S. Department of Energy, http://www.energysavers.gov/your_home/appliances/index.cfm/mytopic=10020.
3. "Wise Water Use," Environment Canada, http://www.ec.gc.ca/eau-water/default.asp?lang=En&n=F25C70EC-1.
4. *Good Stuff? A Behind-the-Scenes Guide to the Things We Buy*, Worldwatch Institute, http://www.worldwatch.org/node/1493.

5. Compiled from Nancy Conner, *Living Green: The Missing Manual* (Sebastopol, Calif.: O'Reilly Media, 2009); David Gershon, *Low Carbon Diet: A 30 Day Program to Lose 5000 Pounds* (Woodstock, NY: Empowerment Institute, 2006); and Brangien Davis, ed., *Wake Up and Smell the Planet* (Seattle: Mountaineers Books, 2007).
6. "Fire Your Clothes Dryer," *Green America*, Summer 2009, posted at http://www.greenamericatoday.org/pubs/realgreen/articles/dryer.cfm.
7. Compiled from Nancy Conner, *Living Green*; Michael Abbaté, *Gardening Eden* (Colorado Springs: WaterBrook Press, 2009); Nancy Sleeth, *Go Green, Save Green* (Carol Stream, Ill.: Tyndale, 2009); Matthew Sleeth, *Serve God, Save the Planet* (Grand Rapids, Mich.: Zondervan, 2006).

13: Gardens, Farms, and Markets

1. "The Grass is Greener . . . and Safer!" OrganicLawnCare101.com, 2006, http://www.organiclawncare101.com.
2. Compiled in part from information obtained from the U.S. Environmental Protection Agency, http://www.epa.gov/wastes/conserve/rrr/composting/basic.htm.
3. David Gershon, *Low Carbon Diet: A 30 Day Program to Lose 5000 Pounds* (Woodstock, NY: Empowerment Institute, 2006).
4. Compiled from information obtained from the U.S. Environmental Protection Agency, Union of Concerned Scientists, and Greg Bowman.

14: Cooking and Eating

1. Michael Pollan, *In Defense of Food: An Eater's Manifesto* (New York: Penguin, 2008), 8.
2. Adam Voiland, "Eat at Home for Your Own Good," *U.S. News and World Report*, December 25, 2006, posted at http://health.usnews.com/usnews/health/articles/061217/25eat.health.htm.
3. Nancy Gibbs, "The Magic of the Family Meal," *Time*, June 4, 2006, posted at http://www.time.com/time/magazine/article/0,9171,1200760,00.html.
4. Nancy Conner, *Living Green: The Missing Manual* (Sebastopol, Calif.: O'Reilly Media, 2009), 75.
5. Holly Hill, "Food Miles: Background and Marketing," *National Sustainable Agriculture Information Service*, June 23, 2010, http://attra.ncat.org/attra-pub/foodmiles.html.

15: Clothes and Bodies

1. "A Closet Obsession," *Time*, October 24, 2005, posted at http://www.time.com/time/magazine/article/0,9171,1122026-1,00.html.

2. The figure comes from "End-Use Consumption of Electricity, 2001," U.S. Energy Information Administration, http://www.eia.doe.gov/emeu/recs/recs2001/enduse2001/enduse2001.html.
3. This section has been moved to this location from Longacre's "Nurturing People" chapter.
4. Current information comes from Danae King, et al., "Adherence to Healthy Lifestyle Habits in US Adults, 1988–2006," *The American Journal of Medicine* 122, no. 6 (2009): 528–34. Interestingly, the journal also reports that adherence to these five habits decreased from 1988 to 2006, with documented decreases in three of the five habits.
5. "The Great Diaper Debate," *Envirozine: Environment Canada's Online Newsmagazine* 45, posted at http://www.ec.gc.ca/envirozine/default.asp?lang=En&n=250EEDD7-1.

16: Transportation and Travel

1. Data to produce this graph is from the U.S. Department of Census and the U.S. Department of Transportation and is available at http://www.bts.gov/publications/national_transportation_statistics/html/table_01_37.html and http://www.census.gov/popest/states/NST-ann-est2008.html and http://www.census.gov/popest/archives/1990s/nat-total.txt. Keep in mind that expressing these miles in per-person terms takes population growth into account.
2. Steven E. Polzin, PhD, "The Case for Moderate Growth in Vehicle Miles of Travel: A Critical Juncture in U.S. Travel Behavior Trends," University of Florida Center for Urban Transportation Research, 2006, http://cutr.us/pub/files/The%20Case%20for%20Moderate%20Growth%20in%20VMT-%202006%20Final.pdf.
3. *Good Stuff? A Behind-the-Scenes Guide to the Things We Buy*, Worldwatch Institute, http://www.worldwatch.org/node/1480.
4. Ibid.

17: Recreation and Schedules

1. Robert Putnam, *Bowling Alone: The Collapse and Revival of American Community* (New York: Simon & Schuster, 2000), 189.
2. "Running Out of Time: Kids Today are Busier than Ever Before," *Junior Scholastic*, September 3, 2001.

18: Celebrations and Life Passages

1. Center for a New American Dream, "Simplify the Holidays," 2009, http://www.newdream.org/holiday/brochure.php.
2. "Wedding Trends in Canada," Wedding Bells, based on an online survey from February 18 to March 12, 2010, http://www.weddingbells.ca/results/.
3. "Cocoa Campaign," International Labor Rights Forum, http://www.laborrights.org/stop-child-labor/cocoa-campaign.

4. "Reducing Holiday Waste," U.S. Environmental Protection Agency, posted at http://www.epa.gov/wastes/wycd/funfacts/winter.htm.

19: Technology and Media

1. "Study Tallies Environmental Cost of Computer Boom," United Nations University Update, May–June 2004, posted at http://update. unu.edu/archive/issue31_5.htm.
2. Fredric Jameson, *Postmodernism, or, The Cultural Logic of Late Capitalism* (Durham, N.C.: Duke University Press, 1991), 314–15.
3. The Enough Project, www.enoughproject.org.
4. Tamar Lewin, "If Your Kids Are Awake, They're Probably Online," *New York Times*, January 20, 2010, http://www.nytimes.com/2010/01/20/education/20wired.html.
5. "Affluent Spend Most Time Online," E-Marketer, September 16, 2008, http://www.emarketer.com/Article.aspx?id=1006541.
6. "American Time Use Survey Summary," U.S. Bureau of Labor Statistics, June 22, 2010, http://www.bls.gov/news.release/atus.nr0.htm.
7. "Computer Manufacturing Soaks Up Fossil Fuels, UN University Study Says," United Nations News Centre, March 8, 2004, http://www. un.org/apps/news/story.asp?NewsID=10007&Cr=computer&Cr1.

20: Meetinghouses and Churches

1. "Bottom Line Ministries that Matter," a report of the National Council of Churches Eco-Justice Program (Washington, D.C.: National Council of Churches USA), 1.

21: Strengthening Each Other and Organizing Communities

1. Global Humanitarian Forum, Geneva, "Human Impact Report: Climate Change—The Anatomy of a Silent Crisis," 2009, 1. Available at http://www.humansecuritygateway.com/documents/GHF_Human-ImpactReport_AnatomySilentCrisis.pdf.
2. The environmentalist is Bill McKibben, author of *Eaarth: Making a Life on a Tough New Planet* (New York: Henry Holt, 2010). McKibben sounded one of the first alarms about global warming with his book *The End of Nature* in 1988. This history of global warming is based in part on information from his book *Eaarth*.
3. Rich Pirog and Andrew Benjamin, "Checking the Food Odometer: Comparing Food Miles for Local Versus Conventional Produce Sales in Iowa Institutions," Leopold Center for Sustainable Agriculture, July 2003, http://www.leopold.iastate.edu/pubs/staff/files/food_travel072103.pdf.
4. Bill McKibben, *Maybe One: A Personal and Environmental Argument for Single-Child Families* (New York: Simon & Schuster, 1998), 107.

The Author

Doris Janzen Longacre was the author of *Living More with Less* (1980) and the *More-with-Less Cookbook* (1976). Doris died from cancer on November 10, 1979, at the age of thirty-nine, before she was able to finish the *Living More with Less* manuscript. She is survived by her husband, Paul, and daughters, Cara and Marta.

The Editor

Valerie Weaver-Zercher is a writer and editor in Mechanicsburg, Pennsylvania. Her work has appeared in *Orion, Sojourners, The Christian Century, Christianity Today, Publishers Weekly, The Los Angeles Times*, and *The Mennonite*, among others. She is a contributing editor to *Sojourners* and a book reviewer for *Christian Century*, and her work has been nominated for and received special mention for a Pushcart Prize. Valerie and her husband and three children attend Slate Hill Mennonite Church.

"*Living More with Less* is about a way of living rooted in the Christian faith. It's about following Jesus who cared for the poor. It tells the stories of those who live with less—a countercultural move in a society of excess. Our planet is groaning and we desperately need the kind of thoughtful essays and tips in this book to show us the way forward."
—Ron Sider, founder and president of Evangelicals for Social Action

"In recent years global interconnectedness has made us more aware of worldwide injustices; consumer culture, environmental changes, and energy crises have only heightened our sense that things are not as they should be. The collective wisdom of *Living More with Less* is a tremendous gift to us in that it articulates a holistic vision for a better way as well as practical insights for making that life a reality."
—Albert Y. Hsu, author of *The Suburban Christian*

"As someone who wants to pattern my life after the person of Jesus in very practical and contemporary ways, *Living More with Less* is a volume to underline and dog-ear and highlight and bookmark. I highly recommend it for those who aspire to live well."
—Margot Starbuck, author of *The Girl in the Orange Dress* and *Unsqueezed*